THINKING SPAN[ISH]
TRANSLATION

For details of the Teachers' Handbook and cassette of oral texts please write to:

ROUTLEDGE LTD
ITPS
CHERITON HOUSE
NORTH WAY
ANDOVER
HANTS SP10 5BE

ROUTLEDGE INC.
29 WEST 35TH STREET
NEW YORK
NY 10001
USA

TITLES OF RELATED INTEREST

Thinking Translation: A Course in Translation Method: French to English
Sándor Hervey and Ian Higgins

In Other Words: A Coursebook on Translation
Mona Baker

Redefining Translation
Lance Hewson and Jacky Martin

Translation Studies
Susan Bassnett

Colloquial Spanish
Untza Otaola Alday

Colloquial Spanish of Latin America
Roberto Rodríguez-Saona

Manual of Business Spanish
Michael Gorman and María-Luisa Henson

Spanish Business Situations
Michael Gorman and María-Luisa Henson

The Linguistics Encyclopedia
Kirsten Malmkjær, ed.

THINKING SPANISH TRANSLATION

A Course in Translation Method: Spanish to English

Sándor Hervey
Reader in Linguistics, University of St Andrews

Ian Higgins
Senior Lecturer in French, University of St Andrews

Louise M. Haywood
Lecturer in Spanish, University of St Andrews

London and New York

First published in 1995
by Routledge
11 New Fetter Lane, London EC4P 4EE

Simultaneously published in the USA and Canada
by Routledge
29 West 35th Street, New York, NY 10001

Typeset in Times by Michael Mepham, Frome, Somerset
Printed and bound in Great Britain by
T.J. Press (Padstow) Ltd, Padstow, Cornwall

British Library Cataloguing in Publication Data
A catalogue record for this book is available from the British Library

Library of Congress Cataloguing in Publication Data
A catalogue record for this book has been requested

ISBN 0–415–11658–9 (hbk)
ISBN 0–415–11659–7 (pbk)

Contents

Acknowledgements

We owe a debt of gratitude to a number of friends and colleagues who helped us in the elaboration of *Thinking Spanish Translation*: José Barroso Castro, Bernard Bentley, Maggie Bolton, Mercedes Clarasó, Cathy Davies, Marta Gómez Mata, Esther Gómez Sierra, Adrian Gratwick, John Minchinton, Alan Paterson, Raquel de Pedro and Ralph Penny. We are particularly grateful to Gustavo San Román, who read the entire typescript and made many helpful suggestions for its improvement. We also owe a considerable debt to the many students whose critical and creative participation in the successive versions of the course have helped to give it its present shape. Finally, we would like to thank our editor, Jane Dennis, for her alertness, forbearance and good-humoured help.

Introduction

This book is a revised version of a course in translation methodology taught mainly to third- and fourth-year undergraduates of Spanish at the University of St Andrews. A course of this type was first designed for students of French; the French–English version was published by Routledge in 1992 under the title of *Thinking Translation*. However, long before this publication, parallel courses were also developed for German–English and Spanish–English. These courses are also currently taught at St Andrews.

The present volume is a fully developed Spanish–English version of the course. (A German–English version is being published concurrently.) While it will be found, in many respects, to correspond to the 1992 version of *Thinking Translation*, it is a self-contained, 'parallel' coursebook for English-speaking students of Spanish, with both major and minor departures from the 1992 version. Some of these departures spring from specific differences between Spanish and French (for instance the 'contrastive topics' in Chapters 16 to 19). Others result from the inevitable process by which ideas are refined through continued application and practice (for instance the section on 'oral genres' in Chapter 11). The most evident area of revision is to the course structure. This consists in the inversion of the order in which 'textual levels' are presented. In the 1992 version we opted for what Mona Baker (1992, p. 6) calls a 'top-to-bottom' arrangement: that is to say, textual levels were discussed starting with the broadest and most general level and ending with the level of the smallest, most particular units of language. However, the St Andrews Spanish–English course has always been taught using a 'bottom-to-top' approach (the approach which, incidentally, Mona Baker favours). Our experience has confirmed that students prefer to work from the particular to the general. Therefore, in the present volume we follow a 'bottom-to-top' approach.

Let us now briefly outline a few basic assumptions underlying our approach. First, this course is not a disguised version of the traditional 'grammar-and-translation' method of language teaching. Our focus is on how to *translate* from Spanish, not how to communicate in Spanish. We assume that students already have the considerable linguistic resources in Spanish needed to benefit from the course and that they already possess basic dictionary and research skills. Naturally, in using these resources and skills to produce good translations, they inevitably extend and improve their competence in Spanish. This is an important fringe benefit; but, as we have said, our main interest lies in developing useful translation skills and, generally, in improving *quality* in translation work. It should not be forgotten that this quality depends on the translator's command of English as much as of Spanish; indeed, Birgit Rommel, head of the Übersetzer- und Dolmetscherschule Zürich, has lamented the lack of mother-tongue training in universities, concluding that: 'Great stress is laid on improving foreign language proficiency, but excellence in the mother-tongue – the translator's target language – is, quite wrongly, taken for granted' (Rommel, 1987, p. 12). Rommel's comment is a qualified reminder of the common assumption that higher quality can be expected when translating into the mother-tongue than into a foreign language. The predominance in this course of unidirectional translation from Spanish into English reflects our acceptance of this assumption in its qualified form: excellence in the mother-tongue is not taken for granted, but constitutes one of the objectives of the course.

Second, the course is not intended as a disguised version of translation theory, or of linguistics. This does not mean that we avoid technical discussion of linguistic or translation-theoretical issues. However, such issues are not treated out of theoretical interest, but out of direct concern with specific types of problem encountered in translating. That is, our approach is *methodological* and practical: where the discussion of theoretical issues facilitates and rationalizes methodological problems of translation, we have freely borrowed theoretical notions from translation theory and linguistics. Throughout the course, we have provided instant and simple exemplification of each theoretical notion invoked, and have tried to link these notions instantly and directly to practical issues in translation.

Third, the course has a progressive overall structure and thematic organization. After setting out the fundamental issues, options and alternatives of which a translator must be aware, it examines a series of layers that are of textual importance in translation ('upwards' from the nuts and bolts of phonic and graphic details to the generalities of intertextuality and culture). It then moves on, via a series of semantic and stylistic topics (literal meaning, connotation and language variety), to a consideration of textual genres and the demands of translating texts in a range of different genres. If literary genres have, on balance, a higher profile than 'commercial' ones, this is partly offset by the use of non-literary texts of various kinds throughout the course (such as speed translation exercises). In any case, 'commercial' texts tend to present translation difficulties that are far too narrowly specific in subject matter to be suitable for a general coursebook on translation method. Our aim has been to produce an integrated, non-specialized approach to the various aspects that need to be discussed in the context of a general methodology of translation. While we cannot claim that this approach is exhaustive, it does have wide scope and a coherent organization, and it is applicable to virtually any type of text likely to be encountered by graduates who go on to translate professionally.

Finally, our claim that the course systematically and progressively builds up a methodical approach to translation practice should not be taken to mean that we are offering a way of 'mechanizing' the process of translation, or attempting to provide rules and recipes to be followed. On the contrary, we believe translation to be a highly creative activity in which the translator's personal responsibility is constantly to the forefront. We have, therefore, tried to emphasize throughout the need to recognize options and alternatives, the need for rational discussion, and the need for decision-making. All the material in the course – expository and practical alike – is intended not for silent consumption, but for animated discussion between students and between students and tutor. (In fact, we have found that many of the practicals are best done by students working in small groups and reporting their findings to the class.) Each chapter is, therefore, intended for tutor-student discussion at an early stage in the corresponding practical; this is because we are not trying to inculcate this or that particular theory or method, but simply to foster the general principle that, whatever approach the translator adopts, it should be self-aware and methodical.

While the course we are presenting is a progressively designed whole, it is divided into a series of successive units intended to fit into an academic timetable. Each unit consists of a chapter outlining a set of related notions and problems, and an accompanying practical in which students are given a concrete translation task, working on textual material to which the notions and problems outlined in the chapter are particularly relevant. The first fifteen units are designed to be dealt with progressively, in numerical order. There are, however, four further units, which can be studied at whatever points in the course seem most appropriate to local conditions. These are Chapters 16–19, devoted to four different 'contrastive linguistic' topics. In these four units, the proportion of expository material to practical exercises varies from chapter to chapter.

With the exception of some of the 'contrastive' chapters, each unit needs between ninety minutes' and two hours' class time, and students are also required to prepare in advance for class discussion of the chapter. It is important that each student should have the necessary reference books in class: a monolingual Spanish dictionary, a Spanish–English/English–Spanish dictionary, an English dictionary and an English thesaurus. Some of the practicals will be done at home – sometimes individually, sometimes in groups – and handed in for comment by the tutor. How often this is done will depend on local conditions; in our situation we have found that once a fortnight works well. When an exercise is done at home, this implies that some time should be devoted in the following class to discussion of the issues raised. (Fuller suggestions for teaching and assessment can be found in the *Teachers' Handbook*.)

From consideration of the progressive overall structure of the course and its modular arrangement, it is easy to see how versions of the same course outline can be designed for languages other than French, German and Spanish. With the exception of the contrastive topics in Chapters 16–19 (which, for each other language, need to be replaced by different contrastive topics dealing with problems that loom large for that language), adapting the course involves the provision of illustrative material for each chapter and suitable texts for the practicals.

NB (1) A number of the practicals in the course involve work on texts that are not contained in the present volume, but intended for distribution in class. These texts are found in S. Hervey, I. Higgins and L. M. Haywood, *Thinking Spanish Translation: Teachers' Handbook* (Routledge, 1995), which can be obtained from the addresses given on the opening page of this book. (2) The oral texts for use in practicals are available on a cassette: S. Hervey, I. Higgins and L. M. Haywood, *Thinking Spanish Translation* which can also be obtained from the addresses given on the opening page.

1

Preliminaries to translation as a process

It is often said that skill in translation cannot be learned and, especially, cannot be taught. Underlying this attitude is the assumption that certain people are born with the gift of being good translators or interpreters, whereas others simply do not have this knack; in other words, skill in translation is an inborn talent: either you've got it or you haven't.

Up to a point, we would accept this view. No doubt it is true, for instance, that some people take to mathematics or physics, whereas others have little aptitude for such subjects, being more inclined towards the humanities. There is no reason why things should be otherwise for translation; some are 'naturally' good at it, others find it difficult; some enjoy translating and others do not.

The twin assumptions behind this book are that it will help its users acquire proficiency in translation, and that we are addressing ourselves to people who do enjoy translating, and would like to improve their translation skills. Indeed, enjoyment is a vital ingredient in acquiring proficiency as a translator. This, again, is quite normal: elements of enjoyment and job satisfaction play an important role in any skilled activity that might be pursued as a career, from music to computer technology. Note, however, that when we talk of proficiency in translation we are no longer thinking merely of the basic natural talent an individual may have, but of a skill and facility that require learning, technique, practice and experience. Ideally, translators should combine their natural talent with acquired skill. The answer to anyone who is sceptical about the formal teaching of translation is twofold: students with a gift for translation invariably find it useful in building their native talent into a fully developed proficiency; students without a gift for translation invariably acquire some degree of proficiency.

Since this is a course on translation method, it cannot avoid introducing a number of technical terms and methodological notions bordering on the theoretical. (These are set in bold type when they are first explained in the text, and are listed in the Glossary on pp. 219–25.) Our aims are primarily methodological and practical rather than theoretical, but we believe that methods and practices are at their best when underpinned by thoughtful consideration of a rationale behind them. This book is, therefore, only theoretical to the extent that it encourages a thoughtful consideration of the rationale behind solutions to practical problems encountered in the process of translation or in evaluating translations as texts serving particular purposes.

Throughout the course, our aim is to accustom students to making two interrelated sets of decisions. The first set are what we shall call **strategic decisions**. These are general decisions which, ideally, the translator should make before actually attempting a translation, in response to such questions as 'what are the salient linguistic characteristics of this text?'; 'what are its principal effects?'; 'what genre does it belong to and what audience is it aimed at?'; 'what are the functions and intended audience of my translation?'; 'what are the implications of these factors?'; and 'which, among all such factors, are the ones that most need to be respected in translating this particular text?'. The other set of decisions may be called **decisions of detail**. These are arrived at in the light of the strategic decisions, but they concern the specific problems of grammar, lexis and so on encountered in translating particular expressions in their particular context. We have found that students tend to start by thinking about decisions of detail which they then try to make piecemeal without realizing the crucial prior role of strategic decisions. The result tends to be a translation that is bitty and uneven. This is why, in the practicals, students will usually be asked first to consider the strategic problems confronting the translator of a given text, and subsequently to discuss and explain the decisions of detail they have made in translating it. Naturally, they will sometimes find during translating that problems of detail arise which lead them to refine the original strategy, the refined strategy in turn entailing changes to some of the decisions of detail already taken. This is a fact of life in translation, and should be recognized as such, but it is no reason not to elaborate an initial strategy: on the contrary, without the strategy many potential problems go unseen until the reader of the translated text trips up over the inconsistencies and the obscurities of detail.

TRANSLATION AS A PROCESS

The aim of this preliminary chapter is to look at translation as a process – that is, to examine carefully what it is that a translator actually does. Before we do this, however, we should note a few basic terms that will be used throughout the course. Defining these now will clarify and simplify further discussion:

Text Any given stretch of speech or writing produced in a given language and assumed to make a coherent, self-contained whole. A minimal text may consist of no more than a single word – for example, ¡Basta! – preceded and followed by a period of silence. A maximal text may run into volumes – for example, Pérez Galdós's *Episodios nacionales*.

Source language (SL) The language in which the text requiring translation is couched.
Target language (TL) The language into which the original text is to be translated.
Source text (ST) The text requiring translation.
Target text (TT) The text which is a translation of the ST.

With these terms in mind, the translation process can, in crude terms, be broken down into two types of activity: understanding a ST and formulating a TT. While they are different in kind, these two types of process occur not successively, but simultaneously; in fact, one may not even realize that one has imperfectly understood the ST until one comes up against a problem in formulating or evaluating a TT. In such a case, one may need to go back to square one, so as to reconstrue the ST in the light of one's new understanding of it (just as a translation strategy may need to be modified in the light of specific, unforeseen problems of detail). In this way, ST interpretation and TT formulation go hand in hand. Nevertheless, for the purposes of discussion, it is useful to think of them as different, separable, processes.

The component processes of translation are not qualitatively different from certain ordinary and familiar processes that all speakers perform in the normal course of their daily lives. In this sense, translation is not an extraordinary process. For a start, comprehension and interpretation of texts are commonplace processes that we all perform whenever we listen to or read a piece of linguistically imparted information. The act of understanding even the simplest message potentially involves all the beliefs, suppositions, inferences and expectations that are the stuff of personal, social and cultural life. Understanding everyday messages is therefore not all that different from what a translator must do when first confronting a ST – and it is certainly no less complicated. It is, however, true that messages may be understood with varying degrees of precision. For instance, suppose that a mother asked her son to get the blue biro from the top left-hand drawer of the bureau, and he responded by giving her a black biro that happened to be handy. She would be justified in thinking that he had not understood her message fully, as he had evidently not paid attention to a number of details in it. Yet he could not be accused of a total lack of comprehension, because he did register and respond to the one salient fact that he had been asked for a biro.

In everyday communication, evidence that a message has been understood may come from appropriate practical response. Another measure of how precisely a message has been understood is appropriate *linguistic* response. Appropriate linguistic response includes such basic things as returning a greeting appropriately, giving a satisfactory answer to a question, or filling in a form correctly. While none of these are translation-like processes, they do show that the element of comprehension and interpretation within the translation process involves what can be a perfectly ordinary, everyday activity requiring no special skill or power of intellect, only an average native command of the language used.

There is, however, another kind of ordinary, everyday linguistic response that is rather similar to translation proper. Here is a commonplace example:

BOY Ask your Dad if I can take you to the disco tonight.
GIRL OK (*Exit to find her father*; *to father*) Dad, there's a disco on at the YMCA tonight. Can I go?
DAD Just a minute. Who are you going with?
GIRL Guess who.
DAD Oh, I see. And what time does it start?
GIRL Eight o'clock – and it finishes at midnight.
DAD Right. If you make sure you get your homework done by seven and get what's-his-name to bring you home the moment the thing finishes, you can go. But I want you back here by 12.15 at the latest, and no messing around going round to friends on the way, or whatever it is you lot get up to in the middle of the night. And you come right in and go to bed when you get home, is that clear? No hanging around at the door saying goodnight for hours on end.
GIRL OK, Dad. Thanks. (*Goes back to find Boy*)
BOY Well? What did your Dad say?
GIRL He says we can go as long as we come straight back at quarter past midnight – and as long as we behave ourselves.

In this commonplace verbal exchange, the girl gives ample evidence of having understood very precisely what her father has said. She does so, not by appropriate practical response, or by making the appropriate reply, but by a process of *interpreting* her father's words (including managing to read skilfully between the lines), and then *reporting the gist* of her father's intended message *in her own words*.

This twofold process is strongly reminiscent of translation proper. Extracting information (by way of comprehension and interpretation) from a given text, and then re-expressing the details of that information in another text using a different form of words is what translators do. We can even distinguish in the example between a ST (the words used by Dad) and a TT (the girl's reply to 'What did your Dad say?'). The only real difference between this example and translation proper is that both ST and TT are in English. We shall follow Jakobson in referring to the reporting or **rephrasing** of a text in the same language as **intralingual translation** (Jakobson, 1971, pp. 260–6).

Jakobson also talks of **inter-semiotic translation** (ibid.). This is another commonplace, everyday process, as can be shown in a banal example:

A What does that road sign say?
B It says 'end of speed limit'.

Of course, the road sign does not actually *say* anything: the words 'end of speed limit' are just a verbal rendering of a message conveyed by the device of a black oblique bar on a white circular field. Verbalizing this non-linguistic message is simply a way of *translating*, not from one language to another, but from a non-linguistic communication system (road signs) to a linguistic one. The common denominator between the two is that they are both 'semiotic systems' (that is, systems for communication), and Jakobson rightly calls the process inter-semiotic translation: something we do all the time without even thinking about it. This is another reason, then, for arguing that everybody is a translator of a sort.

Another common process of interpretation that bears a similarity to translation proper is an intra-linguistic process whereby one expands on a particular text and its contents. A good example would be an explanatory commentary on the Lord's Prayer, which might expand and expound the message contained in the single phrase 'Our Father' to read as follows:

> When we pray, we should not pray by ourselves and only ourselves; prayer should always be a corporate activity (compare 'Wherever two or three of you are gathered together ...'). This, we may say, is the significance of the word 'our': a first person plural inclusive pronoun.
>
> In using the word 'Father', Jesus is suggesting forcefully that one should think of God not as an abstraction, but as a person, and not as a distant, unapproachable one at that, but as a person having some of the attributes associated with a father-figure: head of the household, strict, caring, loving, provident, and so on.

This type of expository interpretation can, as here, easily develop into a full-scale textual exegesis that tries to analyse and explain the implications of a text (perhaps with the addition of cross-references, allusions, footnotes and so on). This process may not tally with everyone's view of translation, but it does share some common features with translation proper, especially with certain kinds of academic translation: both cases involve a ST which is subjected to interpretation, and a TT which is the result of a creative (extended and expository) reformulation of the ST.

The first and third examples above represent two extremes on a continuum of translation-like processes. At one end, the TT expresses only a condensed version of the ST message; we shall call this **gist translation**. At the other end, the TT is far more wordy than the ST, explaining and expanding it; we shall call this **exegetic translation**. Both gist translation and exegetic translation are, of course, matters of degree.

Half-way between these two extremes there is, in principle at least, a process that adds nothing to, and omits nothing from, the message content of the ST, while couching it in terms that are radically different from those of the ST. In *form of expression* ST and TT are quite different, but in *message content* they are as close to one another as possible. We shall call this ideal process **rephrasing**. Thus, we can say that 'Stop!' is a rephrasing of 'red traffic light', and 'yours truly consumed a small quantity of alcohol approximately sixty minutes ago' is a rephrasing of 'I had a little drink about an hour ago'.

The attainability of ideally precise rephrasing is a controversial question that will continue to occupy us in what follows. From the examples just cited, it is clear that precision is a relative matter. 'Stop!' is perhaps a successful inter-semiotic rephrasing of 'red traffic light' (but it omits the associations of danger and the law), while 'yours truly consumed a small quantity of alcohol' is a distinctly less exact (intralingual) rephrasing of 'I had a little drink'. These examples illustrate what is surely a fundamental maxim of translation, namely that rephrasing never allows a *precise reproduction* of the total message content of the ST, because of the very fact that the two forms of expression are different, and difference of form always entails a difference in communicative impact. We shall return to this in Chapter 2, in discussing the concept of translation loss.

So far, then, we have suggested that there are three basic types of translation-like process, defined according to the degree in which the TT abstracts from, adds to, or tries to reproduce faithfully, the details contained in the ST message.

It should be added that there are two important respects in which these three types of process are on an equal footing with one another, as well as with translation proper. First, they all require intelligence, mental effort and linguistic skill; there can be no substitute for a close knowledge of the subject matter and context of the ST, and a careful examination and analysis of its contents. Second, in all three cases, mastery of the TL is a prerequisite. It is salutary to remember that the majority of English mother-tongue applicants for translation posts in the European Commission fail *because of the poor quality of their English* (McCluskey, 1987, p. 17). In a translation course, TL competence needs as close attention as SL competence. There is, after all, not much point in people who do not have the skill to rephrase texts in their native language trying their hand at translation proper into their mother-tongue. Consequently, synopsis-writing, reported speech, intralingual rephrasing and exegesis are excellent exercises for a translator, because they develop technique in finding, and choosing between, alternative means of expressing a given message content. That is why the first practical exercise in this course is a piece of intralingual translation in English.

PRACTICAL 1

1.1 Intralingual translation

Assignment

(i) Assess the purpose of the text given below.
(ii) Recast the story in different words, adapting it for a specific purpose and a specific type of audience (define carefully what these are).
(iii) Discuss the textual changes you found it necessary to make, and the reasons for these alterations. (Do this by inserting into your TT a superscript note-

number after each point you intend to discuss, and then discussing the points in order on a fresh sheet of paper. Whenever you annotate your TT, this is the system you should use.)

Text

AND the whole earth was of one language, and of one speech.

And it came to pass, as they journeyed from the east, that they found a plain in the land of Shinar; and they dwelt there.

And they said one to another, Go to, let us make brick, and burn them throughly. And they had brick for stone, and slime had they for morter.

And they said, Go to, let us build us a city and a tower, whose top may reach unto heaven; and let us make us a name, lest we be scattered abroad upon the face of the whole earth.

And the LORD came down to see the city and the tower, which the children of men builded.

And the LORD said, Behold, the people is one, and they have all one language; and this they begin to do: and now nothing will be restrained from them, which they have imagined to do.

Go to, let us go down, and there confound their language, that they may not understand one another's speech.

So the LORD scattered them abroad from thence upon the face of all the earth: and they left off to build the city.

Therefore is the name of it called Babel; because the LORD did there confound the language of all the earth: and from thence did the LORD scatter them abroad upon the face of all the earth.

(Genesis 11, v. 1–9. Extracts from the Authorized Version of the Bible (The King James Bible), the rights in which are vested in the Crown, are reproduced by permission of the Crown's Patentee, Cambridge University Press.)

1.2 Gist translation

Assignment

You will be asked to produce a gist translation of a passage given to you in class by your tutor. The tutor will give you any necessary contextual information, and tell you how long you should take over the translation.

2

Preliminaries to translation as a product

As we saw in Chapter 1, translation can be viewed as a process. It can, however, also be viewed as a product: and that is how we shall look at it in this chapter. Here, too, it is useful to start by examining two diametric opposites, in this case two opposed types of translation, one showing extreme SL bias, the other extreme TL bias.

At the extreme of SL bias is **interlineal translation**, where the TT attempts to respect the details of SL grammar by having grammatical units corresponding point for point to every grammatical unit of the ST. Interlineal translation is rare and exists only to fulfil specialized purposes in, say, language teaching, descriptive linguistics or in certain kinds of ethnographic transcript. Since it is of little practical use to us, we shall not, in fact, give it much consideration, other than to note its position as the furthest degree of SL bias. Interlineal translation is actually an extreme form of the much more common **literal translation**, where the literal meaning of words is taken as if from the dictionary (that is, out of context), but TL grammar is respected. (Literal meaning will be discussed as a topic in Chapter 7.) For our purposes, we shall take literal translation as the practical extreme of SL bias.

At the extreme of TL bias is completely **free translation**, where there is only a global correspondence between the textual units of the ST and those of the TT. The following example contrasts a literal and a free translation of a stock conversation in Chinese between two people who have just been introduced:

	Literal TT		Free TT
A	Sir, are you well?	A	How do you do?
B	Are you well?	B	Pleased to meet you.
A	Sir comes from where?	A	Do you come here often?
B	I come from England.	B	No, this is my first visit.
A	How many persons in your family?	A	Nice weather for the time of year.

Literal TT	Free TT
B Wife and five children. And you?	B Yes, it's been quite warm lately.

The type of extreme freedom seen in the second version is known as **communicative translation**, which is characterized as follows: where, in a given situation (like introducing oneself to a stranger), the ST uses a SL expression standard for that situation, the TT uses a TL expression standard for an analogous target culture situation. This degree of freedom is no more to be recommended as general practice than interlineal translation. (Translators have to use their own judgement about when communicative translation is appropriate.) Communicative translation is, however, mandatory for many culturally conventional formulas that do not allow literal translation. Public notices, proverbs and conversational clichés illustrate this particularly clearly, as in:

Prohibido el paso.	No entry.
Antes que te cases, mira lo que haces.	Marry in haste, repent at leisure.
¿Qué hay?	How's it going?

For further examples, see p. 24 below.

Between the two extremes of literal and free translation, one may imagine an infinite number of degrees, including some sort of a compromise or ideal half-way point between the two. Whether this ideal is actually attainable is the question that lies behind our discussion of 'equivalence' and 'translation loss' below. For the moment, we simply suggest that translations can be usefully judged on a parameter between the two polarities of extreme SL bias and extreme TL bias. Five points on this parameter are schematized in the following diagram adapted from Newmark (1982, p. 39):

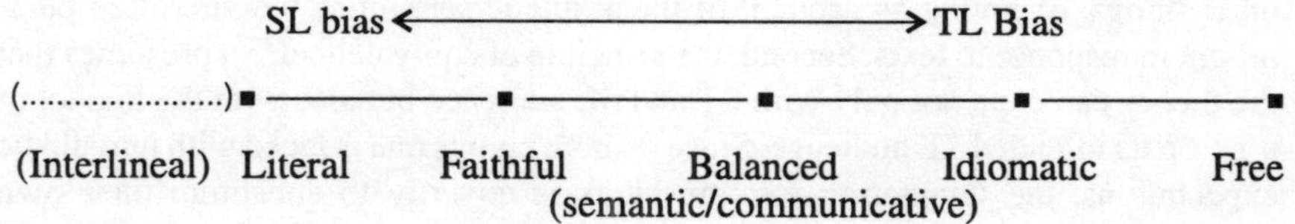

Between the literal and free extremes, the Chinese conversation given above might be rendered at the three intermediate points as follows:

Faithful TT	Balanced TT (semantic/communicative)	Idiomatic TT
A Are you well, Sir?	A How do you do?	A Hello.
B Are you well?	B How do you do?	B Hi.
A Where do you come from?	A Where are you from?	A Where are you from, then?

	Faithful TT		Balanced TT		Idiomatic TT
B	I come from England.	B	England.	B	I'm English.
A	How big a family do you have?	A	Have you any family?	A	Got a family?
B	A wife and five children. And yourself?	B	Yes, a wife and five children. Have you?	B	Wife and five kids. How about you?

EQUIVALENCE

In characterizing communicative translation, we used the term 'analogous target culture situation'. Before going any further, we should make it clear what we mean – or rather, what we do not mean – by the terms 'equivalent' and 'equivalence'.

The literature on translation studies has generated a great deal of discussion of what is generally known as *the principle of equivalent effect*.

In so far as 'equivalence' is taken as a synonym of 'sameness' (which is often the case), the concept runs into serious philosophical objections, which we will not go into here (for a good recent discussion see, for example, Snell-Hornby, 1988). The claim that ST and TT effects and features are 'equivalent' in the sense of 'the same' is in any case unhelpful and misleading for the purposes of translation methodology, for two main reasons.

First, the requirement that the TT should affect its recipients in the same way as the ST does (or did) its original audience raises the difficult problem of how any one particular recipient responds to a text, and of the extent to which texts have constant interpretations even for the same person on two different occasions. Before one could objectively assess textual effects, one would need to have recourse to a fairly detailed and exact theory of psychological effect, a theory capable, among other things, of giving an account of the aesthetic sensations that are often paramount in response to texts. Second, the principle of equivalent effect presumes that the theory can cope not only with ST and SL audience but also with the impact of a TT on its intended TL audience. Since on both counts one is faced with unrealistic expectations, the temptation for translators is covertly to substitute their own subjective interpretation for the effects of the ST on recipients in general, and also for the anticipated impact of the TT on its intended audience.

It seems obvious, then, that if good translation is defined in terms of 'equivalence', this is not an *objective* equivalence, because the translator remains ultimately the only arbiter of the imagined effects of both the ST and the TT. Under these circumstances, even a relatively objective assessment of 'equivalent effect' is hard to envisage.

More fundamentally still, unlike intralingual translation, translation proper has the task of bridging the cultural gap between monolingual speakers of different languages. The backgrounds, shared knowledge, cultural assumptions and learnt responses of monolingual TL speakers are inevitably culture-bound. Given this fact, SL speakers' responses to the ST are never likely to be replicated exactly by effects on members of a different culture. The notion of cross-cultural 'sameness' of psychological effect is a hopeless ideal. Even a small cultural distance between the ST audience and the TT audience is bound to produce *fundamental* dissimilarity between the effects of the ST and those of the TT – such effects can at best be vaguely similar in a global and limited sense; they can never be 'the same'.

To take a simple example: a translator who decides that the effect of a given ST is to make its audience laugh can replicate that effect by producing a TT that makes its audience laugh. However, claiming 'sameness' of effect in this instance would only be at the expense of a gross reduction of the effects of a text to a single effect. In fact, of course, few texts can be attributed such a monolithic singleness of purpose, and as soon as a ST is acknowledged to have multiple effects, it is unlikely that the TT will be able to replicate them all. (In any case, humour itself is a highly culture-bound phenomenon, which means that even the genuine cross-cultural equivalence of laughter is questionable.)

Another point one must query about the principle of objective equivalent effect concerns the requirement that the TT should replicate the effects of the ST on its *original* audience. This might conceivably be possible for a contemporary ST, but for a work of any appreciable age it may not be feasible or even desirable. It may not be possible for the translator to determine how audiences responded to the ST when it was first produced. But even if one assumes that such effects can be determined through historical research, one is still faced with a dilemma: should the effects of the TT be matched to those of the ST on its *original* audience, or on a present-day audience? The extract from Teresa de Jesús's *Su vida* used in Practical 7 is a good example of these problems. Even if it were translated into early modern English, could one ever know if the TT would produce the same effects on an English-speaking readership in the 1990s as the ST did on its contemporary Spanish readers? The choice between modernizing a TT or making it archaic is fraught with difficulties whatever one decides: on the one hand, the TT may be rendered trivial without the effects it produced on its original audience; on the other, the original cultural impact of the ST may even be incomprehensible, or unpalatable, to a modern TL audience. For example, in the case of Fernando de Rojas's *Tragicomedia de Calisto y Melibea*, many people in his contemporary audience would have appreciated the rhetoric in Pleberio's lament for its own sake, as well as the ideas and feelings expressed; but today, few readers in Spain – or in Britain – have enough knowledge of rhetoric to be able to appreciate it as Rojas's original audiences must have done.

In short, we find the principle of equivalent effect, in so far as it implies 'sameness', too vague to be useful in a methodology of translation. At best, a good TT produces a carefully fabricated approximation to some of the manifest properties of the ST. This means that a sound attitude to translation methodology should avoid an absolutist attempt at *maximizing sameness* in things that are crucially different (ST and TT), in favour of a relativist attempt at *minimizing relevant dissimilarities* between things that are clearly understood to be different. Once the latter approach is accepted, there is no objection to using the term 'equivalence' as a shorthand for 'not dissimilar in certain relevant respects'. It is in this everyday sense of the word that we use it in this book.

TRANSLATION LOSS

Our position is best explained in terms of an analogy with engineering. All engineering is based on the premise that the transfer of energy in any mechanical device is necessarily subject to a certain degree of 'energy loss'. A machine that permits energy loss is not a theoretical anomaly in engineering: engineers are not puzzled as to why they have not achieved perpetual motion, and their attention is directed, instead, at trying to design machines with increased efficiency, by reducing energy loss. By analogy, believing in translation equivalence in the sense of 'sameness' encourages translators to believe in the elusive concept of a perfect translation, representing an ideal mean between SL bias and TL bias. But it is far more realistic to start by admitting that the transfer of meaning from ST to TT is necessarily subject to a certain degree of **translation loss**; that is, a TT will always lack certain culturally relevant features that are present in the ST. The analogy with energy loss is, of course, imperfect. While energy loss is a loss *of* energy, translation loss is not a loss *of* translation, but of exact ST-TT correspondence *in* (the process of) translation. Similarly, the very factors that make it impossible to achieve 'sameness' in translation also make it impossible to measure translation loss absolutely and objectively. Nevertheless, once one accepts the concept of inevitable translation loss, a TT that is not a replica of its ST is no longer seen as a theoretical anomaly, and the translator can concentrate on the realistic aim of reducing translation loss, rather than on the unrealistic one of seeking *the* definitive translation of the ST.

It is important to note that translation loss embraces *any* failure to replicate a ST exactly, whether this involves *losing* features in the TT or *adding* them. Our concept of translation loss is, therefore, not opposed to a concept of translation *gain*; where the TT gains features not present in the ST, this is a form of translation loss. For example, in rendering 'brasero' as 'electric element heater', an obvious translation loss is that the TT lacks the concision of the ST, as well as its cultural specificity (even though there is a gain in explicitness); but rendering 'electric element heater' by 'brasero' entails an equally obvious translation loss, in that the TT does not have the explicitness of the ST (even though there is a gain in concision and vividness, as well as cultural appropriateness). Similarly, translating 'tuerto' as 'blind in one eye' is an instance of translation loss, even though the TT is not only literally exact, but has 'gained' several words *and* makes explicit reference to blindness and to eyes. A third example exhibits still more sorts of translation loss: the translation of 'capital transfer tax' by 'impuesto sobre plusvalía de cesión'. The English is more concise, but its grammar is a potential source of ambiguity for the unwary; for instance, is this a transfer tax that is capital, or a tax that is a capital transfer, or a tax on transfers that are capital, or a tax on the transfer of capital? The grammar of the Spanish expression eliminates all such ambiguity, but it is more cumbersome than the English. As these three examples show, translation loss, in the way we have defined it, is inevitable, even where the TT gains in, say, economy, vividness, cultural specificity or avoidance of ambiguity. The challenge to the translator is, therefore, not to eliminate translation loss altogether, but to reduce it by deciding which of the relevant features in the ST it is most important to respect, and which can most legitimately be sacrificed in doing so.

For all translators, but particularly for students, there are two great advantages in the notion that translation loss is inevitable, and that a so-called gain is actually a loss. First, they are relieved of the inhibiting, demoralizing supposition that, if only they were clever enough or lucky enough to find it, the perfect TT is just round the corner; and, second, they are less tempted to try crudely to *outweigh* losses in their TT with a greater volume of gains.

Our approach assumes, then, that the translator's ambition is not an absolutist one to maximize sameness, but a relativist one to minimize difference: to look, not for what one is to put into the TT, but for what one might save from the ST, and therefore to forget the mirage of gain and to concentrate instead of the real benefits of compensation. (We shall discuss compensation in the next chapter.) Once this approach is adopted, the culturally relevant features in the ST will tend to present themselves to the translator in a certain hierarchical order. The most immediately obvious features which may prove impossible to preserve in a TT are 'cultural' in a very general sense, arising from the simple fact of transferring messages from one culture to another – references or allusions to the source culture's history, geography, literature, folklore and so on. We shall, therefore, discuss such issues in the next chapter. The second step will be to analyse the objectively ostensible formal properties of the ST – syntax, lexis and so on; we shall suggest a systematic framework for discussing these properties in Chapters 4–6. Subsequent ST features which will inevitably be lacking, or changed, in any TT will have to do with nuances of literal or connotative meaning; yet others will stem from such aspects of language variety as dialect, sociolect and register. We shall be discussing literal and connotative meaning in Chapters 7 and 8 respectively, and questions of language variety in Chapters 9 and 10.

PRACTICAL 2

2.1 Strategic decisions and decisions of detail; translation loss

Assignment

(i) Discuss the strategic problems confronting the translator of the following text, and outline your own strategy for translating it.
(ii) Translate the text into English.

(iii) Explain the significant decisions of detail you made in producing your TT, paying special attention to the question of translation loss.

Contextual information

The passage is from Julio Cortázar's short story 'Estación de la mano' (1967). (Students are advised to investigate the context of the full text before translating the passage.)

Text

Le puse nombres: me gustaba llamarla Dg, porque era un nombre que sólo se dejaba pensar. Incité su probable vanidad olvidando anillos y brazaletes sobre las repisas, espiando su actitud con secreta constancia. Alguna vez creí que se adornaría con las joyas, pero ella las estudiaba dando vueltas en torno y sin tocarlas, a semejanza de una araña desconfiada; y aunque un día llegó a ponerse un anillo de amatista fue sólo por un instante, y lo abandonó como si le quemara. Me apresuré entonces a esconder las joyas en su ausencia y desde entonces me pareció que estaba más contenta.

Así declinaron las estaciones, unas esbeltas y otras con semanas teñidas de luces violetas, sin que sus llamadas premiosas llegaran hasta nuestro ámbito. Todas las tardes volvía la mano, mojada con frecuencia por las lluvias otoñales, y la veía tenderse de espaldas sobre la alfombra, secarse prolijamente un dedo con otro, a veces con menudos saltos de cosa satisfecha. En los atardeceres de frío su sombra se teñía de violeta. Yo encendía entonces un brasero a mis pies y ella se acurrucaba y apenas bullía, salvo para recibir, displicente, un álbum con grabados o un ovillo de lana que le gustaba anudar y retorcer. Era incapaz, lo advertí pronto, de estarse largo rato quieta. Un día encontró una artesa con arcilla y se precipitó sobre ella; horas y horas modeló la arcilla mientras yo, de espaldas, fingía no preocuparme por su tarea. Naturalmente, modeló una mano. La dejé secar y la puse sobre el escritorio para probarle que su obra me agradaba. Era un error: a Dg terminó por molestarle la contemplación de ese autorretrato rígido y algo convulso. Cuando lo escondí, fingió por pudor no haberlo advertido.

Mi interés se tornó bien pronto analítico. Cansado de maravillarme, quise saber, invariable y funesto fin de toda aventura. Surgían las preguntas acerca de mi huésped: ¿Vegetaba, sentía, comprendía, amaba? Tendí lazos, apronté experimentos. Había advertido que la mano, aunque capaz de leer, jamás escribía. Una tarde abrí la ventana y puse sobre la mesa un lapicero, cuartillas en blanco y cuando entró Dg me marché para no pesar sobre su timidez. Por el ojo de la cerradura la vi cumplir sus paseos habituales; luego, vacilante, fue hasta el escritorio y tomó el lapicero. Oí el arañar de la pluma, y después de un tiempo ansioso entré en el estudio. En diagonal y con letra perfilada, Dg había escrito: *Esta resolución anula todas las anteriores hasta nueva orden*. Jamás pude lograr que volviese a escribir.

2.2 Speed translation

Assignment

You will be asked to produce a 125-word article in English based on a 166-word Spanish ST given to you in class by your tutor. The tutor will tell you how long you have for the exercise. This assignment combines an element of gist translation with an introduction to one of the main demands made of professional translators: working under pressure and at speed.

3

Cultural issues in translation; compromise and compensation

The first part of this chapter brings together a number of issues directly connected with the fact that translation proper involves not just a transfer of information between two languages, but a transfer from one culture to another. The second part looks at two related translation techniques necessitated by the translation loss attendant on the transfer from one cultural mode of expression to another: compromise and compensation.

CULTURAL TRANSPOSITION

We shall use the term **cultural transposition** as a cover-term for any degree of departure from purely literal, word-for-word translation that a translator may resort to in an attempt to transfer the contents of a ST into the context of a target culture. That is to say, the various kinds of cultural transposition we are about to discuss are all alternatives to a strictly SL-biased literal translation. Any degree of cultural transposition involves, therefore, the choice of features indigenous to the TL and the target culture in preference to features rooted in the source culture. The result is the minimizing of 'foreign', that is to say markedly SL-specific, features in the TT. By suppressing reminders of its SL origins, the TT is to some extent 'naturalized' into the TL and its cultural setting.

The various degrees of cultural transposition can be visualized as points along a scale between the extremes of **exoticism** and **cultural transplantation**:

Exoticism	Cultural borrowing	Calque	Communicative translation	Cultural transplantation

Some of the most straightforward examples of the basic issues involved in cultural transposition are offered by place-names and proper names. Translating names is not usually a major concern, and certainly does not pose great difficulties for translators, but a brief look at the question will provide a simple introduction to what are often complex problems.

Translating names

In translating a name there are, in principle, at least two alternatives. Either the name can be taken over unchanged from the ST to the TT, or it can be adapted to conform to the phonic/graphic conventions of the TL. The first alternative is tantamount to literal translation, and involves no cultural transposition. It is a form of 'exoticism' in the sense that the foreign name stands out in the TT as a signal of extra-cultural origins. This alternative may be impracticable if, as with Chinese or Russian names, it creates problems of pronounceability and comprehension in an oral TT, or problems of spelling, printing and memorization in a written one. The second alternative, **transliteration**, is less extreme: conversional conventions are used to alter the phonic/graphic shape of the ST name bringing it more in line with TL patterns of pronunciation and spelling. The result is that the transliterated name stands out less clearly as a reminder of foreign and culturally strange elements in the TT. Transliteration is the standard way of coping with, for example, Chinese or Arabic names in English texts.

How a name is transliterated may be entirely up to the translator, if there is no established precedent for transcribing the name in question and no strictly laid down system of transliterational conventions. Alternatively, it may be a matter of using a standard transliteration created by earlier translators. Standard transliterations vary, of course, from language to language. Examples are common in the translation of place-names: 'Zaragoza/Saragossa'; 'Córdoba/Cordova'; 'MOCKBA/Moscow/Moscú'; 'Bruxelles/Brussel/Brussels/Bruselas', and so on.

Some names are not normally transliterated, but have instead standard indigenous communicative equivalents in the TL. For example, Flemish 'Luik' = French 'Liège' = German 'Lüttich'; German 'Aachen' = French 'Aix-la-Chapelle' = Spanish 'Aquisgrán'; Spanish 'San Esteban' = English 'St Stephen' = Hungarian 'Szent István'. Where such conventional communicative equivalents exist, the translator may feel constrained to use them. Not to do so would either display ignorance, or be interpreted as a significant stylistic choice. As an example of the latter, deliberately using 'España' instead of 'Spain' in an English TT (for instance, of a popular song) would be a form of exoticism, a stylistic device for enhancing the Spanishness of the text.

For some names, particularly place-names, a standard TL equivalent may exist in the form of a **calque**. Here the structure of the TL name imitates that of the SL name, but grammatical slots in it are filled with TL units translating the individual meaningful units of the SL name. For example, 'la Casa Blanca' is a standard calque translation of 'the White House'. In the absence of a standard calque translation, the option of *creating* a calque may sometimes be open to the translator. For example, in principle at least, in an English translation of a tourist brochure for the 'Costa del Sol', the name might plausibly be rendered as 'Coast of the Sun'. However, calque translations of names must be used with care in order not to sound stilted; for example, the calque element through which, in a Colombian tourist brochure, 'Colombia: país de Eldorado' has been rendered as 'Colombia: the country of Eldorado' would be more consistently and idiomatically rendered as 'Colombia: the Land of Eldorado'.

A further alternative in translating names is cultural transplantation. This is the extreme degree of cultural transposition. SL names are replaced by indigenous TL names that are not their referential equivalents, but have similar cultural connotations. Thus, for instance, where in a Spanish ST someone is referred to as 'don Fulano', the corresponding English TT might usefully refer to 'Joe Bloggs' or 'Mr Average' in a British context, or to 'John Doe' in an American one. Taking a different kind of example, careful consideration would need to be given in an English TT of Rosa Montero's *Te trataré como a una reina* (1983) to the translation of 'Isabel López', chosen as a stereotypical name for a bolero singer in a nightclub, as well as of 'Antonio and Antonia Ortiz' used for comic effect as stereotypical names for a civil servant and his sister. Should, for instance, 'Isabel López' become, by cultural transplantation, 'Liza Johnson', and 'Antonio and Antonia Ortiz' be transformed into 'Julian and Julia Smythe'? These solutions would allow some of the stereotyping, and comic effect, to be preserved in the TT, at the expense of the characters' inherent Spanishness. The examples show clearly why cultural transplantation of names is such a risky option. For example, if 'Liza Johnson' continued to be nicknamed as 'La Bella' (as she is in the ST), and if Julian Smythe were portrayed as having lived all his life in Madrid, or as a keen *aficionado* of bullfighting, the effect would be incongruous.

When translating names, one must, therefore, be aware of three things: first, the full range of possible options for translating a particular name; second, the implications of following a particular option (for example, if 'Low Dung Fang' were a character in a novel written in Chinese, an English translator might want to alter the name sufficiently to avoid its undesirable connotations); and third, all the implications of a choice between exoticism, transliteration, communicative translation and cultural transplantation.

We will now look at issues raised by the various degrees of cultural transposition in more complex units than names.

Exoticism

In general, the extreme options in signalling cultural foreignness in a TT fall into the category of exoticism. A TT translated in a deliberately exotic manner is one which constantly resorts to linguistic and cultural features imported from the ST into the TT with minimal adaptation, and which contains constant reminders of the exotic source culture and its cultural strangeness. Of course, this may be one of the TT's chief attractions, as with some translations of Icelandic sagas or Arabic poetry that deliberately trade on exoticism. However, such a TT has an impact on TL audiences which the ST could never have on a SL audience, for whom the text has none of the features of an alien culture. As a strategic option, exoticism needs to be carefully handled: there is always a danger that audiences will find the TT's eccentricities more irritating than charming. Furthermore, if a culturally distant exotic TT is to be understood, many of the terms used in it may need to be explained; yet the constant intrusion of glosses, footnotes and academic explanations of exotic features in a TT is likely to reduce its attractiveness. This may present a serious dilemma for the translator.

Cultural transplantation

At the opposite end of the scale from exoticism is cultural transplantation, whose extreme forms are hardly to be recognized as translations at all, but are more like adaptations – the wholesale transplanting of the entire setting of the ST, resulting in the text being completely reinvented in an indigenous target culture setting. Examples include *Carmen Jones*, the American version of Bizet's *Carmen* – which in turn is a reworking of Mérimée's novelette of the same title – and Saura's film adaptation of *Carmen* into a Spanish flamenco setting. Another well-known, and extreme, example is the transplantation of Rostand's *Cyrano de Bergerac* into the film *Roxanne*. These are not different in kind from the intralingual adaptation of *Romeo and Juliet* into the musical *West Side Story*, or of Shaw's *Pygmalion* into *My Fair Lady*. Examples involving Spanish texts include the musical *Man of the Mancha* based on *Don Quixote* and Lou Stein's *Salsa Celestina* (1993), which re-enacts Rojas's tragicomedy in a modern Cuban nightclub setting. As these examples show, cultural transplantation on this scale can produce highly successful texts, but it is not normal translation practice. However, on certain points of detail – as long as they do not have knock-on effects that make the TT incongruous – cultural transplantation may be considered as a serious option.

By and large, normal, middle-of-the-road translation practice avoids both wholesale exoticism and wholesale cultural transplantation. In attempting to avoid the two extremes, the translator may have to consider the alternatives lying between them on the scale given on p. 20.

Cultural borrowing

The first alternative is to transfer a ST expression verbatim into the TT. This process is termed **cultural borrowing**. The translator resorts to it when it proves impossible to find a suitable indigenous expression in the TL for translating the ST expression. 'Guerilla' is an example: first attested in English in 1809, it is defined in the OED as 'one engaged in irregular warfare carried on by small bodies of men acting independently'.

A vital condition for the success of cultural borrowing in a TT is that the textual context of the TT should make the meaning of the borrowed expression clear.

Cultural borrowing will be most frequent in texts on history, or philosophy, or on social, political or anthropological matters, where the simplest solution is to give a definition of terms like 'glasnost', 'perestroika', 'mesnada', 'tapas', 'estoque', 'picador' or 'mestizo', and then to use the original SL word in the TT.

Of course, cultural borrowing only presents translators with an open and free choice in cases where previous translation practice has not already set up a precedent for the verbatim borrowing of the ST expression. The Saussurean linguistic terms 'langue' and 'parole' are good examples of this issue. The option of translating 'langue' and 'parole' as 'language' and 'speaking' does exist, but the fact that specialist English texts frequently resort to the borrowed terms 'langue' and 'parole' in the precise linguistic sense prejudices the issue in favour of borrowing. Furthermore, where terms with SL origins have already passed into common usage in the TL without significant change of meaning, thus constituting standard conventional equivalents of the original SL terms borrowed, the translator may not be faced with a significant decision at all. So, for example, such expressions as 'hacienda', 'pueblo', '*joie de vivre*', '*savoir-faire*', 'flamenco', 'kindergarten', 'schnapps', 'bonsai', 'totem' or 'taboo' can be treated as standard conventional equivalents of the corresponding foreign expressions from which they originate. Unless special considerations of style can be invoked, there is little reason not to render such terms verbatim in an English TT. On occasion it may even seem perverse not to do so.

Communicative translation

In contrast with cultural borrowing, the translator may opt for communicative translation. As we saw briefly in Chapter 2 (p. 13), this is often mandatory for culturally conventional formulas where a literal rendering would be inappropriate.

For example, many proverbs, idioms and clichés have readily identifiable communicative equivalents in the TL. Only special contextual reasons can justify opting against a standard communicative translation in such cases. Otherwise the result is likely to be a piece of ludicrous translationese, as in the deliberately comic rendering '¡Bondad graciosa!' in *Asterix en Bretaña* (Goscinny and Uderzo, 1967, *passim*) calqued on 'Bonté gracieuse!' (in *Astérix chez les Bretons* (Goscinny and Uderzo, 1966, *passim*)), which is, in turn, calqued on English 'Goodness gracious'. The translator has virtually no freedom of choice in rendering stock institutionalized phrases like the following: 'Prohibido el paso/No entry/Kein Eintritt'; 'Rebajas/Sale/Soldes'; 'Sentido único/One way/Sens unique'; 'Compraventa/Second hand'; 'gravamen/encumbrance, lien'. Similarly, only for reasons of blatant exoticism, or (again) for special contextual reasons, could one avoid a communicative translation of 'charlar por los codos' as 'talk one's head off', or of 'tonto del bote' as something like 'thick as two planks', 'crazy as a coot' or 'daft as a brush'. The very fact that the ST uses a set phrase or idiom is usually part and parcel of its stylistic effect, and if the TT does not use corresponding TL set phrases or idioms this stylistic effect will be lost.

However, it often happens that set phrases in the ST do not have readily identifiable communicative TL equivalents. In such cases, the translator has a genuine choice between a literal rendering and some kind of attempt at communicative translation. Assuming that a communicative translation is strategically appropriate in the context, it can only be achieved by rendering the situational impact of the ST phrase in question with a TT expression that, while not a cliché, is nevertheless plausible in the context defined by the TT. An example of this choice and its implications can be drawn from translating a Hungarian ST into English. (We choose Hungarian because it is unfamiliar to most readers, and therefore capable of giving a genuinely exotic impression.) Waking on the first morning of the holiday, the children are disappointed to find that it is raining heavily. Their mother comforts them with a proverb, suggesting that it will soon clear up: 'Nem baj! Reggeli vendég nem maradandó.' Compare these three translations of her words:

Literal 'No problem! The morning guest never stays long.'

Communicative equivalent 'Never mind! Sun before seven, rain before eleven.'

Communicative paraphrase 'Never mind! It'll soon stop raining.'

The only possible advantage of the literal translation is its exoticism, but this advantage is cancelled by two things: the obscurity of the TT, and its lack of contextual plausibility. If there were good reasons for preserving the exoticism, one could mitigate these disadvantages by obliquely signalling in the TT that the mother is using what is, for TL readers, an exotic proverb: 'Never mind! You know the saying: the morning guest never stays long.'

The communicative equivalent has the advantage of rendering proverb for proverb. However, in the circumstances, the communicative equivalent is incongruous – what the narrative context requires is 'rain before seven, sun before eleven', but this is not a universally recognized form of the English proverb.

The communicative paraphrase has the advantage of being idiomatic and plausible in the TT – it is the kind of thing the children's mother might plausibly say in English in the situation. It has the disadvantage of losing the stylistic flavour of 'speaking in proverbs' (which might be an important feature of the way the mother speaks).

Which solution is deemed best will naturally depend on contextual factors outside the scope of this example. Nevertheless, the example illustrates very well the alternatives in cultural transposition, including the one we have yet to discuss, namely calque.

Calque

'The morning guest never stays long' is a calque, an expression that consists of TL words and respects TL syntax, but is unidiomatic in the TL because it is modelled on the structure of a SL expression. In essence, then, calque is a form of literal translation. A bad calque imitates ST structure to the point of being ungrammatical in the TL; a good calque manages to compromise between imitating a ST structure and not offending against the grammar of the TL.

Calquing may also be seen as a form of cultural borrowing, although, instead of verbatim borrowing of expressions, only the model of SL grammatical structures is borrowed. For example, if ST 'Santa Teresa del Niño Jesús' is rendered in the TT as '*Santa Teresa del Niño Jesús*', this is cultural borrowing proper, whereas TT 'Saint Teresa of the Child Jesus' is a calque. Like cultural borrowing proper, and for similar reasons, translation by creating calques does occur in practice. Furthermore, as also happens with cultural borrowing proper, some originally calqued expressions become standard TL cultural equivalents of their SL originals. Examples are Spanish 'peso mosca' calqued on English 'flyweight'; English 'world-view', calqued on German 'Weltanschauung' (also existing as a verbatim borrowing); Spanish 'jardín de infancia', calqued on French 'jardin d'enfants' (in turn calqued on German 'Kindergarten') and American English 'ants in the pants' calqued (by popular etymology) on German 'Angst in den Hosen'.

Clearly, there are certain dangers in using calque as a translation device. The major one is that the meaning of calqued phrases may not be clear in the TT. In the worst cases, calques are not even recognizable for what they are, but are merely puzzling bits of gibberish for the reader or listener. This is why, in our Hungarian example, we suggested using a device like 'you know the saying' as a means of signalling the calquing process in the TT. But, of course, it is not sufficient for the TT to make it clear that a particular phrase is an intentional calque. The meaning of the calqued phrase must also be transparent in the TT context. The most successful calques need no explanation; less successful ones may need to be explained, perhaps in a footnote or a glossary.

Like all forms of cross-cultural borrowing, calque exhibits a certain degree of exoticism, bringing into the TT a flavour of the cultural foreignness and strangeness of the source culture. Consequently, it should generally be avoided in texts where exoticism is strategically inappropriate, such as an instruction manual, whose prime function is to give clear and explicit information. In any text, one should also definitely avoid unintentional calquing resulting from too slavish a simulation of the grammatical structures of the ST. At best, such calques will give the TT an unidiomatic flavour as in 'Very sure you have read *One Hundred Years of Solitude*, that famous novel by the Colombian García Márquez', calqued on 'Seguramente usted leyó *Cien años de soledad*, aquella novela tan famosa del colombiano García Márquez'. At worst, the TT may become ungrammatical to the point of gibberish, as in 'where girls fly and the deads keep on tied up to the trees or stroll through the old mansions' calqued on 'donde las muchachas vuelan y los muertos permanecen atados a los árboles o deambulan por las casonas'. (These examples are from a Colombian tourist brochure.)

In brief summary of the discussion so far: where standard communicative equivalents exist for a ST expression, the translator should give these first preference, and only reject them if there are particular reasons for doing so. Where standard communicative equivalents are lacking, and also a particular ST concept is alien to the target culture, preference should be given to cultural borrowing, *unless* there are particular reasons against it.

The emphasis in the preceding paragraph on solutions being preferable unless certain conditions militate against them draws attention to the need to balance one set of considerations against another. This is, indeed, a general feature of the translation process, and remarking on it in the context of a choice between literal translation, communicative translation, cultural transplantation and so on brings us to a discussion of compromises made necessary by this feature.

COMPROMISE AND COMPENSATION

Throughout this course, it will be obvious that translation is fraught with compromise. Compromise in translation means reconciling oneself to the fact that, while one would like to do full justice to the 'richness' of the ST, one's final TT inevitably suffers from various translation losses. Often one allows these losses unhesitatingly. For instance, a translator of prose (particularly in the commercial sector) may without any qualms sacrifice the phonic and prosodic properties of a ST in order to make its literal meaning perfectly clear, while a translator of verse (for instance, song lyrics) may equally happily sacrifice much of the ST's literal meaning in order to achieve certain desired metric and phonic effects. These are just two examples of the many kinds of compromise translators make every day.

Compromises should be the result of deliberate decisions taken in the light not only of what latitudes are allowed by the SL and TL respectively, but also of all the factors that can play a determining role in translation: the nature of the ST, its relationship to SL audiences, the purpose of the TT, its putative audience, and so forth. Only then can the translator have a firm grasp of which aspects of the ST can be sacrificed with the least detriment to the effectiveness of the TT, both as a rendering of the ST and as a TL text in its own right. Much of the material in this book will in fact draw attention, in both principle and practice, to the different kinds of compromise suggested – perhaps even dictated – by different types of text.

The issue of undesirable, yet inevitable, translation losses raises a special problem for the translator. The problem consists in knowing that the loss of certain features sacrificed in translation does have detrimental effects on the quality of the TT, but seeing no way of avoiding these unacceptable compromises. So, for instance, 'sword' is admittedly far from being an exact translation of the literal meaning of 'estoque'; it lacks the association with the weapon's ceremonial use in bullfighting which is so much part of the meaning of the word. Nevertheless, translating 'estoque' as 'sword' may be an acceptable compromise if the ST merely makes casual mention of it. However, this is less acceptable in, say, an anthropological text examining the aesthetic and ideological aspects of the bullfight; and such a compromise is quite unacceptable if 'estoque' is the sole means by which the cultural context of bullfighting is evoked in the ST.

It is when faced with apparently inevitable, yet unacceptable, compromises that translators may feel the need to resort to techniques referred to as **compensation** – that is, techniques of making up for the loss of important ST features through replicating ST effects approximately in the TT by means other than those used in the ST. For methodological purposes it is useful to distinguish four different aspects of compensation (while remembering that these aspects frequently occur together).

Compensation in kind

The first aspect we shall call **compensation in kind**. This refers to making up for one type of textual effect in the ST by another type in the TT. One area where compensation in kind is often needed is in the differences between 'gender' in Spanish and English. The contrast in Spanish between masculine and feminine forms of the definite article is one that frequently causes problems. The definite article in English does not permit the expressive power that a Spanish ST may derive from the contrast between feminine and masculine gender. Thus, the opening sentence of Dora Alonso's short story 'Los gatos' (Alonso, 1980, pp. 133–4), 'La gata dilataba las pupilas en la oscuridad' – which, if encountered in a gender-neutral text might harmlessly be rendered as 'The cat's eyes grew large/dilated in the darkness' – would almost certainly not be adequately translated without some reference to female gender in the context of this feminist ST. As 'The cat's eyes grew large/dilated in the darkness' cannot create the gender-based link between feline motherhood and human motherhood which is such a crucial motif of the ST, this option represents an unacceptable translation loss. One way of overcoming this loss might be to compensate in kind, by translating 'La gata dilataba las pupilas en la oscuridad' as ' The pupils of the *she-cat* grew large/dilated in the darkness' (but 'she-cat' might be perceived as translationese), or even as 'The *mother* cat's pupils grew large/dilated in the darkness'. Alternatively, mention of feminine gender may have to be delayed to a subsequent sentence in the TT where it can be signalled by anaphoric 'she'.

Compensation in kind can be further illustrated by three of its most typical forms. First, explicit meanings in the ST may be compensated for by implicit meanings in the TT. In the following example from poem LXXVII of Machado's *Soledades, galerías y otros poemas* (1903), the Predmore version (Machado, 1987) represents a literal rendering, whereas in the Trueblood translation (Machado, 1982b) the literal meaning of Spanish 'usual' is compensated for by the connotations of tedium carried by 'same old':

y es esta vieja angustia	and it's this old anguish
que habita mi usual hipocondría.	that inhabits my usual hypochondria.
(Machado, 1982a, p. 125)	(Machado, 1987, p. 207)
	The old distress is back,
	Stirring inside the same old fancied ills.
	(Machado, 1982b)

Second, connotative meanings in the ST may be compensated for by literal meanings in the TT. This type of compensation can be illustrated by comparing two translations of another extract from Machado (poem LX). Once again, the Predmore translation (Machado, 1987) represents a literal rendering of 'noria', occasioning a loss in the TT of the connotative oxymoron implicit in the ST's juxtaposition of 'seca' and 'noria', whereas the Trueblood translation (Machado, 1982b) restores the oxymoron by explicitly referring to 'water wheel', thus juxtaposing 'water' and 'dry':

Colmenares de mis sueños	Beehives of my dreams,
¿ya no labráis? ¿Está seca	do you work no more? Has
la noria del pensamiento ...	the noria of my thought run dry ...
(Machado, 1982a, p. 117)	(Machado, 1987, p. 179)
	Have the beehives of my dreams
	stopped working, the water wheel
	of the mind run dry ...
	(Machado, 1982b)

(We shall discuss literal and connotative meaning in Chapters 7 and 8.)

Third, where, for example, the humour of the ST hinges on the comic use of calque, the TT may have to derive its humour from other sources, such as a play on words. Successful examples of this sort of compensation in kind abound in the Astérix books; compare, for instance, *Astérix chez les Bretons* with *Asterix en Bretaña*:

OBELIX Pourquoi parlez-vous à l'envers?	OBELIX ¿Por qué habla al revés?
JOLITORAX Je demande votre pardon?	BUENTORAX Le ruego me perdone.
(Goscinny and Uderzo, 1966, p. 9)	(Goscinny and Uderzo, 1967, p. 9)

In the ST, the comic effect of Jolitorax's anglicism is achieved by the substitution of a calque on English 'I beg your pardon' for 'Plaît-il?' or 'Comment?': (the ST expression in fact means 'I ask your forgiveness'. In the Spanish TT, where '¿Que?' or '¿Como?' would be expected (cf. 'Comment?'), the comic effect hinges on the generic incongruity of a phrase only found in business correspondence, never in speech; that is, the translator has compensated for the element of humour by means other than those used in the ST.

Compensation in place

Compensation in place consists in making up for the loss of a particular effect found at a given place in the ST by creating a corresponding effect at an earlier or later place in the TT. A simple example of compensation in place is that of compensating for a comic effect in the ST by constructing a similar comic effect at a different place in the TT, as in *Asterix en Bretaña* (p. 9):

JOLITORAX Je serai ravi, j'en suis sûr, *d'aller dans la vôtre maison*!	BUENTORAX *Me gustará*, estoy seguro, ir a vuestra casa.
(Goscinny and Uderzo, 1966; our italics)	(Goscinny and Uderzo 1967; our italics)

One of the comic effects of the ST is achieved by the grammatical incongruity of 'aller dans la vôtre maison'. In the Spanish TT the corresponding 'ir a vuestra casa' is grammatically correct, but contextually inappropriate, and the comic effect is transferred to the incongruous 'me gustará'. Compensation in place is also needed in translating the phrase 'un galán maduro, algo calvo', probably best rendered as 'a mature gentleman, handsome but slightly balding'. This example illustrates the relationship between **grammatical transposition** – the reorganization of a ST grammatical structure into a different, more idiomatic, structure in the TT – and the notion of compensation in place: grammatical transposition is, in fact, a type of compensation in place.

Compensation in place is frequently a necessary device in translating verse. Thus, for instance, an adequate TT could not afford to lose all trace of the salient and insistent sound-symbolic effects in the following extract from Nicolás Guillén's 'Mulata' (*Motivos de son*, 1930):

Tanto tren con tu cueppo,
tanto tren;
tanto tren con tu boca,
tanto tren;
tanto tren con tu sojo,
tanto tren.

(Guillén, 1976, p. 104)

Here the element of sound symbolism that is so central to the poem as a whole is reinforced by alliterations and assonances which concentrate particularly, on the one hand, on the consonants [t] and [n], and, on the other, on the vowel [o]. This phonetic reinforcement cannot be precisely, and equally intensively, replicated in an English TT because the key words do not alliterate in the required ways. The following TT attempts at least partly to compensate for this by using phonetic reinforcement distributed in different places from where it occurs in the ST:

> **S**o m**u**ch f**uss** **'bou**t you' **b**ody
> so m**u**ch **fuss**;
> so m**u**ch **fuss** **'bou**t you' m**ou**th,
> so m**u**ch **fuss**;
> so m**u**ch **fuss** **'bou**t you' eyes,
> so m**u**ch **fuss**.

(unpublished translation by Gustavo San Román)

Compensation by merging

The technique of **compensation by merging** is to condense ST features carried over a relatively long stretch of text (say, a complex phrase or a compound word) into a relatively short stretch of the TT (say, a simple phrase or a single word). In some cases, compensation by merging is the only way to strike a fair balance between doing justice to the literal meaning of a piece of ST and constructing an idiomatic TT, as in the example 'estuvo bastante tiempo sin resolverse'. An accurate literal translation of this phrase might be produced by translating word for word; but the resulting TT phrase would be far too long-winded and ponderous to be suitable in most contexts, and certainly out of place in a colloquial one. The semantic contents of the ST expression are rendered accurately, and in a more streamlined fashion, through compensation by merging, as 'he shilly-shallied'.

The following item provides two examples where compensation by merging offers the most plausible solution ('es necesario que' merged into 'should' and 'de aspecto deportivo' merged into 'sporty-looking'):

> Es necesario que al paso de un joven de aspecto deportivo cualquier señorita musite: '¡Adiós, Pirri! ¿Quieres que sea la Sonia Bruno de tu existencia?'

This piece of text presents other interesting problems of compensation and cultural transposition and would repay a short discussion and attempted translation in class.

Compensation by splitting

Compensation by splitting may be resorted to, if the context allows, where there is no single TL word that covers the same range of meaning as a given ST word. A simple example is furnished by the Spanish verb 'escasear', which, for literal exactitude, has to be translated as 'to be in short supply'.

The following example is more complex, but no less typical. In most contexts 'el toreo' can be effectively rendered as 'bullfighting' (a solution which, in itself, represents a degree of culturally necessary circumlocution; that is, compensation by splitting). In certain contexts, however – for instance where a Spanish ST deals with the exposition of the ethics and aesthetics of the 'toreo' – the English reader needs, for obvious cultural reasons, to be reminded that 'bullfighting' should be seen as more than a mere sport or a mere popular spectacle. In such contexts, compensation by splitting may be appropriate, leading to a rendering of 'el toreo' as '*the art of* bullfighting'.

As well as illustrating compensation by splitting, this rendering is also an example of compensation in kind: the ST's implicitly (culturally) connoted notion of bullfighting as an art form is rendered in the TT by literal means through the explicit addition of 'the art of'. We will not pursue this any further, because what is involved is the question of literal versus connotative meaning, and these questions are not addressed until Chapters 7 and 8. Suffice it to say that the TT exhibits the substitution of literal meaning for connotative meaning.

The four types of compensation discussed above can, of course, take many different forms; and, as our last example indicates, it also often happens that a single case of compensation belongs to more than one category at the same time. Good examples of multiple compensation will be found in the texts set for analysis in Practical 3.

We conclude with a word of caution: while compensation exercises the translator's ingenuity, the effort it requires should not be wasted on textually unimportant features. The aim is to reduce some of the more serious and undesirable translation losses that necessarily result from the fundamental structural and cultural differences between SL and TL.

PRACTICAL 3

3.1 Cultural transposition; compensation

Assignment

(i) Discuss the strategic problems confronting the translator of the following text, and outline your own strategy for translating it.
(ii) Translate the text into English.
(iii) Explain the main decisions of detail you made in producing your TT.

Contextual information

The text appears as part of a two-page advertisement (in colour) in the *Anuario El País 1992*. The advertisement is sponsored by the Sociedad para la Promoción y Reconversión Industrial (SPRI), the Diputación Foral de Bizkaia, and the Ayuntamiento de Zamudio.

Text

PARQUE TECNOLOGICO DEL PAIS VASCO

Lista la primera fase

El Parque Tecnológico del País Vasco ha concluido la construcción de su Primera Fase.

6.000 millones de inversión en tres años se han transformado en 140.000 m^2 de superficie (32.000 de ellos edificables) a disposición exclusiva de las empresas de alta tecnología con decidida vocación innovadora.

Con todos los servicios, tanto generales como particulares, disponibles.

Y con las máximas ayudas institucionales de la Comunidad Autónoma del País Vasco y todos los incentivos fiscales establecidos por la Diputación Foral de Bizkaia.

Espacios y dependencias se ceden en régimen de alquiler, con posibilidad de opción de compra a los 12 años.

Infraestructura

Carretera de acceso al Parque y viales de enlace, urbanización completa de la zona, tendido eléctrico (acometida, centro de maniobra y centro de distribución), traída de agua (red primaria, red general de abastecimiento, red interna, aguas residuales, depuradora y aguas pluviales), sistema anti-incendios, telefonía y gas natural, con canalizaciones acondicionadas para la inserción de conductores de fibra óptica.

Edificios

- 'ESTRELLA', de 4.500 m^2, propiedad del Parque, para acoger empresas de pequeño tamaño, ya existentes, que desarrollen su actividad en sectores de futuro.
- 'NIDO', de 2.500 m^2, propiedad del Parque, para actuar como incubadora de empresas de nueva creación que pretenden desarrollar actividades tecnológicas.
- 'BARCO', de 6.900 m^2, propiedad del Parque, acoge a las Oficinas Centrales y Servicios, disponiendo también de grandes pabellones para la instalación de empresas de mediana dimensión.
- 'INDELEC', empresa fabricante de radioteléfonos móviles (6.865 m^2).
- 'INGELECTRIC', empresa de ingeniería eléctrica (4.535 m^2).

En breve, dispondrán también de sus propios edificios las empresas Degremont (Tratamiento de aguas, 4.000 m^2) y ABB (I+D, 2.700 m^2). Existe, igualmente, una superficie de 2.000 m^2 en trámite de adjudicación a Inser Robótica.

Empresas

Hasta el momento han solicitado su admisión en el Parque 80 empresas, pertenecientes fundamentalmente a actividades relacionadas con la electrónica, robótica, automatización, informática, ingeniería...

En régimen de alquiler se encuentran ya instaladas en el Parque las siguientes empresas: SPRITEL, JKC SISTEMAS, BEMBS, NEXTEL, MICROA, LANDATA, NAFAR, HITE, ERABIDE, ONDOAN, TELION y 2-3 DIMENSION.

Avance segunda fase (Conclusión 1991)

- 190.000 m^2, con 52.000 edificables.
- Infraestructura viaria ya realizada y urbanización en ejecución.
- Construcción de 4 nuevos edificios de 3.000 m^2 cada uno: 2 para parcelar y alquilar y 2 para instalación de empresas de tamaño pequeño.
- Conclusión del edificio Ingemat (Ingeniería y Sistemas de Automatización y Robótica), de 2.800 m^2.
- Conclusión del complejo adquirido por la Diputación Foral de Bizkaia para ubicación de las sociedades y grupos de carácter tecnológico dependientes del Departamento de Promoción y Desarrollo de dicho Organismo Foral.
- Conclusión del Telepuerto, construido por Telefónica en colaboración con la SPRI, para regir, desde él, todo el sistema de telecomunicaciones del País Vasco.

(turn to p. 35)

3.2 Compensation

Assignment

Working in groups, analyse the various cases of cultural transposition and of compensation in the TT on pp. 37 and 39. Give your own version where you can improve on the published TT.

Contextual information

The ST is an extract from Juan Goytisolo's *Señas de identidad*, first published in 1966. It is the first volume in a trilogy of works which experiment with narrative technique. In this volume the protagonist reflects on his own identity and experience. Goytisolo was a bitter opponent of Franco's regime and his early novels were banned in Spain. He has lived the life of a political and cultural exile. The TT is from *Marks of Identity*, Gregory Rabassa's translation of *Señas de identidad*, published in 1988 by Serpent's Tail (Goytisolo, 1988).

Source text

en el centro
en medio de un cuadrado de césped señalado por cuatro mojones
un zócalo sobrio realzaba la estatua ecuestre de un guerrero en bronce regalo de la Ciudad
eso decía la lápida
a su Caudillo Libertador
buscaste refugio a la sombra de los pórticos
los turistas discurrían en grupos compactos hacia el museo del Ejército fotografiaban la estatua ecuestre se aglomeraban a la entrada de las tiendas de souvenirs hacían girar los torniquetes de tarjetas postales visitaban el almacén de Antigüedades Heráldica Soldados de Plomo

ENTRADA LIBRE
ENTRÉE LIBRE
FREE ENTRANCE
EINTRITT FREI

el cartel anunciador de una corrida de toros atrajo bruscamente tu atención

SOUVENIR SOUVENIR
DE ESPAÑA DE ESPAÑA
Plaza de Toros Monumental
Grandiosa corrida de toros
6 Hermosos y Bravos Toros 6
con la divisa rosa y verde de
la renombrada ganadería de
Don Baltasar Iban de Madrid
para los grandes espadas
LUIS MIGUEL DOMINGUÍN
ICI VOTRE NOM – HERE, YOUR NAME – HIER, IHRE NAMEN
ANTONIO ORDÓÑEZ
con sus correspondientes cuadrillas
Amenizará el espectáculo la Banda
'La popular Sansense'

pasaste de largo
una multitud de curiosos examinaba dos composiciones fotográficas en las que un torero (sin cabeza) clavaba (con estampa de maestro) un par de banderillas y una gitana (sin cabeza igualmente) se abanicaba (muy chula ella) frente a una maqueta de la Giralda

Target text

in the center
in the middle of a square of grass marked off by four stones
a somber base held up the equestrian statue of a bronze warrior the gift of the City
the plaque said so
to its Liberator and Caudillo
you took refuge in the shade of the porticos
the tourists were going through in compact groups toward the Army museum they were photographing the equestrian statue they were clustered around the souvenir stands they were turning the card racks they were going into the shop with Antiques Heraldic Material Lead Soldiers

ENTRADA LIBRE
ENTRÉE LIBRE
ENTRANCE FREE
EINTRITT FREI

the bullfight poster suddenly drew your attention

SOUVENIR SOUVENIR
OF SPAIN OF SPAIN
Monumental Bullring
Great Bullfight
6 Beautiful and Brave Bulls 6
with the pink and green colors
of the famous ranch of
Don Baltasar Iban of Madrid
for the great bullfighters
LUIS MIGUEL DOMINGUÍN
ICI VOTRE NOM – YOUR NAME. HERE – HIER, IHRE NAMEN
ANTONIO ORDÓÑEZ
with their respective teams
music furnished by the Band of
'La Popular Sansense'

you passed by quickly
a crowd of curious people was examining the photographic compositions in which a bullfighter (headless) was placing (with the stamp of a master) a pair of *banderillas* and a Gypsy woman (also headless) was fanning herself (very flashy she was) opposite a mock-up of the Giralda

en endiablado esperanto un caracterizado ejemplar de hombrecillo español de la estepa explicaba que se trataba de una imagen trucada con la que los señores y caballeros messieurs et dames ladies and gentlemen aquí presentes podrían sorprender a sus amistades y conocidos vestidos de toreros y gitanas toreadors et gitanes matadors and gypsies de regreso a sus respectivos países vos pays d'origine your native countries y afirmar así su personalidad affimer votre personnalité your personality con el relato de sus aventuras españolas aventures espagnoles spanish adventures

Reprinted by kind permission from Juan Goytisolo, *Señas de identidad* (Barcelona: Seix Barral, 1976, pp. 407–9), copyright © Juan Goytisolo, 1966.

in a devilish Esperanto a characteristic example of a little Spaniard from the steppe was explaining that it was a matter of a cut-off image with which the señoras y caballeros messieurs et dames ladies and gentlemen here present could surprise their friends and acquaintances dressed as bullfighters and Gypsies when they returned to sus respectivos países leur pays d'origine your native countries and afirmar así su personalidad affirmer leur personalité show your personality with the story of your aventuras españolas aventures espagnoles Spanish adventures

Reprinted by kind permission from Juan Goytisolo, *Marks of Identity*, translated by Gregory Rabassa (London: Serpent's Tail, 1988, pp. 340–1).

3.3 Cultural transposition; compensation

Assignment

Working in groups:

(i) Discuss the strategic problems confronting the translator of the following ST, and say what your own strategy would be.

(ii) In the light of your findings in (i), translate the text into English, paying particular attention to cultural transposition and compensation.

(iii) Explain the main decisions of detail you made in producing your TT.

Contextual information

The text is an official information leaflet explaining arrangements for postal votes in the 1983 local elections.

Text

ELECCIONES LOCALES 1983

VOTO POR CORREO

CUANDO ALGUN ELECTOR PREVEA QUE EN LA FECHA DE VOTACION NO SE HALLARA EN EL LUGAR EN QUE LE CORRESPONDA EJERCER SU DERECHO DE SUFRAGIO, PODRA EMITIR SU VOTO POR CORREO. (ARTICULO 57 DEL REAL DECRETO-LEY 20/1977, SOBRE NORMAS ELECTORALES.)

FORMA DE VOTAR

1°. Solicitud del CERTIFICADO DE INSCRIPCION EN EL CENSO.

a) Personándose en la Junta Electoral de Zona se solicitará el IMPRESO DE SOLICITUD DE LA CERTIFICACION.

Una vez cumplimentado se entregará personalmente en dicha Junta Electoral de Zona, previa identificación mediante el Documento Nacional de Identidad y cotejo por el funcionario de la firma de ambos documentos.

b) La solicitud también puede ser efectuada en nombre del elector, por persona debidamente autorizada, previa acreditación de su identidad y representación con documento autenticado por Notario o Cónsul.

Si el elector fuese funcionario del Estado, la solicitud puede ser efectuada en su nombre por persona debidamente autorizada, previa acreditación de su identidad y representación con documento autorizado por el Jefe del Centro o Dependencia administrativa donde el elector preste sus servicios.

c) Asimismo, y de acuerdo con lo establecido en el artículo 66, apartados uno, tres y cuatro, de la Ley de Procedimiento Administrativo, podrá formularse la solicitud dirigida a la Junta Electoral de Zona de donde resida el elector, de la forma siguiente:

— A través del Gobierno Civil de su provincia o de cualquier otra.

— De las oficinas de Correos, siempre que se presente la solicitud en sobre abierto, para ser fechada y sellada por el funcionario de Correos, antes de ser certificada.

— De las representaciones diplomáticas o consulares españolas correspondientes, si el elector se encuentra en el extranjero.

En todos los casos, el funcionario encargado de la recepción de la solicitud exigirá del interesado la exhibición del Documento Nacional de Identidad, a fin de comprobar la identidad del mismo y la coincidencia de firma de ambos documentos.

TIEMPO HABIL PARA LA SOLICITUD

Desde el día siguiente al de la Convocatoria de las Elecciones Locales hasta cinco días antes de la votación.

2°. RECEPCION DE LA DOCUMENTACION

La Junta Electoral de Zona, previas las comprobaciones y anotaciones oportunas, remitirá al elector y a su domicilio:

— CERTIFICADO DE INSCRIPCION EN EL CENSO ELECTORAL.

— UN SOBRE CON LA DIRECCION DE LA MESA QUE CORRESPONDE VOTAR.

— LAS PAPELETAS ELECTORALES DE TODAS LAS OPCIONES Y VOTACIONES EN SU CASO.

— LOS SOBRES NECESARIOS CON LAS INDICACIONES OPORTUNAS PARA INTRODUCIR LAS PAPELETAS DE VOTACION.

TIEMPO HABIL PARA RECEPCION DE LA DOCUMENTACION

Desde el inicio de la campaña de propaganda electoral hasta tres días antes de la votación.

3°. REMISION DE LA DOCUMENTACION

El elector introducirá la papeleta o papeletas, en su caso, por él elegidas en el sobre o sobres correspondientes.

A continuación introducirá lo anterior y el certificado de inscripción en el Censo Electoral, en el sobre que tiene la dirección de la Mesa Electoral en que debe votar. Una vez cerrado, lo remitirá por correo certificado a la Mesa Electoral, procurando hacerlo con la antelación necesaria, a fin de que sea recibido por la Mesa el día de la votación.

4

The formal properties of texts: phonic/graphic and prosodic problems in translating

If the challenge of translation is not to replicate a ST in the TL but rather to reduce translation loss, the immediate problem that arises after the general cultural issues have been assessed is that of the ST's objectively ostensible formal properties. There are, doubtless, insurmountable problems in establishing objectively what the ostensible properties of a text are, but it can at least be said that whatever effects, meanings and reactions are triggered by a text must originate from features concretely present in it. It is, therefore, necessary for the translator to look at the text as a linguistic object.

THE FORMAL PROPERTIES OF TEXTS

In trying to assess the formal properties of texts, one can usefully turn to some fundamental notions in linguistics. There is no need for a detailed incursion into linguistic theory, but linguistics does offer a hierarchically ordered series of systematically isolated and complementary *levels* on which the formal properties of texts can be located for the purposes of a methodical discussion.

It is true of any text that there are various points on which it could have been different. For instance, where there is an allusion to the Bible, there might have been a quotation from Shakespeare; or where there is a question mark there might have been an exclamation mark (compare 'Was he drinking?' and 'Was he drinking!'); or where the text has a letter 'c' there might have been a letter 'n' (compare 'This is a cosy little nook' and 'This is a nosy little cook'). All these points of detail, no matter how large or small, where a text could have been different (that is, where it could have been *another* text) are designated as **textual variables**. It is these textual variables that the series of levels defined in linguistics makes it possible to identify.

Taking the linguistic levels one at a time has two main advantages. First, looking at textual variables on an organized series of isolated levels enables one to see which textual variables are important in the ST and which are less important. As we have seen, some of the ST features that fall prey to translation loss may not be worth the effort of compensation. It is, therefore, excellent strategy to decide which of the textual variables are indispensable, and which can be ignored, for the purpose of formulating a good TT. (In general, as we shall see, the more prominently a particular textual variable contributes to triggering effects and meanings in a text, and the more it coincides in this with other textual variables conveying related meanings and effects, the more important it is.)

Second, one can assess a TT, whether one's own or somebody else's, by isolating and comparing the formal variables of both ST and TT. This enables the translator to identify what textual variables of the ST are absent from the TT, and vice versa. That is, although translation loss is by definition not ultimately quantifiable, it is possible to make a relatively precise accounting of translation losses on each level. This also permits a more self-aware and methodical way of evaluating TTs and of reducing details of translation loss.

We propose six levels of textual variables, hierarchically arranged from lowest to highest; hierarchically in the sense that each level is, as it were, built on top of the previous one. Naturally, other schemes could have been offered, but arguing about alternative theoretical frameworks is beyond the scope of this coursebook, as it would involve a deeper plunge into linguistic theory than is useful for our purposes. In this chapter and the next two, we shall work our way up through the levels, showing what kinds of textual variable can be found on each, and how they may function in a text. Together, the six levels constitute a kind of 'filter' through which the translator can pass a text to determine what levels and formal properties are important in it and most need to be respected in the TT. Surprising as it may seem at this early stage, this method does not imply a plodding or piecemeal approach to texts: applying this filter (and others) quickly becomes automatic and very effective in translation practice. (A schematic representation of all the filters we are suggesting can be found on p. 216.)

THE PHONIC/GRAPHIC LEVEL

The most basic level of textual variables is the **phonic/graphic level**. Taking a text on this level means looking at it as a sequence of sound segments (*phonemes*) if it is an oral text, or as a sequence of letters (*graphemes*) if it is a written one. Although phonemes and graphemes are different things, they are on the same basic level of textual variables: phonemes are to oral texts as graphemes are to written ones. To help keep this in mind, we shall refer to the 'phonic/graphic level' regardless of whether the text in question is an oral one or a written one.

Every text is a unique configuration of phonemes/graphemes, these configurations being restricted by, among other things, the conventions of a particular language. This is why, in general, no text in a given language can reproduce exactly the same sequence of sound segments/letters as any text in another language. Occasional coincidences apart (which may be cited as curiosities, such as the sequence 'I VITELLI DEI ROMANI SONO BELLI' which can be read alternatively, and with two completely different meanings, in either Latin or Italian: as 'Go, Vitellus, to the martial sound of the god of Rome', or as 'the calves of the Romans are beautiful', respectively), ST and TT will always consist of markedly different sequences. This always and automatically constitutes a source of translation loss. The real question for the translator, however, is whether this loss matters at all. Could we not simply put it down as a necessary consequence of the transition from one language to another, and forget about it?

The suggestion that the translator should not bother with the sound/letter sequences in texts echoes Lewis Carroll's jocular translation maxim: 'Take care of the sense and the sounds will take care of themselves.' We may give two initial answers to this maxim. First, some translators have been known to pay special attention to recreating phonic/graphic effects of the ST, at times even to the detriment of the sense. Second, some texts would lose much of their point (and meaning) if deprived of their special phonic/graphic properties.

As a matter of fact, even in the most ordinary, prosaic text one may come across problems of translation that have to do specifically with the phonic/graphic level. The transcription of names is a prime example. When looking, in the last chapter, at the possibilities for cultural transposition of names, we noted that it is a matter of conventional equivalence that accounts for the translation of Spanish 'Zaragoza' as English 'Saragossa', Russian 'MOCKBA' as English 'Moscow' and Spanish 'Moscú', and so on. Equally conventional is the standard English transliteration 'Mao Tse-tung'. This transliteration in fact occasions a phonic distortion (from Chinese [mɑwdzduŋ] to English [mawtsit'uŋ]), which does not much matter even to the few people who are aware of it. On the other hand, if 'C. O. JONES' COUGH SWEETS' were the brand name of an export product, one might well be reluctant, for word-associative reasons, to retain this brand name when advertising the product in Spain. Certainly, similar word-associative reasons account for the reported lack of success of the Chevrolet Nova ('no va') in Puerto Rico: a reaction that might well have been foreseen by General Motors.

As these examples show, a measure of phonic/graphic inventiveness and decision-making may be involved in the process of translation. These resources are, of course, called upon to a much greater degree in translating a ST that makes important and self-conscious use of phonic/graphic variables for *special effects*. We mean by such special effects the patterned use of phonic/graphic features in order to create or – more usually – to reinforce a thematic motif or mood within a text.

The simplest example of such special effects is onomatopoeia. Onomatopoeia is either directly *iconic* – that is, the phonic form of a word impressionistically imitates a sound which is the referent of the word – or *iconically motivated* – that is, the phonic form of the word imitates a sound associated with the referent of the word (for example, 'cuckoo'). If it has a thematically important function, onomatopoeia may require care in translation. Some examples are straightforward, of course, as in those instances where Spanish 'tintinear' is appropriately rendered by 'tinkle', which presents little difficulty or translation loss. Others, while still straightforward, are potentially more problematic, as in the conventional translation of Spanish 'retintín' into English 'ringing', where there is slightly more phonic translation loss and that loss could conceivably be significant in certain contexts. Even greater and more potentially significant phonic translation loss might be occasioned by the usual translation of 'boom', when describing the sound of a gun, as 'resonar' or 'retumbar'.

Cross-cultural variations in onomatopoeia are common – compare, for example, Spanish '¡pum!' with English 'bang!'. What is more, many SL onomatopoeic words do not have one-to-one TL counterparts. For instance, 'squeak' may be rendered in Spanish as 'chillido' or 'grito' (if a mouse is making the noise), as 'chirrido' (if it is a badly oiled door, or wheel) or 'crujido' (if it is a shoe); Spanish 'silbido' may be rendered as 'whistling', 'hiss', 'wheeze', 'whine', 'whizz', 'swish' or even 'hum', depending on who or what is making the noise and in what circumstances; similarly, Spanish '¡pum!' may translate alternatively as 'bang!', 'pop!' or 'thud!'. In these and many other cases the range of reference of the SL word does not coincide exactly with that of its nearest TL counterpart. These types of cross-cultural difference are phonic in nature, and are in themselves potential sources of translation problems.

Onomatopoeia may cause more of a translation problem where the nearest semantic counterparts to an onomatopoeic SL word in the TL are not onomatopoeic. For instance, English 'peewit' is onomatopoeic, but its Spanish rendering as 'avefría' is clearly not. Conversely, Spanish 'búho' has an onomatopoeic quality, but its English rendering 'long-eared owl' does not. To the extent that the very fact of onomatopoeia is an effect contributing to textual meaning, its loss in the TT is a translation loss that the translator may have reason to regret.

Other translation difficulties may be caused by onomatopoeia where cross-cultural differences arise on a grammatical as well as the phonic/graphic level. Words like '¡pum!', '¡bee!' and '¡zas!' are onomatopoeia at its most basic: sound-imitative interjections, not onomatopoeic nouns. Spanish 'miau' is a directly onomatopoeic noun denoting the sound made by a cat; translating it as 'miaow' involves virtually no translation loss at all. 'Cuclillo' is an indirectly onomatopoeic noun; translating it as 'cuckoo' involves very little translation loss. Translating 'zumbador' (in a Central American context) as 'humming-bird', on the other hand, involves a greater degree of phonic translation loss, which could be significant in certain contexts.

Some onomatopoeic words can be used not only as interjections, but also as nouns or verbs: for example, Spanish '¡tictac!' and '¡crujido!' can double as nouns and interjections, while English 'bang!', 'splash!' and 'squeak!' are even more grammatically versatile since they can also be used as both nouns and verbs. Where cross-linguistic onomatopoeic counterparts of equal grammatical versatility exist, translation loss is limited to minor losses on the phonic/graphic level. Take, however, a hypothetical case where 'she climbed the stairs slowly, her high heels clacking' is to be translated into Spanish. In order to retain in the Spanish TT the onomatopoeia of 'clacking', the translator might be tempted to resort to rendering this word as 'tictaquear'. The option 'subió las escaleras lentamente, sus tacones tictaqueando' is, on balance, to be rejected due to connotative associations, as is the equally appealing 'teclear', because both directly conjure the image of inappropriate concrete objects, a clock and a typewriter, respectively. In addition, 'subió las escaleras lentamente con un tictaquear' may be objected to on the grounds that Spanish 'tictac' exists only as an interjection and as a noun but does not lend itself readily to the formation of the verb 'tictaquear'. An alternative is to reject a strongly onomatopoeic rendering of 'clacking' and resort to the referentially and associatively appropriate 'taconear', used in either a verbal or a nominal form. While reasonably acceptable, 'subió las escaleras lentamente con un taconear', lacks a sufficient degree of phonic reinforcement. On the other hand, the insistent acoustic quality of the footsteps described is sound-symbolically reinforced in 'subió las escaleras lentamente con un taconeo de tacones'. This compensation by alliteration and repetition of the stem 'tacon-' may even be overemphatic, depending on the context. Perhaps a more acceptable solution might be to coin 'claquetear' or 'claqueteo' from the noun 'clac', itself a French borrowing, and render the sentence as 'subió las escaleras lentamente con un claquetear/claqueteo de tacones'. The example typifies a common translation problem: that of a single thematic clue combining with onomatopoeia or the recurrence of phonic/graphic variables to give connotative force to a TT expression.

Even something as simple as onomatopoeia, then, may need attention in translating. The same is true, in fact, of any type of word-play that hinges on phonic/graphic similarities between expressions with different meanings. For example, the more obviously a pun or a spoonerism is not accidental or incidental in the ST, the more it is in need of translating. A major strategic decision will then be whether to seek appropriate puns or spoonerisms for the TT, or whether to resort to some form of compensation. Typical problems of this kind will be found in Practicals 4 and 8.

A frequently encountered area of phonic/graphic special effects is alliteration and assonance. We define **alliteration** as the recurrence of the same sound/letter or sound/letter cluster at the beginning of words (for example, '**m**any **m**ighty **m**idgets') and **assonance** as the recurrence, within words, of the same sound/letter or sound/letter cluster (for example, 'their cr**aft**y hi**st**ory-m**ast**er's b**ath**t**u**b'). It is important to remember a vital difference between alliteration/assonance and onomatopoeia. Alliteration and assonance do not involve an imitation of sounds (unless they happen to coincide with onomatopoeia, as would be the case in 'ten tall clocks tock'). We have already seen something of how alliteration and assonance work, in the stanza from Nicolás Guillén's 'Mulata' discussed in Chapter 3, and we shall meet a further example in the Hebrew text discussed in Chapter 5. As we shall see, the crucial associative feature in the pattern underlying that text is the X–Z–R phonic/graphic root (involving a combination of alliteration and assonance). Every time this root recurs in the text, it coincides with a vital moment in the narrative, so that it very soon acquires emphatic force, underlining crucial narrative and thematic points. A major strategic decision for the translator of this story arises on the phonic/graphic level, but also affects the grammatical level (as we shall see in more detail in Chapter 5). This decision is whether to create a corresponding pattern of lexical items in the TT for underlining crucial points in the narrative and, if so, whether to make systematic phonic/graphic recurrences the hub of that TT pattern.

This example makes clear why the problems raised by phonic/graphic special effects can be so hard to solve. It is common to find that the literal sense and the mood of a text are reinforced by some of the phonic qualities of the text (so-called 'sound symbolism'). This makes it all the easier to forget the contribution of the reader/listener's subjectivity to the textual effect. This subjective input is relatively minor in the case of onomatopoeia, but it is greater in texts like the Hebrew story where the pattern of phonic/graphic special effects may easily be overlooked by the casual or unsophisticated reader, and greater still where alliteration and assonance are more varied and objectively less obtrusive. The important thing to keep in mind is that, onomatopoeia aside, the sound-symbolic effect of words is not intrinsic to them, but operates in conjunction with their literal and connotative meanings in the context.

For example, persistent repetition of the sound [l] does not, in and of itself, suggest a sudden burst of spiritual illumination, or a flood of bright daylight, or a cacophony of voices instrumental in ridiculing petty officialdom. Yet it may be said to suggest the first of these things in the opening lines of Jorge Guillén's *Cántico*:

(E**l** a**l**ma vue**l**ve a**l** cuerpo,
Se dirige a **l**os ojos
Y choca.) – ¡**L**uz! Me invade...
(Guillén, 1950, p. 16)

It may be said to connote the second in the opening lines of Jorge Guillén's 'Del alba a la aurora':

¿**L**uz de **l**una? No es **l**a **l**una
Quien va azu**l**ando **l**a ca**ll**e...
(Guillén, 1950, p. 460)

And it has been noted as carrying the third set of connotations in the same author's 'Coro de burocracia' :

La **l**ey **l**evanta
Frente a**l** oficia**l** cacumen

La sacrosanta
Letra que todos consumen.
(Guillén, 1968, p. 576)

In each case, [l] draws its suggestive power from four things in particular: first, the lexical meanings of the words in which it occurs; second, the lexical meanings of the words associated with those in which it occurs; third, other phonetic qualities of both those groups of words; and, fourth, the many other types of connotative meaning at work in these texts, as in any other. (We shall discuss connotative meaning as such in Chapter 8.)

In the last of these examples, sound symbolism clearly has such an important textual role that to translate the texts without some attempt at producing appropriate sound-symbolic effects in the TT would be to incur severe translation loss. The more a text depends for its very existence on the interplay of onomatopoeia, alliteration and assonance, the more true this is – and the more difficult the translator's task becomes, because, as our examples show, sound symbolism is not only largely language-specific, but a very subjective matter as well.

By far the most widespread textual effects arising from the use of phonic/graphic variables involve the exploitation of *recurrences*. Apart from alliteration and assonance, rhyme is the most obvious example. When such recurrences are organized into recognizable patterns on a large scale, for example in a regularly repeated rhyme scheme, they are clearly not accidental or incidental. At this point, the translator is forced to take the resulting phonic/graphic special effects into serious consideration. However, this does not mean that one is obliged, or even well advised, to reproduce the exact patterns of recurrence found in the ST. In fact, opinions are divided among translators of verse about the extent to which even such obvious devices as rhyme scheme should be reproduced in the TT. In English, for example, blank verse is a widespread genre with at least as high a prestige as rhyming verse, so that there is often a case for translating rhyming STs from other languages into blank verse in English. In the end, this is a decision for individual translators to make in individual cases; often the genre of the ST and the availability of TL genres as 'models' will be a crucial factor in the decision. (We shall consider at length the importance of genre as a factor in translation in Chapter 11.)

We can conclude so far that the phonic/graphic level of textual variables *may* merit the translator's attention, and that translation losses on this level *may* be serious. There is no suggestion here that attention to sounds should be to the detriment of sense; on the contrary, it is where ignoring the contribution of phonic/graphic features would damage the sense of the text that they are considered important.

There is, however, a style of translation that actually more or less reverses the maxim quoted from Lewis Carroll; that is, it concentrates on taking care of the sounds and allows the sense to emerge as a kind of vaguely suggested impression. This technique is generally known as **phonemic translation**. An extraordinary example, whose authors seem to take their method perfectly seriously, is a translation of Catullus's poetry by Celia and Louis Zukovsky. Here is part of one poem, followed by (i) the phonemic translation and (ii) a literal prose translation:

> Ille mi par esse deo videtur,
> Ille, si fas est, superare divos,
> qui sedens adversus identidem te
> spectat et audit
> dulce ridentem, misero quod omnis
> eripit sensus mihi; [...]

(i) He'll hie me, par *is* he? the God divide her,
he'll hie, see fastest, superior deity,
quiz – sitting adverse identity – mate, in-
spect it and audit –
you'll care ridden then, misery holds omens,
air rip the senses from me; [...]
(Zukovsky, 1969, poem 51)

(ii) He seems to me to be equal to a god, he seems to me,
if it is lawful, to surpass the gods, who, sitting
opposite to you, keeps looking at you and hearing you
sweetly laugh; but this tears away all my senses,
wretch that I am.

We shall not dwell on this example, beyond saying that it perfectly illustrates the technique of phonemic translation: to imitate as closely as possible the actual phonic sequence of the ST, while suggesting in a vague and impressionistic way something of its literal content.

As a matter of fact, it is difficult, if not impossible, for a TT to retain a close similarity to the actual phonic sequences of the ST and still retain anything more than a tenuous connection with any kind of coherent meaning, let alone the meaning of the ST. This difficulty is ensured by the classic 'arbitrariness' of languages, not to mention the language-specific and contextual factors which, as we have seen in discussing onomatopoeia, alliteration and assonance, make phonic effect such a relative and subjective matter.

Entertaining illustrations of the way phonic imitation in a TT renders the sense of the ST unrecognizable are Van Rooten's *Mots d'heures: gousses, rames* (*Mother Goose Rhymes*!) and John Hulme's *Mörder Guss Reims* which consist in a playful imitation of English nursery rhymes in French and in German, respectively. Here, for example, the text of 'Humpty-Dumpty' is reproduced in French as:

Un petit d'un petit
S'étonne aux Halles,
Un petit d'un petit
À degrés te fallent.
(Van Rooten, 1968, poem 1)

and in German as 'Um die Dumm' die Saturn Aval;/Um die Dumm' die Ader Grät' fahl' (Hulme, 1981, p. 4).

While providing an entertaining pastiche, for which we have unfortunately found no Spanish counterpart, *Mots d'heures: gousses, rames* and *Mörder Guss Reims* do not really count as phonemic translation proper: there is no attempt at all to render anything of the literal meaning of the ST. What we have here is a form of humorous pastiche which consists in the cross-linguistic phonic imitation of a well-known text.

Although phonemic translation cannot be recommended as a technique for serious translation of sensible texts, there are texts that are not intended to be sensible in the original and which qualify as suitable objects for a degree of phonemic translation. Nonsense rhymes, like Lewis Carroll's 'Jabberwocky', are a good example. Here, by way of illustration, is a sample of a Spanish TT of 'Jabberwocky':

JABBERWOCKY	GALIMATAZO
'Twas brillig, and the slithy toves Did gyre and gimble in the wabe: All mimsy were the borogoves, And the mome raths outgrabe.	Brillaba, brumeando negro, el sol; agiliscosos giroscaban los limazones banerrando por las váparas lejanas; mimosos se fruncían los borogobios mientras el momio rantas murgiflaba.

Finally, though they are less common than sound symbolism, special effects may also be contrived through the spatial layout of written texts. Such cases illustrate the potential importance of specifically *graphic* textual variables. An obvious example is the acrostic, a text in which, say, reading the first letter of each line spells out, vertically, a hidden word. Another is concrete poetry, where the visual form of the text is used to convey meaning. A simple example of this, and one which would pose no great translation problems in English, is the calligram 'Cabellera' by Guillermo de Torre (1900–71):

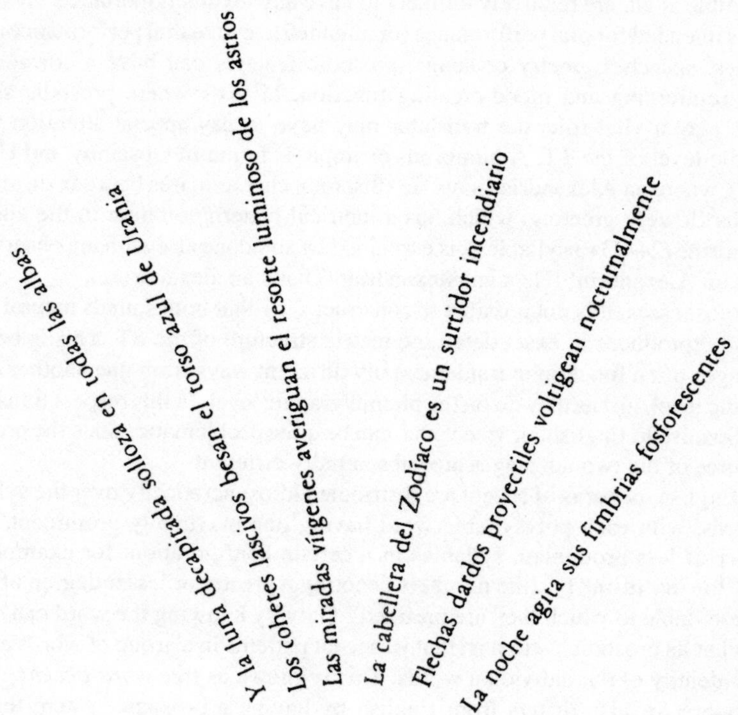

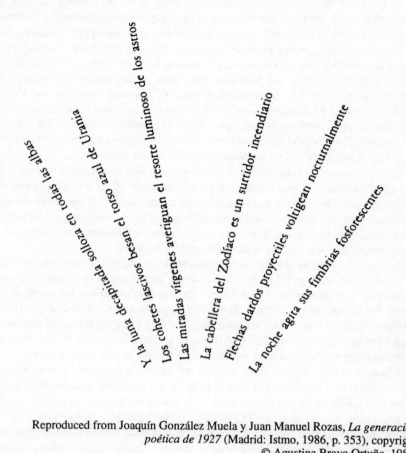

Reproduced from Joaquín González Muela y Juan Manuel Rozas, *La generación poética de 1927* (Madrid: Istmo, 1986, p. 353), copyright © Agustina Bravo Ortuña, 1986.

The text in Practical 4, from the same source, is also a good example; just as onomatopoeia is iconic phonically, this text – like much concrete poetry – is iconic graphically, imitating visually what it describes referentially.

THE PROSODIC LEVEL

On the **prosodic level**, utterances count as 'metrically' structured stretches, within which syllables have varying degrees of prominence according to accent, stress and emphasis, varying melodic qualities in terms of pitch modulation, and varying qualities of rhythm, length and tempo. Groups of syllables may, on this level, form *contrastive* prosodic patterns (for example, the alternation of a short, staccato, fast section with a long, slow, smooth one), or *recurrent* ones, or both.

In texts not designed to be read aloud, such prosodic patterns, if they are discernible at all, are relatively unlikely to have any textual importance. However, in texts intended for oral performance (or intended to evoke oral performance), such as plays, speeches, poetry or songs, prosodic features can have a considerable theme-reinforcing and mood-creating function. In texts where prosodic special effects play a vital role, the translator may have to pay special attention to the prosodic level of the TT. A humorous example is found in Goscinny and Uderzo (1965), where an Alexandrian says 'Je suis, mon cher ami, très heureux de te voir', and this flowery greeting, which has a metrical pattern common in the classical alexandrine (2+4/3+3 syllables), is explained by someone else with the observation 'C'est un Alexandrin' (He's an Alexandrian/That's an alexandrine).

In most cases, it is not possible to construct a TT that both sounds natural in the TL and reproduces in exact detail the metric structure of the ST. This is because languages often function in fundamentally different ways from one another on the prosodic level, just as they do on the phonic/graphic level. In this respect translating from Spanish to English, or vice versa, can be quite problematic, since the prosodic structures of the two languages are substantially different.

In English, patterns of accent are distributed idiosyncratically over the syllables of words, with each polysyllabic word having one maximally prominent, and a number of less prominent, syllables in a certain configuration: for example, the word '^{1}un^{2}na^{1}tu^{1}ral^{0}ly' (the numbers denoting a greater or lesser degree of stress on the syllable to which they are prefixed). Only by knowing the word can one be sure what its prosodic pattern is; that is, accent patterns in a group of words are tied to the identity of the individual words. This is known as *free word-accent*.

Modern Spanish differs from English by having a prosodic system that is a combination of a *fixed word-accent*, falling on the penultimate syllable of words, as in '^{1}tor^{1}ce^{2}du^{1}ra' and a *free word-accent*, placed on a non-penultimate syllable in particular words, such as '^{2}tó^{1}ni^{1}ca', '^{1}to^{2}pó^{1}gra^{1}fo', '^{1}to^{1}po^{2}grá^{1}fi^{1}co'. In effect, this means that free word-accent applies to both Spanish and English with the proviso that penultimate syllable stress predominates in Spanish and is regarded as the norm. These differences between the English and Spanish prosodic systems may in themselves sometimes give rise to translation problems in prose and verse alike. They are not, however, the main source of metrical difficulties in verse translation: these stem rather from the fact that, as we shall see below, Spanish verse is syllabic while English verse operates with units (feet) consisting of two or more syllables each.

RUDIMENTS OF SPANISH AND ENGLISH VERSIFICATION

We have seen that on the phonic/graphic level, translators of verse often have to pay special attention to patterns of recurrence in a text. The same is true on the prosodic level. The difference between Spanish and English versification constitutes a major problem in verse translation. We shall deal here in elementary terms with the basics of the two systems, so that they can be compared. Such metrical structure is the main feature of the patterned use of recurrences on the prosodic level. (It does not, however, exhaust the entire field of prosody, since it ignores tempo and melodic pitch, which may also constitute vital textual variables in an oral text.) We shall not discuss free verse, which would need too detailed a study for the purposes of this course. However, in so far as free verse is defined by its difference from fixed-form verse, our analysis will help translators isolate the relevant features of STs in free verse.

In translating verse, one strategic decision that needs to be made is on the prosodic level: assuming (and this is a big assumption) that the TT is to be in verse, should it attempt to reproduce the metric recurrences of the ST? This decision will depend ultimately on the textual function of metre in the ST, and on whether creating metric recurrences in the TT would lead to unacceptable translation losses on other levels.

In discussing one's decision, it is useful to have a basic notation for describing metric structure. For English, there is a well-tried system, which we adopt here. For Spanish, we suggest a simple notation below. The notation brings out clearly and concisely the metric patterns, and the variations in them, which are so fertile a source of special textual effects. Only when these patterns have been identified in a ST, and their effects pinpointed, can the translator begin to face the decision as to what – if any – TL prosodic patterns might be appropriate in the TT. That there will need to be prosodic patterns in the translation of a prosodically patterned ST is virtually certain; that they will hardly ever replicate those of the ST is even more certain. The challenge to the translator is to find appropriate compromises.

Spanish

Spanish verse is *syllabic*. That is, the writer does not have to choose among conventional configurations of stressed and unstressed syllables, as is the case in traditional English or German verse. A line of verse in Spanish is defined in terms of the number of syllables it contains, and the pattern of stresses may vary greatly within that framework. However, syllable counting is not an entirely straightforward matter. When working out the syllabic pattern of Spanish verse, a particular difficulty arises from the fact that elision may, but does not necessarily, occur between a word ending in a vowel and a following word which begins with a vowel (or a silent h). Normal practice is to use the symbol ‿ to indicate elision, as here:

cuan/do‿en/ la/ mar/ so/se/ga/da = 8
pre/so‿y / for/za/do‿y / so/lo‿en / tie/rra‿a/je/na = 11
que/ jun/tos/ tan/tos/ ma/les/ me‿han/ lle/va/do = 11
No/ hay/ ti/em/po/ que/ per/der = 8

Two vowels which occur together may count as part of the same syllable even if they do not usually occur as diphthongs in prose (for example, trisyllabic ma/est/ro may become bisyllabic mae/stro). Likewise, diphthongs may sometimes be separated into two separate vocalic elements (as in ti/em/po above). When the last word of a line has a stressed final syllable (^{1}cor^{2}tés), an additional syllable is counted, and when the rhyme word is stressed on the antepenultimate syllable (^{1}es^{2}drú^{1}ju^{1}la, ^{1}fo^{2}tó^{1}gra^{1}fo), one less is counted. It is useful to think of Spanish verse forms as being of two basic types: those which have lines of eight syllables or less ('arte menor') and those which have nine or more ('arte mayor'). Those with nine or more syllables often have a mid-line pause.

The metric structure of a line of Spanish verse can be worked out and notated through a combination of syllable counting and registering groups of stressed and unstressed syllables separated by junctures marked by a pause. These structures are, of course, not intended to lay down a rigid and immutable rule of scansion; they merely suggest and represent plausible oral readings of the lines concerned. Difficult decisions, such as whether to read 'No hay tiempo que perder' as six, seven or eight syllables, can often only be taken in the light of thematic considerations and of the overall metric structure of a poem. For practical purposes, the following simple system is an adequate way of notating metric structure in Spanish verse:

˘ ˘ ˘ˋ ˘ ˘ ˘ ˋ
No hay tiempo que perder = 8

˘ ˘˘ˋ ˘ / ˘ ˘ ˘ ˘ ˋ ˘
Al horitaña / de la montazonte = 11

˘ ˋ / ˘ ˘ ˋ ˘ ˘ ˋ ˘ ˘ ˋ ˘
El mar / como‿un vasto cristal azogado = 12

˘ ˋ ˘ ˘ ˋ ˘ ˘ / ˘ ˋ ˘ ˘ ˋ
refleja la lámina / de‿un cielo de zinc; = 12

In this notation, the following symbols are used: [˘] denotes an unstressed syllable, [ˋ] a stressed one; [/] denotes a pause.

Rhyme. In modern Spanish verse, assonance and full rhyme are equally likely to appear and are of equal value. The most common verse forms are: the *romance* (ballad) which has an undetermined number of octosyllabic lines assonating in every second line; the sonnet; the *redondilla* which has any number of stanzas of four octosyllabic lines rhyming abba or abab; the *lira* which combines hepta- and hendecasyllabic lines; and the alexandrine, which has 12 syllables.

English

Whereas a line of modern Spanish verse is defined in terms of a syllable count, lines in English verse are conventionally defined in terms of *feet*. A **foot** is a conventional group of stressed and/or unstressed syllables occurring in a specific order, and a line of traditional verse consists of a fixed (conventional) number of particular feet. Take for example:

˘ – ˘ – ˘ – ˘ – ˘ –
The cur | few tolls | the knell | of par | ting day

This line is a *pentameter*: that is, it consists of five feet. Each of the feet in this case is made up of one unstressed syllable followed by one stressed syllable. A foot of this type is an *iamb*, represented as | ˘ – |. A line consisting of five iambic feet is an iambic pentameter. It is the most common English line, found in the work of great playwrights and poets like Shakespeare, Milton and Wordsworth.

A line consisting of three iambs is an iambic *trimeter*; one consisting of four iambs is an iambic *tetrameter*; one consisting of six iambs is an iambic *hexameter*. The shorter lines are more usual than the pentameter in songs, ballads and light verse.

Besides the iamb, the commonest other types of feet are:

– ˘ – ˘ – ˘ – ˘
trochee: Present | mirth brings | present | laughter (trochaic tetrameter)

˘ ˘ – ˘ ˘ – ˘ ˘ – ˘ ˘ –
anapest: With a leap | and a bound | the swift A | napests throng (anapestic tetrameter)

– ˘ ˘ – ˘ ˘ – ˘ ˘ – ˘ ˘
dactyl: Ever to | come up with | Dactyl tri | syllable (dactylic tetrameter)

– – – – – –
spondee: Slow spon | dee stalks | strong foot (spondaic trimeter)

Naturally, following a single rhythmic pattern without variation would quickly become tedious. Hence the sort of variation typified in lines 1 and 6 of Wordsworth's 'Composed upon Westminster Bridge':

(˘ ˘) (– –)
– ˘ ˘ – ˘ – ˘ – ˘ –
Earth has | not a | nything | to show | more fair

– – ˘ – – ˘ ˘ – ˘ –
Ships, tow | ers, domes, | theatres | and temp | les lie

Like the rest of the poem, these lines may be described as iambic, because their rhythm is predominantly iambic; but within this overriding pattern there is considerable variation.

One other sort of English metre is worth mentioning, *strong-stress metre*. This is different from the syllable-and-stress metre described above. Only the stresses count in the scanning, the number of weak syllables being variable. Much modern verse uses this metre, most frequently with four stresses in a line, often in combination with syllable-and-stress metre.

NB Exact metrical analysis and scansion in English and in Spanish are a far more complex and subtle issue than the simple notations we have given here. However, for the purposes of an introduction to translation methodology, only three things are required: a simple method of identifying and notating rhythmic recurrences and variations; a way of assessing their expressive function in the ST; a means of deciding, in the light of these things, what TL verse form (if any) to adopt. Translators who become proficient enough in these skills to want to specialize in verse translation are recommended to consult the books by Malof (1970) and Navarro Tomás (1991) listed in the References.

PRACTICAL 4

4.1 The formal properties of texts; phonic and prosodic

Assignment

(i) With particular reference to its salient formal properties, discuss the strategic problems confronting the translator of the following text, and outline your own strategy for translating it.
(ii) Translate the text into English.
(iii) Explain the main decisions of detail you made in producing your TT.

Contextual information
The ST is an extract from Vicente Huidobro's poem 'La golondrina'. Huidobro (1893–1948) was a Chilean avant-garde poet, best remembered as the inventor of the literary movement known as 'Creacionismo'.

Text

No hay tiempo que perder
Ya viene la golondrina monotémpora
Trae un acento antípoda de lejanías que se acercan
Viene gondoleando la golondrina

Al horitaña de la montazonte
La violondrina y el goloncelo
Descolgada esta mañana de la lunala
Se acerca a todo galope
Ya viene viene la golondrina
Ya viene viene la golonfina
Ya viene la golontrina
Ya viene la goloncima
Viene la golonchina
Viene la golonclima
Ya viene la golonrima
Ya viene la golonrisa
La golonniña
La golongira
La golonlira
La golonbrisa
La golonchilla

Reprinted from Vicente Huidobro, *Obras completas*, ed. B. Arenas (Santiago de Chile: Zig-Zag, 1964, p. 398).

4.2 The formal properties of texts; graphic

Assignment

Working in groups:

(i) Assess the salient formal properties – especially on the *graphic* level of textual variables – of the following text, discuss the strategic problems confronting the translator, and outline your own strategy for translating it.
(ii) In the light of your findings in (i), translate the text with due attention to graphic detail.
(iii) Explain the main decisions of detail you made in producing your TT.

Contextual information

The text is a two-page graphic poem by Guillermo de Torre (1900–71) entitled 'Paisaje plástico'. It is reprinted from *La generación poética de 1927*, edited by J. González Muela and J. M. Rozas and published in 1986, an anthology which also contains other poems experimenting with the iconic relationship between graphic form and poetic content. In common with other graphic poems by Guillermo de Torre, the key to this iconic relationship in the extract below is given by the title.

Mediodía igniscente en el vórtice de la campaña estival

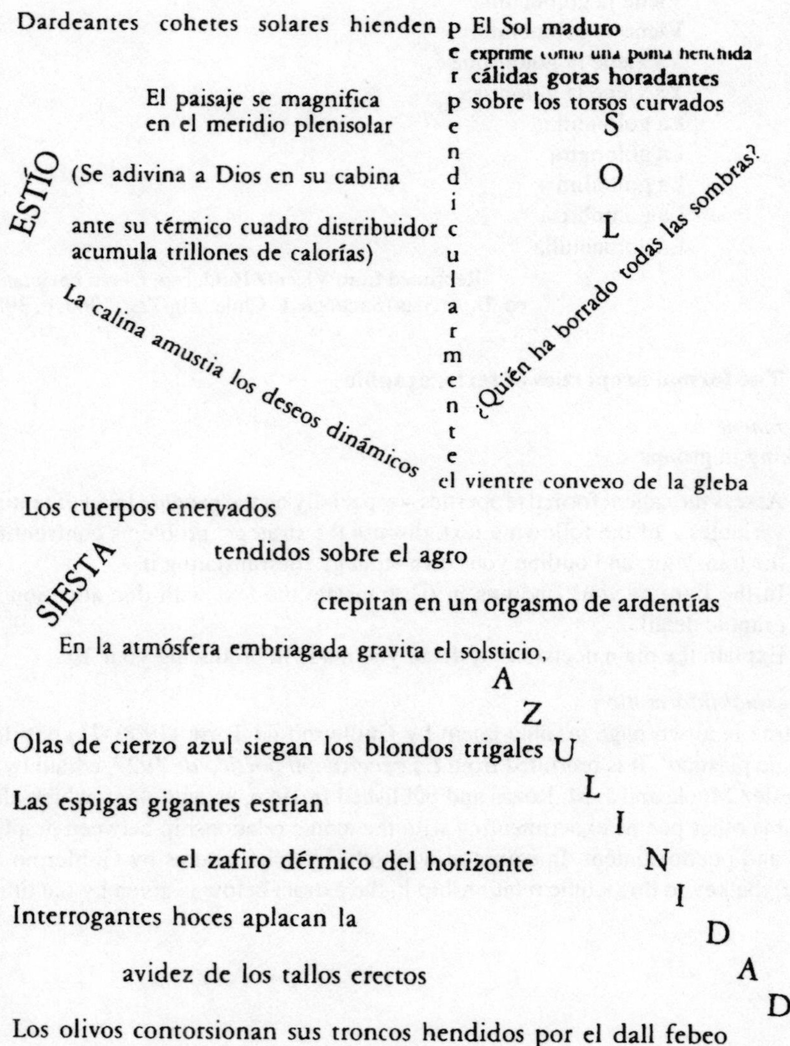

Dardeantes cohetes solares hienden
perpendicularmente
El Sol maduro
exprime como una poma henchida
cálidas gotas horadantes
sobre los torsos curvados
El paisaje se magnifica
en el meridio plenisolar
SOL
ESTÍO
(Se adivina a Dios en su cabina
ante su térmico cuadro distribuidor
acumula trillones de calorías)
¿Quién ha borrado todas las sombras?
La calina amustia los deseos dinámicos
el vientre convexo de la gleba
Los cuerpos enervados
tendidos sobre el agro
SIESTA
crepitan en un orgasmo de ardentías
En la atmósfera embriagada gravita el solsticio,
AZULINIDAD
Olas de cierzo azul siegan los blondos trigales
Las espigas gigantes estrían
el zafiro dérmico del horizonte
Interrogantes hoces aplacan la
avidez de los tallos erectos
Los olivos contorsionan sus troncos hendidos por el dall febeo

Racimos agraces evocan las vendimias saciadoras

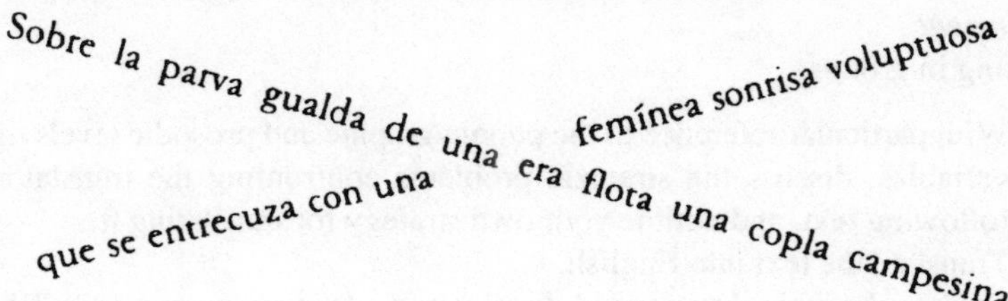

Sobre la parva gualda de una era flota una copla campesina
que se entrecuza con una femínea sonrisa voluptuosa

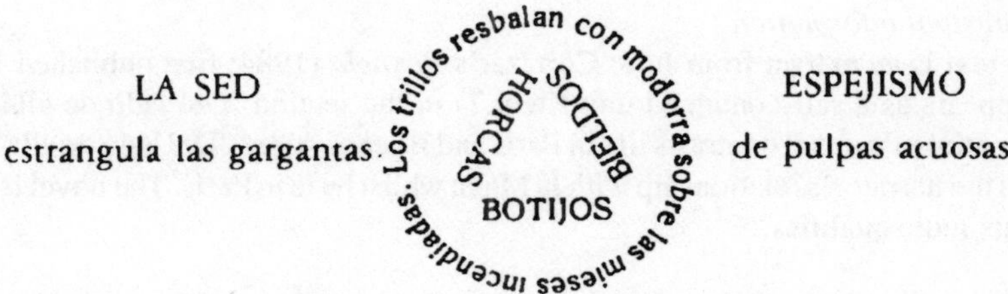

LA SED
estrangula las gargantas
Los trillos resbalan con modorra sobre las mieses incendiadas
HORCAS
BIELDOS
BOTIJOS
ESPEJISMO
de pulpas acuosas

Campesinos jadeantes en su fervor agreste
reciben en la hostia solar la eucaristía triptolémica
Las ranas estridulantes de la alberca
modulan una cansina monodía

El
río
exi
guo

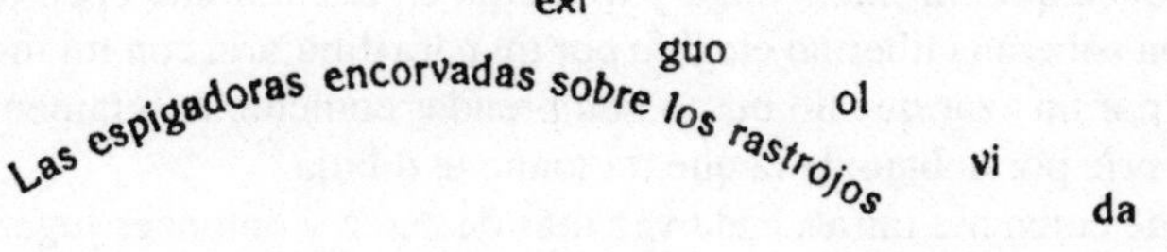

Las espigadoras encorvadas sobre los rastrojos

ol
vi
da
su
cau
ce

se confunden con los sarmientos de las carrascas

HAY UNA CONSTELACIÓN DE GAVILLAS SOBRE LOS PERDIOS RASURADOS

Los barbechos dormitan Bancales barcinos Zahones abandonados
En la alucinación sensorial
bajo la égida meridia
advienen:
ESCUADRILLAS DE AVIONES
QUE AGAVILLAN CON SUS HÉLICES
LAS COSECHAS INFLAMADAS

Y rítmicamente los élitros sonoros de las cigarras ebrias
polarizan la harmonía estival

Reproduced from J. González Muela and J. M. Rozas, *La generación poética de 1927* (Madrid: Istmo, pp. 354–5), copyright © Agustina Bravo Ortuño, 1986.

4.3 The formal properties of texts; phonic/graphic and prosodic

Assignment

Working in groups:

(i) With particular reference to the phonic/graphic and prosodic levels of textual variables, discuss the strategic problems confronting the translator of the following text, and outline your own strategy for translating it.
(ii) Translate the text into English.
(iii) Explain the main decisions of detail you made in producing your TT.

Contextual information

The text is an extract from Julio Cortázar's *Rayuela* (1984; first published 1963). It appears as a self-contained unit (item 7) in the section 'Del lado de allá'. The Argentinian's novel contrasts life in Paris and Buenos Aires. 'Del lado de allá' deals with the narrator's relationship with la Maga whilst he is in Paris. The novel is noted for its ludic qualities.

Text

Toco tu boca, con un dedo toco el borde de tu boca, voy dibujándola como si saliera de mi mano, como si por primera vez tu boca se entreabriera, y me basta cerrar los ojos para deshacerlo todo y recomenzar, hago nacer cada vez la boca que deseo, la boca que mi mano elige y te dibuja en la cara, una boca elegida entre todas, con soberana libertad elegida por mí para dibujarla con mi mano en tu cara, y que por un azar que no busco comprender coincide exactamente con tu boca que sonríe por debajo de la que mi mano te dibuja.

Me miras, de cerca me miras, cada vez más de cerca y entonces jugamos al cíclope, nos miramos cada vez más de cerca y los ojos se agrandan, se acercan entre sí, se superponen y los cíclopes se miran, respirando confundidos, las bocas se encuentran y luchan tibiamente, mordiéndose con los labios, apoyando apenas la lengua en los dientes, jugando en sus recintos donde un aire pesado va y viene con un perfume viejo y un silencio. Entonces mis manos buscan hundirse en tu pelo, acariciar lentamente la profundidad de tu pelo mientras nos besamos como si tuviéramos la boca llena de flores o de peces, de movimientos vivos, de fragancia oscura. Y si nos mordemos el dolor es dulce, y si nos ahogamos en un breve y terrible absorber simultáneo del aliento, esa instántanea muerte es bella. Y hay una sola saliva y un solo sabor a fruta madura, y yo te siento temblar contra mí como una luna en el agua.

5

The formal properties of texts: grammatical and lexical issues in translation

The level of textual variables considered in this chapter is the **grammatical level**. It is useful to divide the contents of this level into two areas: first, grammatical arrangement of meaningful linguistic units into larger units (complex words and syntactic constructions); and second, the actual meaningful linguistic units, in particular the words, that figure in constructions.

A great deal of the explicit literal meaning of a text is carried by the configuration of words and phrases. To interpret any text it is necessary – but, of course, not sufficient – to construe the literal meaning conveyed by its grammatical structures. (Literal meaning as such will be discussed in Chapter 7.) Furthermore, a TT has normally to be constructed by putting words into meaningful grammatical configurations according to the conventions and structures of the TL, and using the lexical means available in the TL. Consequently, translators can never ignore the level of grammatical variables in either the ST or the TT. Let us look at the question of grammatical arrangement first.

GRAMMATICAL ARRANGEMENT

Under this heading we subsume two main types of grammatical structure: first, the patterns by which complex and compound words are formed – that is, affixation/inflection, compounding and word derivation; second, the successive patterns whereby words are linked to form phrases, and phrases can be linked to form yet more complex phrases.

It is important to remember that these structural patterns differ from language to language. Even where apparent cross-linguistic similarities occur, they are often misleading, the structural equivalent of *faux amis*. The following pairs illustrate this point:

estar constipado	to have a cold
embarazada	pregnant
actual	present *(not* actual)
en absoluto	definitely not (*not* absolutely)
no lo sé	I don't know / I have no idea (*not* I don't know it)

In fact, much of what one might be tempted to call the 'ethos' of a typical Spanish, German or classical Chinese text is simply a reflection of preponderant grammatical structures specific to these languages. Thus, to take an obvious example, the potential for complex word formations such as 'Autobahnbrücke' or 'Ungeziefervertilgungsanstalt' (pest control department) is typical of German, and is often absent in other languages. This implies that, for example, a translator into English cannot in principle replicate 'Autobahnbrücke' as a compound word, but must resort to syntactic means, probably using the complex phrase 'motorway bridge', or perhaps 'bridge over the motorway'. The distinction between these two alternatives illustrates a characteristic difference between English and Spanish. While there is a notable tendency for English (under American influence) to move closer to German in the formation of compound words, such as 'failsafe', 'foolproof', 'roadblock' or 'childcare', English abounds in constructions of the type *attributive noun + noun*, for instance 'pleasure boat', 'city wall', 'church roof', 'customs officer'. Spanish, on the other hand, not only has a far greater resistance than English to the 'Germanic' type of compound words, and in fact to compound words in general, but it also tends to prefer prepositional phrases to the *attributive noun + noun* constructions favoured by English. Thus, typically, English 'pleasure-loving' – whose ambiguous status between attributive phrase and compound noun is signalled by the presence of the hyphen – has its closest Spanish counterparts in the prepositional phrases 'amigo de los placeres' and 'amante de placeres', although in some higher register contexts the noun 'sibarita' may offer a plausible alternative. These differences in grammatical tendencies imply that, in translating from Spanish to English, there is a frequent need for grammatical transposition (see p. 185 and Glossary), if one is to avoid translationese. (Other obvious instances of grammatical differences between Spanish and English are the characteristic differences in word order, for example in 'adjectival' constructions such as 'el año pasado' versus 'last year' and verbal constructions such as 'el año que viene' versus 'next year'. These grammatical differences are exploited for comic purposes in *Asterix en Bretaña* (Goscinny and Uderzo, 1967, *passim*), for instance in Buentorax's use of the phrase 'la mágica poción', calqued on English 'the magic potion'. While this calque is not strictly ungrammatical, the word 'mágica' is both lexically incongruous (compare 'encantada') and, because of its position, inappropriately marked for emphasis.

The extent to which grammatical differences between languages can cause major translation loss is dramatically illustrated by 'exotic' languages, for instance by a comparison of English with Chinese. In a normal predicative phrase in Chinese, there are three particularly troublesome grammatical features. First, neither subject nor object need be explicitly singular or plural. Second, there is no definite or indefinite article for either subject or object. Third, there may be no indication of a tense or mood for the predicate. Since all these features are obligatorily present in predicative phrases in English, the Chinese phrase 'rén mǎi shū' (interlineally rendered as 'man buy book') has no exact literal counterpart in English, but has to be rendered, according to what is most plausible in the context, as one of the following combinations:

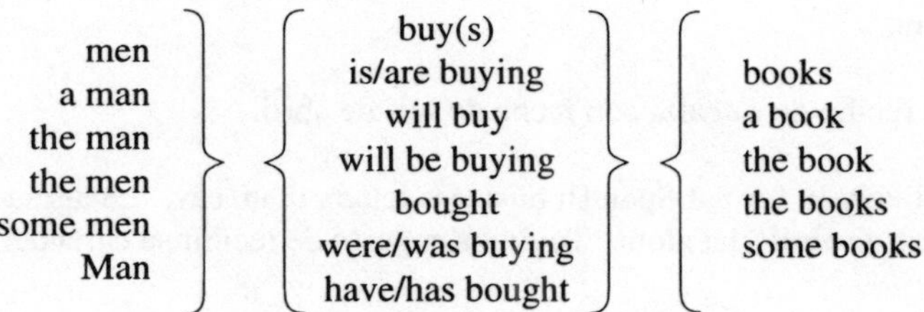

Because English syntax is so different from Chinese, the phrase 'rén mǎi shū' can only be translated if one explicitly specifies in the TT certain details not expressed in the ST – that is, at the cost of considerable, but inevitable, translation loss (as defined in Chapter 2).

Wherever the grammatical structures of the ST cannot be matched by analogous structures in the TT, the translator is faced with the prospect of major translation losses. The problems that may be caused by this are not necessarily serious, but they are complex and many, which means that we can only touch on them briefly here. (Such problems are illustrated in more detail in Chapters 16–19.)

The need for circumlocution in a TT is one of the commonest of these problems. For example, the simple everyday word 'callejear' in Spanish may have to be rendered in English by the circumlocution 'to wander about the streets'. This is an obvious case of translation loss, a neat and compact piece of ST corresponding to a relatively complex and long-winded TT. What may be less obvious is that the converse case of rendering a complex ST word by a simple word in the TT, or a complex ST phrase by a single word, is just as much a translation loss, because the grammatical proportions of the ST are not adhered to in the TT. For example, translating Spanish 'hedonista' by 'pleasure seeker', or English 'obtainable (from)' by Spanish 'estar a la venta', both entail translation loss in terms of grammatical structure. These examples show how, as a rule, *semantic* considerations override considerations of *grammatical* translation loss, priority being given almost automatically to the *mot juste* and to constructing grammatically well-formed, idiomatic TL sentences.

Nevertheless, translators should be aware of grammatical differences between SL and TL, and aware of them as potential sources of translation loss, for there are exceptions to the 'rule' mentioned above, namely STs with salient textual properties manifestly resulting from the manipulation of grammatical structure. Take, for example, this opening sentence from a business letter in English:

> We acknowledge receipt of your letter of 6 April.

This is a more likely formula than 'We have received the letter you sent on 6 April' or 'Thank you for the letter you sent on 6 April'. In putting the sentence into Spanish, the translator should not aim at the simplest, most everyday grammatical structure capable of rendering the literal message of the ST, but should take into consideration the respective effects of 'formality' required in English and Spanish business letters:

> Acusamos recibo de su carta con fecha de seis de abril.

This is more likely in formal Spanish business letters than, say, 'Le agradecemos su carta del seis de abril', let alone 'Tuvimos el gusto de recibir su carta del seis de abril'.

As this example shows, a great deal depends on nuances within the particular TL genre, an issue to which we shall return in Chapters 11–14.

Grammatical structure may assume particular importance in literary translation. A prestigious author's hallmark may partly consist in characteristic grammatical structuring. For example, extreme streamlining of syntax characterizes Lorca's rural tragedies, whereas Góngora's style is known for its extreme syntactic complexity, so much so that the English term 'gongorism' is often used to describe an affected, elaborate literary style. Modern Spanish authors with a reputation for using syntactic complexity as a stylistic device include Martín-Santos (see the extract in Practical 5.2), Goytisolo (see the extract in Practical 5.1) and Cortázar.

We have elected to illustrate the stylistic deployment of syntactic complexity by what is a relatively short sentence from Cortázar's novel *Los premios*:

> Pero aparte de un poco bohemio, López se conducía como un excelente colega, siempre dispuesto a reconocer que los discursos de 9 de julio tenía que pronunciarlos el doctor Restelli, quien acababa rindiéndose modestamente a las solicitaciones del doctor Guglielmetti y a la presión tan cordial como inmerecida de la sala de profesores.
>
> (Cortázar, 1981, p. 10)

Cortázar's elaborate syntactic structure, whose academic preciosity accords well with the theme of academe under discussion, typically contains numerous coordinated phrases, as well as layers of phrases embedded in phrases. To reduce it to a series of small, easily digestible English sentences would be possible, but inappropriate; the resulting TT would fail to convey the feel of Cortázar's style to TL readers. The following version is just such a failure:

> But, apart from being somewhat bohemian, Lopez was an excellent colleague. He was always ready to recognize that it was Dr Restelli who should deliver the Ninth of July speeches. And Dr Restelli, in the end, always yielded modestly to Dr Guglielmetti's solicitations and the extremely cordial, even though unmerited, pressure at the faculty meetings.

The breaking up of the ST sentence into three compact TT sentences occasions a loss of the functional relation between the text's syntactic complexity and its thematic reference. A more stylistically apt TT would need to be syntactically fairly complex and elaborate. Here, for discussion in class, is the Kerrigan translation:

> But apart from being somewhat bohemian, Lopez was an excellent colleague, always ready to recognize that it was Dr Restelli who should deliver the Ninth of July speeches. And Dr Restelli, in the end, always yielded modestly to Dr Guglielmetti's solicitations and the extremely cordial, even though unmerited, pressure at the faculty meetings.
>
> (Cortázar, 1986, p. 4)

While the Kerrigan translation is an improvement on the syntactically fragmented TT above, a still more stylistically satisfying alternative would be one that preserved the syntactic integrity of the ST as a single sentence:

> But, apart from being something of a bohemian, Lopez was an excellent colleague, always disposed to recognize that it was Dr Restelli's right to deliver the Ninth of July Speeches, and the latter would, in the end, invariably yield in all modesty to Dr Guglielmetti's solicitations and to the pressures, no less cordial than unmerited, in the staffroom.

There is another reason why translators must keep a close eye on grammatical structure: contrasts and recurrences in syntactic patterning can be used as devices creating special textual effects. A simple example is seen in the well-known children's rhyme about magpies:

> One for sorrow,
> Two for joy,
> Three for a girl,
> Four for a boy,
> Five for silver,
> Six for gold,
> Seven for a secret that's never been told.

The grammatical patterns underlying this rhyme are schematized as follows:

(part of an ascending series)	number	preposition	abstract noun	(antonyms)
	number	preposition	abstract noun	
	number	preposition	article + common noun	(antonyms)
	number	preposition	article + common noun	
	number	preposition	mass noun	(part of an ascending series)
	number	preposition	mass noun	
	number	preposition	article + abstract noun + relative phrase	

To translate this rhyme into another language, one would have to give careful consideration to the grammatical patterning as schematized above, because the loss of its effects would deprive the text of much of its point; in effect, the structural scheme would be the basis for formulating a TT.

Much less blatantly playful texts, such as rhetorical speeches, may make similar use of devices based on syntactic patterns of contrast and recurrence. In such cases, it would be a serious textual error not to recognize the stylistic importance of these grammatical devices, and a potentially serious translation loss not to try to reconstruct them in the TT. There are also literary texts that amount to a kind of virtuoso performance in syntactic density and complexity; this is a main consideration in translating the Martín-Santos ST in Practical 5.2.

WORDS

For reasons of educational bias (for instance, the paramount use that students make of dictionaries and lexically arranged encyclopedias), people are far more directly aware of individual words than of other units and structures of language. In particular, mentioning 'meaning' or the semantic properties of languages (and therefore also of texts) tends to evoke first and foremost the level of individual words. Yet meanings are certainly not exclusively concentrated in words individually listed in isolation in dictionaries. Any text shows that the combination of words (and their use in contexts) creates meanings that they do not possess in isolation, and even meanings that are not wholly predictable from the literal senses of the words combined.

As our multi-level approach to textual variables indicates, lexical translation losses (such as want of an exact translation for a particular word) are just one kind of translation loss among many. There is no *a priori* reason, as long as the overall sense of the ST is successfully conveyed by the TT, why they should be given a heavier weighting than other kinds of translation loss. In fact, as we saw in Chapter 3, communicative translation is often more important than word-for-word correspondences. For instance, 'no se puede saber' can be plausibly translated in most modern contexts as 'you never can tell', rather than as 'one can never know'; even then, the choice of 'you' instead of 'one', 'a body' or even 'a girl' would be entirely a matter of context.

Lexical translation losses, then, are no more avoidable than other kinds of translation loss. Exact synonymy between SL and TL words is the exception rather than the rule, and problems arising from this should be neither maximized nor minimized, but treated on a par with other translation losses that affect the overall meaning of the TT.

Comparing the lexical meanings of words across languages underlines the fact that lexical translation losses are as likely to result from 'particularization' (where the TT word has a narrower meaning than the ST word) as from 'generalization' (where the TT has a wider meaning than the ST word). So, for example, translating, in a given context, Spanish 'alma' as 'soul', rather than as 'mind' or 'spirit', is an inevitable particularization, because one has to choose one of these three TL words, but each has a narrower range of reference than Spanish 'alma'. Conversely, translating '¡tiene un revólver!' as 'he's got a gun!' is a case of generalization, because 'gun' can also mean 'escopeta', 'pistola', 'fusil' and 'cañón' – that is, it has a wider range of reference than 'revólver'. The translation problems arising from particularization and generalization are very common, and we shall return to them in Chapter 7.

Another reason why, in ordinary language, no TL word is ever likely to replicate precisely the 'meaning' of a given SL word is that, in each language, words form idiosyncratic associations with sets of other words. Such associations may hold by virtue of the forms of words, as in the homonymic association between 'crane' (bird) and 'crane' (machine); or by virtue of the literal meanings of the words, as with the associations of relative value in the series 'gold', 'silver' and 'bronze'; or by virtue of culture-bound prejudices and assumptions, as in the association of 'law and order' (or 'brutality') with 'police'. The exact associative overtones of words in the overall context of a ST are often difficult enough to pinpoint, but it is even more difficult, if not impossible, to find TL words that will, over and above conveying an appropriate literal meaning, also produce exactly the right associative overtones in the context of the TT. This is another source of lexical translation loss, and another potential dilemma between choosing literal meaning at the expense of associative overtones, or vice versa. We shall return to these questions in Chapter 8.

Series of words can be distributed in contrastive and recurrent patterns that signal or reinforce the thematic development of the text. In 'One for sorrow', there are a number of examples of the patterned use of lexical sets over an entire text. In Aphek and Tobin (1988), the term **word system** is used to denote this phenomenon. A word system is a pattern (within a text) of words having an associative common denominator, a pattern which 'nurtures the theme and message of the text with greater intensity' (Aphek and Tobin, 1988, p. 3). Aphek and Tobin illustrate their concept of theme-reinforcing word systems from texts in Hebrew. In Hebrew, words consist of consonantal roots with variable vocalic fillers. Thus, for instance, the word 'XaZiR' ('pig') has the basic consonantal root 'X–Z–R' (an example earlier alluded to in Chapter 4, p. 47). All words with the same consonantal root are perceived in Hebrew as belonging to a single associative set. (This is mainly because of the system of writing, in which vocalic fillers may be omitted.) There is therefore a strongly bonded associative lexical set based on the 'X–Z–R' root, members of which may form a word system distributed over a text in a way that reinforces the theme and message of the text. Aphek and Tobin discern an 'X–Z–R' word system in a twentieth-century Hebrew short story entitled 'The Lady and the Pedlar', in which 'X–Z–R' words are systematically found at various key points in the narrative:

> A Jewish pedlar *makes his rounds* (me XaZeR al ptaxim) in villages.
>
> He meets a gentile woman and he *bows before her repeatedly* (XoZeRet vehishtaxava).
>
> He takes out and *replaces* (maXZiR) his merchandise, but she *goes back* (XoZeRet) indoors.
>
> The man begins to *court* (meXaZeR) the woman and becomes her lover. He forgets to live according to Jewish customs (for example, he eats pork).
>
> Eventually it transpires that the woman is a vampire, and, in a climactic argument, she laughs at the pedlar and calls him a *pig* (XaZiR).
>
> As a turning-point in the story, the man *returns* (XoZeR) to the forest, *returns* (laXZoR) to his religion and *repents* (XoZeR betshuva).
>
> On *returning* (XoZeR) to the house, he finds that the woman has stabbed herself with his knife. She dies.
>
> The pedlar *resumes his rounds* (XiZeR ve-X-XiZeR) *crying* (maXRiZ) his wares *repeatedly* (XoZeR ve-maXRuZ; note the final inversion of X–Z–R to X–R–Z).

The pattern of 'X–Z–R' (and 'X–R–Z') words coincides with salient points in the narrative, thus marking and reinforcing them. It also highlights the important thematic points in the interplay between abandoning Jewish religious observance, eating pork, being a metaphorical pig in the eyes of the vampire woman, and eventual repentance. These points are more tightly bound together by the 'X–Z–R' word system than they would be by the mere narrative sequence of the text.

This example shows that it is worth scanning certain types of text for theme-reinforcing word systems (such as a series of thematic key-words, or phonetic patterns, or an extended metaphor), because such things may be important textual devices. Where a word system is found in the ST, the construction of some analogous word system in the TT may be desirable; if so, this will be a strong factor influencing the translator's lexical choices. In the case of Aphek and Tobin's example, the word system in question hinges on a phonic/graphic common denominator which is highly specific to Hebrew; constructing a similar phonic/graphic word system seems virtually impossible in an English TT. Two of the translator's first strategic decisions will, therefore, be how much priority to give to this type of pattern, and how to construct an appropriate word system in the TT.

PRACTICAL 5

5.1 The formal properties of texts; syntax

Assignment

(i) Examine carefully the word system on which the following passage is based, discuss the strategic problems it raises, and outline your own strategy for translating the passage.
(ii) Translate lines 1–10 of the text (from the start to 'y albricias').
(iii) Explain the main decisions of detail you made in producing your TT.

Contextual information

The passage is taken from Juan Goytisolo's novel *Reivindicación del conde don Julián* (1988b; first published 1970). *Reivindicación* is noted for its audacious style through which Goytisolo breaks down traditional narrative strategies through his manipulation of the first-person point of view in an attempt to throw off some of the restrictions of language. The novel deals thematically with the debt of Spanish to Arabic culture.

Text

y galopando con ellos en desenfrenada razzia saquearás los campos de algodón, algarrobo, alfalfa

vaciarás aljibes y albercas, demolerás almacenes y dársenas, arruinarás alquerías y fondas, pillarás alcobas, alacenas, zaguanes

cargarás con sofás, alfombras, jarros, almohadas

devastarás las aldeas y sacrificarás los rebaños, despojarás a la ilusionada novia de su ajuar, a la dama aristócrata de sus alhajas, al rico estraperlista de su fulana, al hidalgo provecto de su alcurnia

retirarás el ajedrez de los casinos, el alquitrán de las carreteras

prohibirás alborozos y juergas, zalemas y albricias, abolirás las expansivas, eufóricas carcajades

el recio comensal de sanchopancesca glotonería que aborda su bien surtida mesa con un babador randado y, tras la oración de rigor, se dispone a catar los manjares que le sirven maestresalas y pajes, lo amenazarás con tu varilla de ballena, impuesto de la autoridad y el prestigio de tus severos diplomas lexicográficos

no se ha de comer, señor carpeto, sino como es uso y costumbre en las otras ínsulas donde ya he morado : yo, señor, soy gramático, y miro por la pureza del idioma mucho más que por mi vida, estudiando de noche y de día y tanteando la complexión del carpeto para acertar a curarle cuando cayere enfermo : y lo principal que hago es asistir a sus comidas y cenas, y dejarle comer de lo que me parece castizo y quitarle cuanto etimológicamente es extraño : y así mando quitarle estos entremeses porque contienen arroz y aceitunas, y aquellos guisos por ver en ellos alubias, berenjenas y zanahorias

desa manera, aquel plato de perdices que están allí dispuestas, y, a mi parecer bien sazonadas, no me harán algún daño

ésas no comerá el señor carpeto en tanto que yo tuviere vida

pues, ¿por qué?

porque son en adobo y han sido condimentadas con azafrán

si eso es así, vea el señor gramático de cuantos manjares hay en esta mesa cuál me hará más provecho y cuál menos daño y déjeme comer dél sin que me le apalee, porque por vida de carpeto, y así Dios me le deje gozar, que me muero de hambre, y el negarme la comida, aunque le pese al señor gramático y él más me diga, antes será quitarme la vida que aumentármela

vuesa merced tiene razón, señor carpeto : y así me parece que vuesa merced no coma de aquellos conejos guisados que allí están, porque van guarnecidos de alcachofa : de aquella ternera, porque ha sido aderezada con espinaca

aquel platonazo que está más adelante vahando me parece que es olla podrida, que por la diversidad de cosas que en tales ollas podridas hay no podrá dejar de topar con alguna que me sea gusto y provecho

absit! : vaya lejos de nosostros tan mal pensamiento! : no hay cosa peor en el mundo que una olla podrida con albóndigas y unas gotas de aceite : y respecto a los postres de vuesa merced ni uno siquiera le puedo autorizar : el flan, a causa del caramelo : el helado, por contener azúcar : la macedonia, por el jarabe : en cuanto al exquisito sorbete que acaban de servir a vuesa merced, la duda ofende : es etimológicamente foráneo!

Reprinted by kind permission from Juan Goytisolo, *Reivindicación del conde don Julián* (Barcelona: Seix Barral, 1988, pp. 196–8),

5.2 The formal properties of texts

Assignment

(i) With particular reference to salient formal properties, discuss the strategic problems confronting the translator of the following text, and outline your own strategy for translating it.
(ii) Translate the text into English.
(iii) Explain the main decisions of detail you made in producing your TT.

Contextual information

The passage is from Luis Martín-Santos's *Tiempo de silencio*, first published in 1961. The novel has achieved great critical acclaim on account of its innovative narrative strategies. The plot describes the events which surround a young medical researcher who inadvertently becomes involved in an illegal abortion. Although not directly as a result of the researcher's intervention, the patient dies. In the following passage the protagonist-narrator, after a drinking binge, is taken along by his friend, Matías, to visit the brothel where he will later take refuge before finally being caught and held by the police.

Text

Esferoidal, fosforescente, retumbante, oscura-luminosa, fibrosa-táctil, recogida en pliegues, acariciadora, amansante, paralizadora recubierta de pliegues protectores, olorosa, materna, impregnada de alcohol derramado por la boca, capitoné azulada, dorada a veces por una bombilla anémica cuyo resplandor hiere los ojos noctámbulos, arrulladora, sólo apta para el murmullo, denigrante, copa del desprecio de la prostituta para el borracho, lugar donde la patrona vuelve a ser un reverendo padre que confiesa dando claras y rectas normas mediante las que el pecado de la carne es evitable, longitudinal, túnel donde la náusea sube, color tierra cuando el gusano-cuerpo entra en contacto con las masas que aprisionadoramente lo rodean, carente de fuerza gravitatoria como en un experimento todavía no logrado, giroscópica, orientada hacia un norte, elegida para una travesía secreta, laguna estigia, dotada de un banco metálico desde la que el cuerpo alargado y lánguido cae a una blandura apenas inferior, cabina de un vagon-lit a ciento treinta kilómetros por hora a través de las landas bordelesas, cabin-log de un faruest donde ya no quedan cabelleras, camarote agitado por la tempestad del índico cuando los tifones llegan a impedir el vuelo del amarillo cormorán, barquilla hecha de mimbres que montgolfiera, ascensor lanzado hacia la altura de un rascacielos de goma dilatada, calabozo inmóvil donde la soledad del hombre se demuestra, cesto de inmundicia, poso en que reducido a excremento espera el ocupante la llegada del agua negra que le llevará hasta el mar a través de ratas grises y cloacas, calabozo otra vez donde con un clavo lentamente se dibuja con trabajo arrancando trocitos de cal la figura de una sirena con su cola asombrosa de pez hembra, vigilada por una figura gruesa de mujer que la briza, acariciada por una figura blanda de mujer que amamanta, cuna, placenta, meconio, deciduas, matriz, oviducto, ovario puro vacío, aniquilación inversa en que el huevo en un universo antiprotónico se escinde en sus dos entidades previas y Matías ha desempezado a no existir, así la sala de retirada, sala de visitas, sala para los detritus, sala para los borrachos de buena familia que en una noche anegada llegan y encallan en la única puta que no ha podido trabajar y que con mirada incomprensiva los mira mientras que revueltos en las cáscaras de naranjas y en las peladuras de patatas se reconcilian y salvan.

Reprinted by kind permission from Luis Martín-Santos, *Tiempo de silencio* (Barcelona: Seix Barral, 1985, pp. 104–6),

6

The formal properties of texts: sentential, inter-sentential and intertextual issues in translating

Three levels of textual variables will be considered in this chapter: the sentential level, the discourse level and the intertextual level. These levels, which are successively higher in the hierarchy of levels outlined in Chapter 4, will complete our discussion of textual variables.

THE SENTENTIAL LEVEL

The next level of textual variables above the grammatical level is the **sentential level**, on which sentences are considered. By 'sentence' we mean a particular type of linguistic unit that is a complete, self-contained and ready-made vehicle for actual communication: nothing more needs to be added to it before it can be uttered in concrete situations. So, for example, the starter's one-word command 'Go!' or the exclamation 'What bliss!' is a sentence. Words and phrases are mere abstractions from sentences, abstractions stripped of practical communicative purpose, intonation and of other features that make sentences genuine vehicles of linguistic utterance.

For the nature of the textual variables on the sentential level to be grasped, a distinction must be drawn between spoken and written texts, since spoken languages and written languages differ sharply on this level.

A spoken text counts on the sentential level as a sequence of sentences, each with a built-in communicative purpose conveyed by one or more such features as *intonation* (for example the rising pitch that signals a question in English and the fall-rise pitch that signals a question in Spanish); *sequential focus* (for example the word order of 'Him I don't like', which shifts the emphasis on to the object of the sentence); or **illocutionary particles** (for example, the Spanish question-forming particle '¿verdad?', or the particle 'ojalá', which has the force of qualifying a statement as an expression of wishful thinking – in other words, an illocutionary particle tells the listener how to take an utterance). These features do not fit into syntax proper; their function, and 'meaning', consist in marking sentences for particular communicative purposes, and are quite different from the function of syntactic units. Compare, for instance:

'Entiendo muy *bien*' (where 'bien' has a *syntactic* function).
'¡*Bien*, vámonos!' (where 'bien' has a *sentential* function).

Compare also the different functions and different identities of 'ya' in:

'...*Ya* no viene' (where 'ya' has an adverbial *syntactic* function).
'¡*Ya*, cuéntame otro!' (where 'ya' has a *sentential* function of conveying emphasis and impatience).

As we know, a number of different sentences, marked for different purposes, can be created purely through intonation:

'The salt' (with falling intonation: *statement*).
'The salt' (with rising intonation: *question*).
'The salt' (with fall-rise intonation: *emphatic query*).
'The salt' (with high, level intonation: *command*).

Similar effects can be achieved by a combination of intonation and other features with a sentential function:

'That's the salt' (falling intonation: *statement*).
'Surely that's the salt' (illocutionary particle + fall-rise intonation: *question*).
'Is that the salt' (inverted sequence + fall-rise intonation: *question*).
'That's the salt, isn't it' (fall-rise intonation + illocutionary particle: *question*).
'The salt, please' (falling intonation + illocutionary particle: *request*).
'The salt, damn it' (fall-rise intonation + illocutionary particle: *peremptory command*).

The breakdown of a spoken text to its constituent sentences, as indicated by intonation contours, can be vitally important in determining its impact in terms of practical communication. Compare for instance:

'Yes, please pass the salt.' (with a single-sentence intonation)
'Yes. Please pass the salt.' (with a fall and a pause after 'yes')
'Yes, please. Pass the salt.' (with a rise on 'please' followed by a pause)
'Yes. Please. Pass the salt.' (uttered as three sentences)

As these examples suggest, the sentential level of oral languages is extremely rich, with fine shades of intonation distinguishing sentences with subtly different nuances. A lot of these refinements tend to disappear in written texts as a result of the relatively impoverished sentential level in writing systems. Notably, the only ways of conveying intonation in writing are punctuation and typography, which offer far fewer alternatives than the rich nuances of speech. Failing that, the writer has to fall back on explicit information about how particular sentences are spoken, by adding such comments as 'she exclaimed in surprise', 'she said angrily', and so on.

In translating both oral and written texts, then, the sentential level of language demands particular care, so that important nuances of meaning are not missed. Fortunately, sequential focus and illocutionary particles can be represented in written texts, but they are often problematic all the same. For instance, the impact of '¿no?' as an illocutionary particle in 'Estás casado, ¿no?' is not easily rendered in a written English TT: the translator must choose from various alternatives including 'Are you married?', 'You're married, eh?', 'You're married, are you?', 'Surely you're married?' and 'You're married, aren't you?'. Even more difficult is how to convey the intonational nuancing of a TT sentence like 'It makes no difference to me', depending on which of the following spoken STs it is meant to render:

'A mí no me importa' (with gradually falling intonation: *statement*).
'¿A mí?, ¿cómo que no me importa?' (with rise-fall-rise intonation: *indignant question*).
'A mí no me importa' (with intonation and loudness rising sharply far as 'me': *indignant denial*).
'A mí no me importa' (with emphasis on 'mí': *emphatic statement*).
'A mí no me importa' (with emphasis on 'importa': *disclaimer*).
'A mí no me importa' (mumbled with shrug of shoulder: *indifference*).

Languages vary significantly in the sentence-marking features they possess and the way they use them. The frequent use of a wide variety of illocutionary particles is particularly characteristic of German (most of these particles, as for example 'doch', 'aber', 'mal' or 'auch', have no exact English counterparts and are a source of considerable difficulties in translation). The variety and frequency of illocutionary particles in English are relatively low when compared to German, but significantly higher than in Spanish. Because there is a dearth of such particles in Spanish, it is Spanish-speaking students of English rather than English-speaking students of Spanish who experience the greater learning difficulties in the area of the usage of sentential tags and the like. Problems of translation are also more acute in translating from English to Spanish. However, while apparently less acute, the problems are all the more insidious in translating from Spanish to English, as translators are likely to overlook the fact that the most idiomatic rendering of Spanish sentences containing no illocutionary particles is frequently by English sentences marked by illocutionary particles (for instance, 'El chico, ¿dónde está?' idiomatically rendered as 'Where's the boy, *then*?'). In general, because the frequency of illocutionary particles is higher in English than in Spanish, an English TT that contains significantly fewer such particles than the corresponding Spanish ST tends to lack idiomaticity, and might even come across as foreign-sounding. Translators from Spanish into English should, therefore, try to remember the option of rendering the illocutionary impact of Spanish ST sentences by the use of illocutionary particles in the TT.

In translating written TTs, it should also be remembered that there are differences between English and Spanish punctuation, for instance in the use of colons and semi-colons.

Sentence markers are capable of self-conscious, patterned uses as devices contributing to the thematic development of the overall text in which they are distributed. For instance, a dialogue containing persistent recurrences of sentential 'Well ... um ...' may highlight the tentativeness, uncertainty or anxiety typical of a particular character in a novel or play. Recurrences of 'innit, eh?', or Spanish 'con su permiso' (see, for instance, the extract from *Viridiana* used in Practical 12), may have a similar function in the characterization of another protagonist. Or a philosophical argument may be constructed by the regular textual alternation of question and answer. In less obvious cases than these, the progression of a textual theme may be supported or underlined by a patterned progression between sentence types. This can be an effective dramatic device in an introspective monologue or soliloquy. Thus, for instance, in his *Del sentimiento trágico de la vida*, Unamuno addresses the reader directly throughout, concluding:

> Espero lector, que mientras dure nuestra tragedia, en algún entreacto, volvamos a encontrarnos. Y nos reconoceremos. Y perdona si te he molestado más de lo debido e inevitable, más de lo que, al tomar la pluma para distraerte un poco de tus ilusiones, me propuse. ¡Y Dios no te dé paz y sí gloria!
>
> (Unamuno, 1982, p. 271)

Indeed, the tone of direct address is maintained throughout the collection of essays which are structured around rhetorical questions and exclamations. Unamuno himself viewed the essays as closer to soliloquy or 'auto-dialogue' than autobiography or philosophical discourse. The high incidence of rhetorical questions emphasizes this approach and underlines one of the central themes of *Del sentimiento*: that one of the tragic features of human life is the individual's need to search for immortality. Consider the following example from the essay, 'El hambre de la inmortalidad':

> ¿Que sueño...? Dejadme soñar; si ese sueño es mi vida, no me despertéis de él. Creo en el inmortal origen de este anhelo de inmortalidad, que es la sustancia misma de mi alma. ¿Pero de veras creo en ello...? ¿Y para qué quieres ser inmortal?, me preguntas, ¿para qué? No entiendo la pregunta francamente, porque es preguntar la razón de la razón, el fin del fin, el principio del principio.
>
> (Unamuno, 1982, p. 62)

Where the translator finds a clear correlation in the ST between thematic motifs and a patterned use of sentential features, these features are probably not accidental or incidental to the meaning, but devices instrumental in creating it. In such cases it is more or less incumbent on the translator to use appropriate sentential features of the TL as devices enhancing the theme in the TT. Not to do so would be to court unacceptable translation loss.

THE DISCOURSE LEVEL

We now move up one step, to the **discourse level**. The textual variables considered here are the features that distinguish a cohesive and coherent textual flow from a random sequence of unrelated sentences. This level is concerned both with relations between sentences and with relations between larger units: paragraphs, stanzas, chapters, volumes and so on.

Looking at individual sentences in discourse reveals that they often contain 'markers' signalling how sentences relate to one another, markers whose main role is to give a text a transparent inter-sentential organization. Compare, for instance, these two texts:

> I was getting hungry. I went downstairs. I knew the kitchen was on the ground floor. I was pretty sure that the kitchen must be on the ground floor. I don't know why I was certain, but I was. I didn't expect to find the kitchen so easily. I made myself a sandwich.

> I was getting hungry. *So* I went downstairs. *Well* ... I knew the kitchen was on the ground floor. *I mean*, I was pretty sure *it* must be *there*. *Actually*, I don't know why I was *so* certain, but I was. *Still*, I didn't expect to find it so easily. *Anyway*, I made myself a sandwich.

The first text is so devoid of inter-sentential connectives that, if it hangs together at all – that is, if it is *cogent* at all – this is only thanks to the underlying chronological narrative structure. In the second text, however, a rational 'train of thought' is provided by filling in the discourse-connectives (in italics) missing from the first text, which act as markers of a transparent inter-sentential structure. Some of the markers are rather like illocutionary particles, while others are instances of **anaphora** – that is, the replacement of previously used words and phrases by elements such as pronouns or adverbs that refer back to them; here, the anaphoric elements are 'it' (replacing 'the kitchen') and 'there' (replacing 'on the ground floor'). The place of these markers is in individual sentences, but their function would seem to be *outside* them: it is an inter-sentential function linking sentences to one another in a larger text.

As for the larger units of texts mentioned earlier, there are, in written texts at least, some very obvious textual variables whose function is to link parts of a text into clearly recognizable units, and to indicate something about how they are interrelated. Devices like titles, paragraphs, sub-headings, cross-references and so on are typical examples. While such devices may often cause no problems in translating, they may on occasion be subject to cross-cultural differences (we have already seen examples of this in Practical 3.2; further examples will be found in Chapter 14); translators are well advised not to take them too much for granted.

Cogency

The degree to which a text hangs together is known as its **cogency**. The considerable recent research into what it is that makes texts cogent suggests that there may be tacit, yet to some extent conventional, strategies and constraints that regulate cogency. It also suggests that, in so far as they can be isolated, these strategies and constraints are specific to textual genres (see especially Chapters 11 and 12) and vary from culture to culture. This would suggest that rational discourse itself is not a universal concept identical for all language-users in all communities, but a culture-specific and context-specific notion. Assuming this to be the case, translators must be aware of two things.

First, the SL may have different standards of cogency from the TL. Second, what counts for normal, rational cogency in texts of a certain type in one culture may give the appearance of lack of cogency or excessive fussiness to members of another culture, so that a TT that reproduced point for point the discourse structure of the ST, and did not reorganize it in the light of the TL, might appear stilted, poorly organized or over-marked to a TL audience. So, for instance, it is more common in Spanish than in English for texts to be explicitly structured by the use of connectives ('pues', 'entonces', 'luego', 'así', 'sin embargo', 'por otra parte' and so on) that signpost the logical relationships between sentences. Consequently, an English TT that uses explicit connectives to reproduce all those found in a Spanish ST is likely to seem tediously over-marked in discourse structure, and therefore stilted, pedantic or patronizing. This piece of dialogue is a simple example:

– Se encuentran estas cualidades en Picasso.
– En efecto, pensaba en Picasso.

In an oral TT, the 'en efecto' would probably be rendered not with a connective, but either by voice stress and intonation:

–You often get that in Picasso.
– I was *thinking* of Picasso.

or by intonation and sentential focus:

–You often get that in Picasso.
– It was Picasso I had in mind.

In a written TT, one might well render 'en efecto' with a connective: 'I was indeed thinking of Picasso'. The decision will be heavily influenced by the genre of the ST and of the TT: in a novel, italics would probably be used rather than the connective, and in a play one might even consider the alternative 'That's *precisely* who I was thinking about'; but in an academic text, or if the character in the play were a pompous type, the connective 'indeed' would be more appropriate. As this example shows, one cannot lay down a rigid rule for translating connectives. Nevertheless, in the case of emphasis, one can say that written English readily uses italics where Spanish is more likely to use discourse connectives. This difference between Spanish and English is observable even in quite formal written texts.

Cohesion and coherence

Halliday and Hasan (1976) make a useful distinction between two aspects of cogency in discourse: cohesion and coherence.

Cohesion refers to the transparent linking of sentences (and larger sections of text) by the use of explicit discourse connectives like 'then', 'so', 'however' and so on. If correctly used, these act as 'signposts' in following the thread of discourse running through the text. Discourse connectives need careful attention in translating, not just because they are more liberally used in some languages than in others, but because they can be *faux amis* (for instance, 'en absoluto', often wrongly rendered as 'absolutely' where the appropriate rendering would be 'not at all').

As the example of going down to the kitchen suggested, another common way of signalling explicit cohesion is to use grammatical anaphora. It is clear from that example that not using anaphora can make for an absurdly stilted, disjointed text. However, rules of anaphora differ from language to language. This implies that translators should follow the anaphoric norms of the TL, rather than slavishly reproducing ST anaphora. Translating from Spanish, this is vividly illustrated by the anaphoric elements 'en que/en la que/en la cual/de quien'. For example, 'la casa en que/en la que/en la cual vivía' is better rendered as 'the house where I was living' than as the more literal 'the house in which I was living'; and 'la mujer de quien me hablaste' is better rendered as 'the woman you told me about' than as 'the woman about whom you told me'. Preserving the ST anaphora in such cases tends to be at the cost of producing unidiomatic calques.

Coherence is a more difficult concept than cohesion, because it is, by definition, not explicitly marked in a text, but is rather a question of tacit thematic development running through the text. Coherence is best illustrated by contrast with cohesion. Here, first, is an example of a *cohesive* text (units responsible for the explicit cohesion are italicized):

> The oneness of the human species does not demand the arbitrary reduction of diversity to unity; *it* only *demands* that it should be possible to pass from one

> particularity to another, *and that* no effort should be spared in order to elaborate a common language in which each *particularity* can be adequately described.

If we systematically strip this text of all the units on which its explicitly marked cohesion rests, the resultant text, while no longer explicitly cohesive, remains nevertheless *coherent* in terms of its thematic development:

> The oneness of the human species does not demand the arbitrary reduction of diversity to unity. All that is necessary is that it should be possible to pass from one particularity to another. No effort should be spared in order to elaborate a common language in which each individual experience can be adequately described.

While coherence is clearly culture-specific in some respects, it may also vary significantly according to subject matter or textual genre. The coherence of a TT has, by and large, to be judged in TL terms, and must not be ignored by the translator.

THE INTERTEXTUAL LEVEL

The topmost level of textual variables is the **intertextual level**: the level of external relations between a particular text and other texts within a given culture. No text exists in total isolation from other texts. Even an extremely innovative text cannot fail to form part of an overall body of literature by which the impact and originality of individual texts are coloured and defined. The originality of Joyce's *Ulysses*, for instance, is measured and defined by reference to a whole body of literature from Homer onwards, including the most unoriginal of works.

The inevitable relationship any text bears to its neighbours in the SL culture can cause translators notable problems. If the ST is an utterly 'average' specimen of an established SL genre, the translator may feel obliged to produce a similarly unoriginal TT. Formulating a TT that is as unoriginal in the TL as the ST is in the SL has its own difficulties, obliging the translator to identify a TL genre that closely matches the genre of the ST. Such matching is, at best, approximate, and may sometimes be unattainable. The same is true, *a fortiori*, of STs that are predominantly original. For instance, in the context of translating Shakespeare into Spanish, Alarcón or Lope de Vega may be as close Spanish counterparts to Shakespeare as any, but in terms of current prestige and common knowledge, a better counterpart would be Calderón. Conversely, there seems to be no immediately identifiable counterpart to *Don Quixote* in English – certainly none that enjoys the same renown.

If the ST is stylistically innovative, it may be appropriate, where circumstances permit, to formulate a TT that is just as innovative in the SL. Alternatively, it may be necessary to allow the originality of the ST to be lost in translation, for example in the case of technical or scientific texts where the subject matter and thematic content outweigh considerations of style. There are, however, texts (Goytisolo's writings, for instance) where the style and the thematic content together form an indissoluble whole. In such cases, translation cannot do full justice to the ST without trying to recreate the innovative nature of the ST. Whatever the text, these are all matters for strategic evaluation and decision by the translator.

Texts are also in significant relationship with other texts if they directly invoke, by allusion or quotation, parts of other well-known texts, such as Cervantes or the Bible. For instance, in Pérez Galdós's *Miau* (1971b, p. 318) the phrase 'en aquella ciudad provinciana, cuyo nombre no hace al caso' contains a notable allusion to a famous line from the beginning of *Don Quixote*: 'En un lugar de la Mancha, de cuyo nombre no quiero acordarme...'. An intertextual echo is also found in Leopoldo Alas's *La Regenta* which contains direct quotations from *The Barber of Seville*.

The translator must always be on the look-out for such echoes. What to do with them depends on the circumstances. Some cases will simply necessitate finding the appropriate TL passages and integrating them into the TT (although, in the case of the Bible or ancient classics, thought will have to be given to which version to choose). In yet other cases, the echoes are too abstruse or unimportant from the point of view of a TL audience to be worth building into the TT. We shall return to the problem of allusion, with further examples, on pp. 103–4.

Another significant mode of intertextuality is imitation. An entire text may be designed specifically as an imitation of another text or texts, as in pastiche or parody. (An example is the pastiche of Ortega y Gasset's famous perspectives speech in Luis Martín-Santos's *Tiempo de silencio*, 1985, p. 163). Alternatively, sections of a text may deliberately imitate different texts or genres – an example is David Lodge's *The British Museum Is Falling Down*, in which each chapter parodies a different author. Here the overall effect is of a text contrived as a mixture of styles that recall the various genres from which they are copied. A Spanish example is the merging of *novela rosa* and *novela política* in Isabel Allende's *De amor y de sombra* (1984). This aspect of intertextuality has to be borne in mind, because there are STs that can only be fully appreciated if one is aware that they use the device of imitating other texts or genres. Furthermore, to recreate this device in the TT, the translator must be familiar with target culture genres, and have the skill to imitate them. (We shall return to this question in Chapter 11.)

PRACTICAL 6

6.1 The formal properties of texts; the levels of sentence and discourse

Assignment

(i) Discuss the strategic problems confronting the translator of the ST below.
(ii) Translate the extract, paying special attention to its salient formal properties on the sentential and discourse levels.
(iii) Explain the main decisions of detail you made in producing your TT.

Contextual information

The text is an extract from Miguel de Unamuno's *Del sentimiento trágico de la vida*. Unamuno (1864–1936) was an eminent scholar in Classical Studies and Comparative Philology with a prominent involvement in philosophy and in politics. In *Del sentimiento trágico de la vida* he explores, in the form of personal reflections which he himself described as 'auto-dialogues', deep metaphysical issues of human existence: in particular, the conflict between emotion and reason, which he sees as a disease, and at the same time as a powerful driving force behind consciousness.

Text

¿Enfermedad? Tal vez, pero quien no se cuida de la enfermedad, descuida la salud, y el hombre es un animal esencial y sustancialmente enfermo. ¿Enfermedad? Tal vez lo sea como la vida misma a que va presa, y la única salud posible la muerte; pero esa enfermedad es el manantial de toda salud poderosa. De lo hondo de esa congoja, del abismo del sentimiento de nuestra mortalidad, se sale a la luz de otro cielo, como de lo hondo del infierno salió el Dante a volver a ver las estrellas.

e quindi uscimmo a riveder le stelle.

Aunque al pronto nos sea congojosa esta meditación de nuestra mortalidad, nos es al cabo corroboradora. Recógete, lector, en ti mismo, y figúrate un lento deshacerte de ti mismo, en que la luz se te apague, se te enmudezcan las cosas y no te den sonido, envolviéndote en silencio, se te derritan de entre las manos los objetos asideros, se te escurra de bajo los pies el piso, se te desvanezcan como en desmayo los recuerdos, se te vaya disipando todo en nada y disipándote también tú, y ni aun la conciencia de la nada te quede siquiera como fantástico agarradero de una sombra.

He oído contar de un pobre segador muerto en cama de hospital, que al ir el cura a ungirle en extremaunción las manos, se resistía a abrir la diestra con que apuñaba unas sucias monedas, sin percatarse de que muy pronto no sería ya suya su mano ni él de sí mismo. Y así cerramos y apuñamos, no ya la mano, sino el corazón, queriendo apuñar en él al mundo.

Reprinted by kind permission from Miguel de Unamuno, *Del sentimiento trágico de la vida* (Madrid: Espasa-Calpe, 1982, p. 58),

6.2 Speed translation

Assignment

You will be asked to produce an accurate and stylistically appropriate translation of a Spanish ST given to you in class by your tutor. The tutor will tell you how long you have for the exercise. There is no element of gist translation in this assignment – the whole text needs to be translated as it stands.

7

Literal meaning and translation problems

In Chapter 2 we raised objections to using the concept of 'equivalence' in assessing the relationship between a ST and a corresponding TT. This is because it does not seem helpful to say that good translation produces a TT that has 'the same meaning' as the corresponding ST, when such a claim rests on the comparison of two virtually imponderable and indeterminable qualities. The term 'meaning' is especially elastic and indeterminate when applied to an entire text. At one end of the scale, the 'meaning' of a text might designate its putative socio-cultural significance, importance and impact – a historian might define the meaning of *Mein Kampf* in such terms. At the other end of the scale, the 'meaning' might designate the personal, private and emotional impact the text has on a unique individual at a unique point in time – say, the impact of *Mein Kampf* on a German bride presented with a copy of it at her wedding in 1938. Between these two extremes lie many shades of shared conventional meaning intrinsic to the text because of its internal structure and explicit contents, and the relation these bear to the semantic conventions and tendencies of the SL in its ordinary, everyday usage.

Meanings in a text that are fully supported by ordinary semantic conventions (such as the lexical convention that 'window' refers to a particular kind of aperture in a wall or roof) are normally known as **literal** (or 'cognitive') **meanings**. In the case of words, it is this basic literal meaning that is given in dictionary definitions. However, even the dictionary definition of a word, which is meant to crystallize precisely that range of 'things' that a particular word can denote in everyday usage, is not without its problems. This is because the intuitive understanding that native language-users have of the literal meanings of individual words does itself tend to be rather fluid. That is, a dictionary definition imposes, by abstraction and crystallization of a 'core' meaning, a rigidity of meaning that words do not often show in reality. In addition, once words are put into different contexts, their literal meanings become even more flexible. These two facts make it infinitely difficult to pin down the precise literal meaning of any text of any complexity. This difficulty is still further compounded by the fact that literal meanings supported by a consensus of semantic conventions are not the only types of meaning that can function in a text and nuance its interpretations. As we shall see in Chapter 8, there are various connotative tendencies – not sufficiently cut and dried to qualify as conventional meanings accepted by consensus – which can play an important role in how a text is to be interpreted and translated.

SYNONYMY

Although the apparent fixity of literal meaning is something of an illusion, a narrow concept of 'semantic equivalence' is still useful as a measure of correspondence between the literal meanings of isolated linguistic expressions (words or phrases) figuring in texts. If one is prepared to isolate such expressions, one can talk about semantic equivalence as a possible, and fairly objective, relationship between linguistic items that have identical literal meanings (such as 'peewit' and 'lapwing', or 'hoover' and 'vacuum cleaner'). In what follows, we shall discuss ways of comparing degrees of correspondence in literal meaning between STs and TTs, and our discussion will presuppose the type of semantic equivalence defined here.

We make one further basic supposition: that literal meaning is a matter of *categories* into which, through a complex interplay of inclusion and exclusion, a language divides the totality of communicable experience. So, for example, the literal meaning of the word 'page' does not consist in the fact that one can use the word to denote the object you are staring at as you read this. It consists rather in the fact that all over the world (in past, present and future) one may find 'similar' objects each of which is *included in* the category of 'page', as well as countless other objects that are, of course, *excluded from* it. To define a literal meaning, then, is to specify the 'range' covered by a word or phrase in such a way that one knows what items are included in that range or category and what items are excluded from it. The most useful way to visualize literal meanings is by thinking of them as circles, because in this way we can represent intersections between categories, and thus reflect overlaps in literal meaning between different expressions. In exploring correspondence in literal meaning, it is particularly the intersections between categories that are significant; they provide, as it were, a measure of semantic equivalence.

Comparisons of literal meaning made possible by considering overlaps between categories, and visualized as intersections between circles, are usually drawn between linguistic expressions in the same language. They allow, in the semantic description of a language, for an assessment of types and degrees of semantic correspondence between items (for example, lexical items). There is, however, no reason why analogous comparisons may not be made between expressions from two or more different languages, as a way of assessing and representing types and degrees of cross-linguistic semantic equivalence.

To take a simple example of our suggested way of visualizing literal meanings, the expressions 'my mother's father' and 'my maternal grandfather' may be represented as two separate circles. Their two ranges of literal meaning, however, coincide perfectly. This can be visualized as moving the two circles on top of each other and finding that they cover one another exactly, as in Figure 7.1:

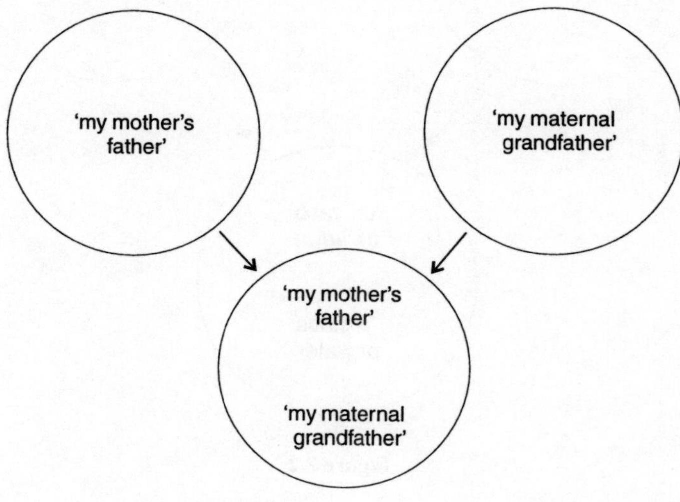

Figure 7.1

Both in general and in every specific instance of use, 'my mother's father' and 'my maternal grandfather' include and exclude exactly the same referents; that is, their literal meanings are identical in range. This exemplifies the strongest form of semantic equivalence: full **synonymy**.

Just as alternative expressions in the same language may be full synonyms, so, in principle at least, there may be full synonymy across two different languages. As one might expect, the closer the SL and the TL are in the way they process and categorize speakers' experiences of the world, the more likely it is that there will be full cross-linguistic synonyms between the two languages. Thus, one can fairly confidently say that 'un vaso de agua' and 'a glass of water' cover exactly the same range of situations, and are, therefore, fully synonymous in their literal meanings, as is seen in Figure 7.2:

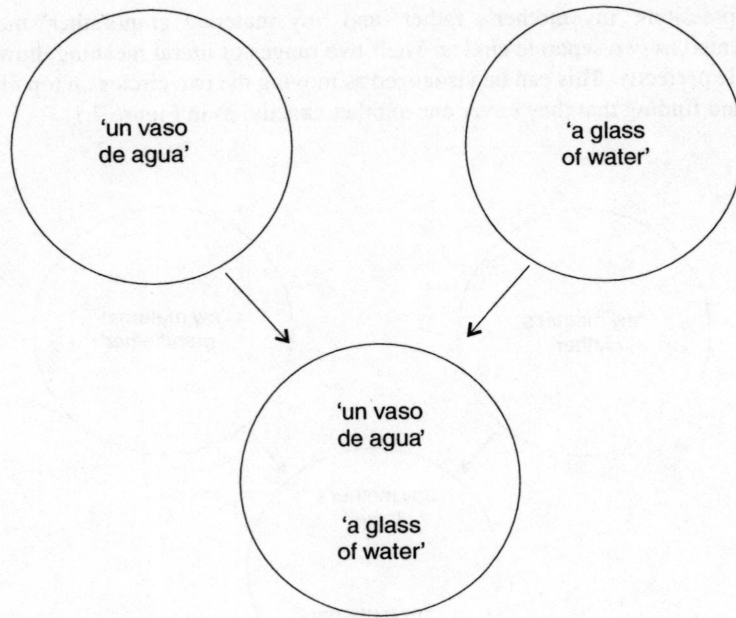

Figure 7.2

HYPERONYMY–HYPONYMY

Unfortunately, full cross-linguistic synonymy is more the exception than the rule, even between historically and culturally related languages. More often than not, the so-called 'nearest equivalent' for translating the literal meaning of a ST expression falls short of being a full TL synonym. Compare, for example, 'el chico abre la ventana' with 'the boy opens the window'. It is at least possible that the Spanish phrase refers to a progressive event reported by the speaker. This would have to be expressed in English by 'the boy *is opening* the window'. That is, 'el chico abre la ventana' and 'the boy opens the window' are not full synonyms, but have non-identical ranges of literal meaning. There is a common element between the two phrases, but the Spanish one covers a wider range of situations, a range that is covered by at least two different expressions in English. This can be shown diagrammatically, as in Figure 7.3:

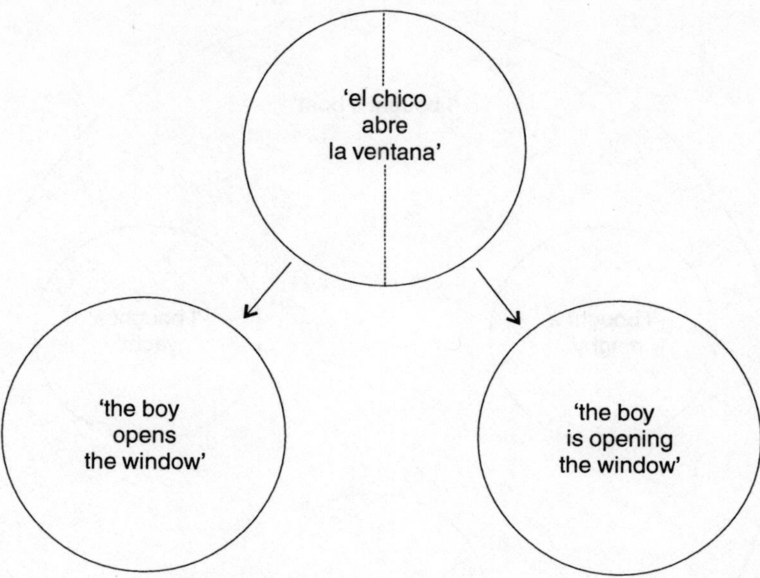

Figure 7.3

The type of relationship between these two phrases can also be instanced within a single language. For example, 'I bought a boat' and 'I bought a dinghy' have a common element of literal meaning, but show a discrepancy in the fact that 'I bought a boat' covers a wider range of situations, including in its literal meaning situations that are excluded from 'I bought a dinghy' – such as 'I bought a yacht', 'I bought a punt', and so on. This is seen diagrammatically in Figure 7.4:

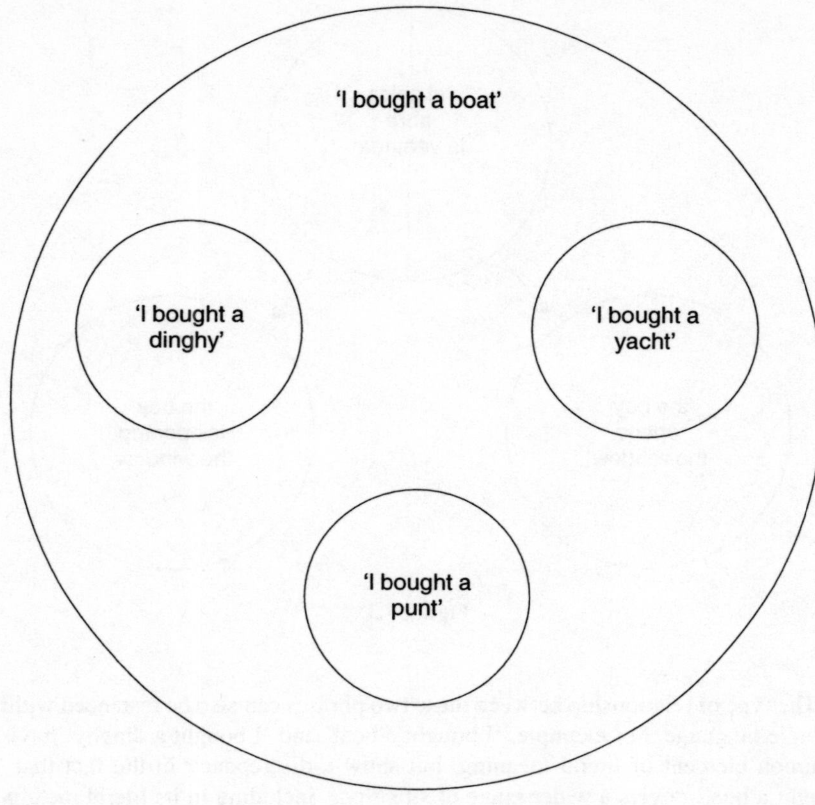

Figure 7.4

The relationship between 'I bought a boat' and 'I bought a dinghy' is known as hyperonymy–hyponymy. The expression with the wider, less specific, range of literal meaning is a **hyperonym** of the one with the narrower and more specific literal meaning. Conversely, the narrower one is a **hyponym** of the wider one. So, 'I bought a boat' is a hyperonym of each of the other three phases, while these are hyponyms of 'I bought a boat'. Similarly, 'el chico abre la ventana' is a hyperonym of both 'the boy opens the window' and 'the boy is opening the window', while these two are hyponyms of the Spanish expression.

Hyperonymy–hyponymy is so widespread in any given language that one can say that the entire fabric of linguistic reference is built up on such relationships. Take, for example, some of the alternative ways in which one can refer to an object – say, a particular biro. If there is a need to particularize, one can use a phrase with a fairly narrow and specific meaning, such as 'the black biro in my hand'. If such detail is unnecessary and one wants to generalize, one can call it 'a writing implement', 'an implement', 'an object' or, even more vaguely, just 'something'.

It is in the very essence of the richness of all languages that they offer a whole set of different expressions, each with a different range of inclusiveness, for designating any object, any situation, anything whatsoever. Thus the series 'the black biro in my hand', 'a biro', 'a writing implement', 'an implement', 'an object', 'something' is a series organized on the basis of successively larger, wider inclusiveness – that is, on the basis of hyperonymy–hyponymy. The series can be visualized as a set of increasingly large concentric circles, larger circles representing hyperonyms, smaller one hyponyms, as in Figure 7.5:

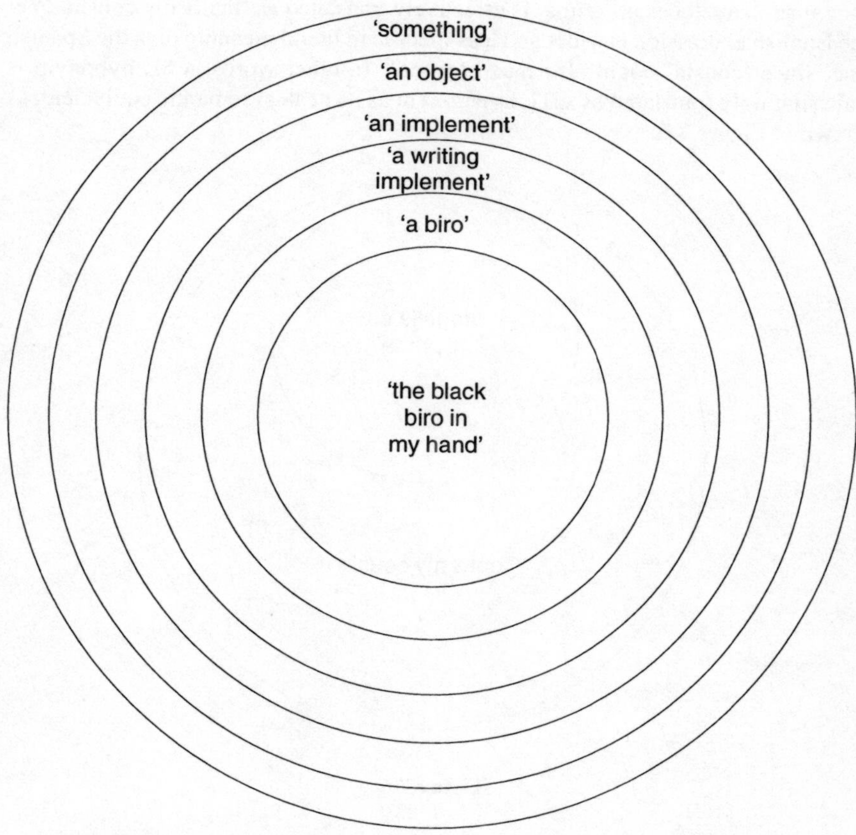

Figure 7.5

As this example shows, the same external reality can be described in an indefinite number of ways, depending on how precise or vague one needs to be.

By its very nature, translation is concerned with rephrasing, and in particular with rephrasing so as to preserve to best advantage the integrity of a ST message, including its degree of precision or vagueness. Therefore, the fact that both a hyperonym and a hyponym can serve for conveying a given message is of great importance to translation practice. It means that, as soon as one acknowledges that there is no full TL synonym for a particular ST expression (for example, 'el chico abre la ventana'), one must start looking for an appropriate TL hyperonym or hyponym. In fact, translators do this automatically, which is why they may see 'the boy opens the window' as the 'nearest' semantic equivalent to 'el chico abre la ventana'; but they do not always do it carefully or successfully. For example, in most contexts, particularly if the person referred to is present at the time of utterance, 'aquella es mi prima' is effectively translated as 'that's my cousin'. Yet the English expression is wider and less specific in literal meaning than the Spanish one, since 'cousin' could also mean 'primo'. In other words, a SL hyponym is unhesitatingly translated by a TL hyperonym as its nearest semantic equivalent, as shown in Figure 7.6:

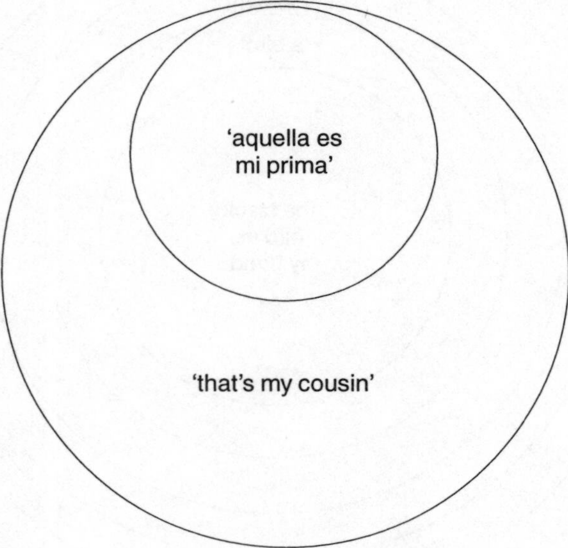

Figure 7.6

Conversely, translating 'el agua está caliente' into English necessarily implies choosing between 'the water is hot' and 'the water is warm'. Of course, contextual and situational clues will normally determine which of the alternatives is appropriate in a given TT. The point, however, is that each of the English phrases designates a different set of circumstances and has a literal meaning distinct from the other.

Whichever alternative is chosen, the translator is rendering a SL hyperonym by a TL hyponym. This can be represented as shown in Figure 7.7:

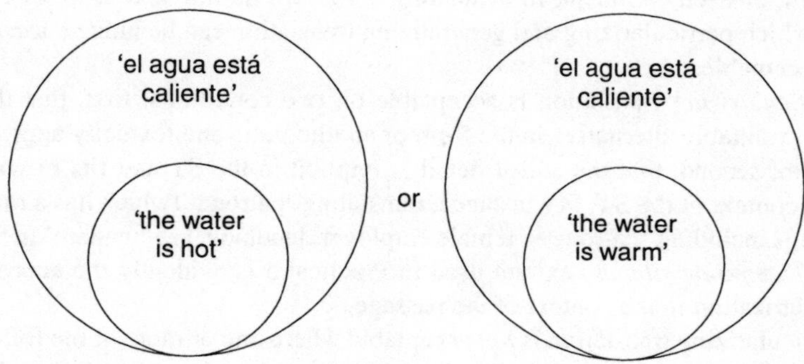

Figure 7.7

Where plausible cross-linguistic synonyms are not available, translating by a hyperonym or a hyponym is standard practice and entirely unremarkable. Indeed, choosing a hyperonym or hyponym even where a synonym does exist may actually be the mark of a good translation. For instance, the term 'toro bravo' is sufficiently current in Spanish usage to be used with discrimination even in non-specialized and non-technical narrative contexts; yet in English, translating it as 'fighting bull', rather than simply using the generic term 'bull', would in some cases be unduly pedantic and cumbersome. Although not a precise synonym, in most contexts, except technical ones, the hyperonym 'bull' is the appropriate translation of 'toro bravo'. It is, then, only when using a TL hyperonym or hyponym is unnecessary, or unnecessarily extreme, or misleading, that a TT can be criticized on this basis.

PARTICULARIZING TRANSLATION AND GENERALIZING TRANSLATION

Translating by a hyponym implies that the TT expression has a narrower and more specific literal meaning than the ST expression. That is, the TT gives *particulars* that are not given by the ST. We shall therefore call this **particularizing translation**, or **particularization** for short. Thus, in our earlier example, 'the water is warm' is a particularizing translation of 'el agua está caliente'.

Conversely, translating by a hyperonym implies that the TT expression has a wider and less specific literal meaning than the ST expression. That is, the TT is more *general*, omitting details that are given by the ST. We shall call this **generalizing translation**, or **generalization** for short. Our example of translating 'prima' as 'cousin' is a case of generalizing translation.

Particularization and generalization both imply a degree of translation loss as we defined it in Chapter 2: detail is either added to, or omitted from, the ST meaning. However, neither the addition nor the omission of detail is necessarily a matter for criticism, or even comment, in evaluating a TT. We outline here a set of criteria under which particularizing and generalizing translation can be judged acceptable or unacceptable.

Particularizing translation is acceptable on two conditions: first, that the TL offers no suitable alternative in the form of an idiomatic and textually appropriate synonym; second, that the added detail is implicit in the ST and fits in with the overall context of the ST. For instance, translating 'patrona' (which has a range of meanings including 'patroness, female employer, landlady') as 'madam' in the TT of the *Tiempo de silencio* extract used in Practical 5 is evidently the appropriate particularization in the context of the passage.

Particularizing translation is *not* acceptable where one or more of the following three conditions hold: first, if the TL does offer a suitable alternative to the addition of unnecessary detail; second, if the added detail creates discrepancies in the TT; third, if the added detail contributes to a misinterpretation of the overall context of the ST. As an example, one may take the following extract from Gaspar Melchor de Jovellanos's eighteenth-century essay 'Ética' (from his *Memoria sobre educación pública*): 'Si volvemos los ojos a nuestras escuelas generales, vemos que [...] la enseñanza de la teología abraza muchas cuestiones de la ética cristiana [...]'. Rendering 'teología' as 'theology' instead of 'religious education' or 'religious studies' would be unacceptable in this context for all three reasons: first, 'religious education' offers a more exact alternative to the unduly particularizing term 'theology'; second, the specification of 'theology' is inconsistent with other details in the TT that clearly indicate the absence of formal theological teaching in the level of education under discussion ('escuelas generales'); third, the specification of 'theology' creates a misleading impression of the educational system described in the overall context of the essay.

Generalizing translation is acceptable on two conditions: first, that the TL offers no suitable alternative; second, that the omitted detail either is clear and can be recovered from the overall context of the TT, or is unimportant to the ST. For example, in the context of the Cortázar passage in Practical 2 (p. 18), translating 'brasero' as 'stove' occasions a harmless, insignificant translation loss.

Generalizing translation is *not* acceptable where one or more of the following three conditions hold: first, if the omitted details are important to the ST; second, if the TL does offer suitable alternatives to the omission of this detail; third, if the omitted detail is not compensated for elsewhere in the TT, and cannot be recovered from the overall context of the TT. Thus, translating Spanish 'hoja de laurel' by the botanically generic term 'laurel', rather than as 'bay leaf', may be relatively harmless in the context of a novel, but it may occasion potentially lethal translation loss in a recipe book.

PARTIALLY OVERLAPPING TRANSLATION

As well as particularizing and generalizing translation, there is another type of semantic near-equivalence. This is more easily illustrated in phrases than in single words. Take the phrase 'The teacher treated brother and sister differently'. 'La profesora trató a los hermanos de un modo distinto' is probably as close a literal rendering into Spanish as possible. Yet in the English phrase the gender of the teacher is not explicitly specified, whereas the Spanish text makes this literally explicit. In respect to the gender of the teacher, the Spanish TT *particularizes* (just as it would have done in specifying 'el profesor'). Conversely, in the English phrase the gender difference between the two siblings is specified unambiguously, whereas the Spanish TT leaves this ambiguous: the Spanish TT *generalizes* here, in that 'los hermanos' is a gender-neutral term, more or less equivalent in its literal meaning to 'siblings'.

In other words, this TT combines particularization with generalization, *adding* a detail not found in the ST and *omitting* a detail that is given in the ST. This is best visualized as two partially overlapping circles, as shown in Figure 7.8:

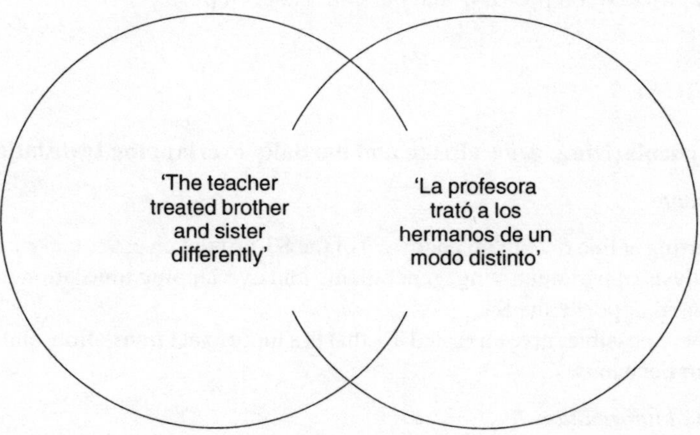
'The teacher
treated brother
and sister
differently'
'La profesora
trató a los
hermanos de un
modo distinto'

Figure 7.8

This type of case is a further category of degree in the translation of literal meaning: along with synonymic, particularizing and generalizing translation, there is **partially overlapping translation**, or **overlapping translation** for short. The concept of overlapping translation applies less obviously, but more importantly, in the case of individual words (as distinct from phrases). For example, if in a particular context Spanish 'profesora' were to be rendered as as 'professor', this would constitute a case of overlapping translation: the common element between ST and TT is the reference to a member of the teaching profession, but the TT *loses* the detail of female gender reference, while it *adds* explicit reference to the teacher's level of employment, English and American uses of 'professor' being limited to tertiary (in particular, university) education.

Once again, overlapping translation may or may not invite comment when one is evaluating a TT. The conditions under which it is acceptable and the criteria for criticizing it are similar to those for particularization and generalization. Overlapping translation is acceptable on two conditions: first, if the TL offers no suitable alternatives in the form of closer semantic equivalents; second, if the *omitted* detail is either unimportant or can be recovered from the overall TT context, and the *added* detail is implicit in, or at least not contradictory to, the overall ST context. For example, 'bullfighter' is an accurate idiomatic rendering of 'matador', but it does *add* explicit reference to bullfighting, and *lose* the reference to 'killing' which is explicit in the ST.

Overlapping translation is *not* acceptable when one or more of the following three conditions hold: first, if the omitted detail is important to the ST but cannot be recovered from the overall context of the TT; second, if the added detail creates discrepancies in the TT; third, if the TL does offer suitable alternatives to avoiding either the omissions or the additions or both. For an example, see the translation of 'ruin' by 'wicked' on pp. 96–7 and our comments on p. 95.

PRACTICAL 7

7.1 Particularizing, generalizing and partially overlapping translation

Assignment

(i) Starting at line 6 ('Era mi padre ...') of the ST printed on p. 96, make a detailed analysis of particularizing, generalizing and overlapping translation in the TT printed opposite the ST.

(ii) Where possible, give an edited TT that is a more exact translation, and explain your decisions.

Contextual information

The passage is taken from the autobiography of St Teresa of Avila (1515–82), *Su vida*. The extract is the opening section of the first chapter in which St Teresa tells of her early childhood. The translation, published in 1957 under the title *The Life of Saint Teresa of Avila by Herself*, is by J. M. Cohen.

NB Here is an example of how to lay out your material for this exercise:

ST 2–4: 'En que trata ... los padres'

1 the omission of a rendering for 'en que trata' constitutes an unnecessary generalization in the TT; it can easily be remedied by adding 'deals with' or 'dealing with' to the edited text.

2 'rouse' is a particularization of 'despertar' ('wake'/'awaken'/'stir up'/ 'arouse'), introducing an element of intensity to the TT which is not present in the ST; 'rouse' is an intensified hyponym of the more neutral 'awaken', which is a more exact, and contextually more appropriate, literal rendering.
3 'her' is an idiomatically necessary particularization of 'esta'; using the literally exact demonstrative pronoun 'this' would have made the TT grammatically stilted.
4 'soul' is a necessary particularization of 'alma' ('soul'/'spirit'/'heart') and is contextually appropriate.
5 'in childhood' is an apt generalization of 'en su niñez'.
6 'to a love of virtue' is an overlapping translation of 'a cosas virtuosas'; the TT loses the reference to individuated objects ('cosas'), but adds the notion of 'love' which is not explicit in the ST. (A contextually plausible solution might be the literally more exact 'to a love of things virtuous'.)
7 'good parents' is a particularizing translation of 'los padres'; the addition of 'good' is a harmless, if somewhat unnecessary, specification of a detail that is implicit in the ST.

Ed TT: In which is told how the Lord started to awaken her soul in childhood to virtuous thoughts, and the help that parents can afford in this respect

ST5–6: 'El tener padres ... ser buena.'

1 'wicked' is an inexact, partially overlapping rendering of 'ruin'; suitable literally more exact alternatives are available, for instance 'base'.
2 'devout' is an unnecessarily narrow particularization of 'virtuosos'; the ST refers to 'moral rectitude' in general, not to its specifically religious forms designated by 'being devout'.
3 'el Señor me favorecía' rendered as 'the favour of God's grace' contains two instances of particularization: the unnecessary duplication of 'grace' and 'favour' renders the TT over-particularized to the point of tautology (as well as grammatically stilted); the unnecessary particularizing of 'Señor' as 'God', where the more literally exact 'Lord' is also more contextually apt.
4 'make me good' is a partially overlapping rendering of 'ser buena'; the TT has lost the element of personal responsibility for good behaviour contained in the ST 'ser' (and the explicit gender reference in 'buena'), but at the same time it has added the notion of a permanent quality of 'goodness', which is not expressed in the ST's reference to good behaviour.

Ed TT: Having virtuous and God-fearing parents, together with the grace of the Lord, should have been enough to ensure that I was good – had I not been so base.

Source text

CAPÍTULO I

EN QUE TRATA CÓMO COMENZÓ EL SEÑOR A DESPERTAR ESTA ALMA EN SU NIÑEZ A COSAS VIRTUOSAS, Y LA AYUDA QUE ES PARA ESTO SERLO LOS PADRES

El tener padres virtuosos y temerosos de Dios me bastara, si yo no fuera tan ruin, con lo que el Señor me favorecía, para ser buena. Era mi padre aficionado a leer buenos libros, y ansí los tenía de romance para que leyesen sus hijos. Éstos, con el cuidado que mi madre tenía de hacernos rezar, y ponernos en ser devotos de Nuestra Señora y de algunos Santos, comenzó a despertarme, de edad, a mi parecer, de seis o siete años. Ayudábame, no ver en mis padres favor sino para la virtud. Tenían muchas. Era mi padre hombre de mucha caridad con los pobres y piadad con los enfermos, y aun con los criados; tanta, que jamás se pudo acabar con él tuviese esclavos, porque los había gran piadad; y estando una vez en casa una de un su hermano, la regalaba como a sus hijos; decía, que de que no era libre, no lo podía sufrir de piadad. Era de gran verdad, jamás nadie le oyó jurar ni murmurar. Muy honesto en gran manera.

Reprinted by kind permission from Santa Teresa de Jesús, *Su vida* (Madrid: Espasa-Calpe, 8th edn, Colección Austral, No. 372, 1978, p. 21),

Target text

CHAPTER 1

How the Lord began to rouse her soul in childhood to a love of virtue, and what a help it is in this respect to have good parents

If I had not been so wicked, the possession of devout and God-fearing parents, together with the favour of God's grace, would have been enough to make me good. My father was fond of reading holy books, and had some in Spanish so that his children might read them too. These, and the pains my mother took in teaching us to pray and educating us in devotion to Our Lady and certain Saints, began to rouse me at the age, I think, of six or seven. It was a help to me that I never saw my parents inclined to anything but virtue, and many virtues they had. My father was most charitable to the poor, and most compassionate to the sick, also to his servants; so much so that he could never be persuaded to keep slaves. He felt such pity for them that when a slave-girl of his brother's was, on one occasion, staying in his house, he treated her like one of his own children. He said that he could not bear the pain of seeing her not free. He was an extremely truthful man and was never heard to swear or speak slander. He was also most rigid in his chastity.

7.2 Speed translation

Assignment

Your tutor will give you a text to be translated in class within a certain time limit. You should try to apply the lessons learned so far, while meeting the demands of speed and accuracy.

8

Connotative meaning and translation problems

As was pointed out in Chapter 7, literal meaning is only one aspect of textual meaning. Understanding the literal reference conventionally attached to verbal signs is a necessary part of unravelling the complex meaning of a text, but it is not, in itself, enough. In actual fact, the meaning of a text comprises a number of different layers: referential content, emotional colouring, cultural associations, social and personal connotations, and so on. The many-layered nature of meaning is something translators must never forget.

Even within a single language, so-called referential synonyms are as a rule different in their overall semantic effects. For instance, in contemporary English, 'homosexual', 'queer' and 'gay' must be rated as synonyms in terms of referential content, but they clearly have different overall meanings. This is because, while 'homosexual' is a relatively neutral expression, 'queer' is usually understood to carry pejorative overtones, and 'gay' meliorative ones. These overtones are not part of literal meaning, but it is evident that to refer to someone as 'queer' could be taken as hostile in a way that the designations 'homosexual' or 'gay' could not. It is impossible to ignore such overtones in responding to messages in one's own language, and one certainly cannot afford to overlook them when it comes to translating. For example, a speaker who refers to a man as 'maricón' does not merely designate a person with certain sexual preferences, but also conveys a certain attitude to him. Consequently, while translating 'maricón' as 'homosexual' would accurately render the literal meaning of the ST, it would fail to render the denigrating attitude connoted by 'maricón' (better translated as 'queer' or 'pansy').

We shall call such overtones **connotative meanings** – that is, associations which, over and above the literal meaning of an expression, form part of its overall meaning. In fact, of course, connotative meanings are many and varied, and it is common for a single piece of text to combine several kinds into a single overall effect. Nevertheless, there are six major types of commonly recognized connotative meaning, which we will examine in turn. We should perhaps add that, by definition, we are only concerned with socially widespread connotations, not private ones – as long as private connotations are recognized for what they are, and not allowed unduly to influence the production of a TT, they are the translator's own affair.

ATTITUDINAL MEANING

Attitudinal meaning is that part of the overall meaning of an expression which consists of some widespread *attitude to the referent*. That is, the expression does not merely denote the referent in a neutral way, but, in addition, hints at some attitude to it on the part of the speaker.

Our example of 'queer' versus 'homosexual' versus 'gay', and 'homosexual' versus 'maricón', are clear cases of attitudinal connotations. As these examples show, attitudinal meanings can be hard to pin down. (For instance, just how hostile is the expression 'queer'? Is it more or less pejorative than 'pansy'? Is 'maricón' less pejorative than 'queer', or perhaps even affectionately derogatory, say as used between teenage boys? How is the pejorative connotation of 'queer' to be reconciled with the contemporary appropriation of that term in queer ideology? Connotations will vary from context to context.) There are two main reasons why attitudinal meanings are generally hard to define. First, being connotations, they are intrinsically intended to be suggestive: the moment they cease to be suggestive, and become fixed by convention, they cease to be connotations and become part of literal meaning. Second, being controlled by the vagaries of usage, they can change very rapidly. Both these factors are illustrated by the evolution of the word 'Tory', originally a term of abuse imported from Irish ('tóriadhe', meaning 'outlaw'), but later proudly adopted by the parties so labelled.

ASSOCIATIVE MEANING

Associative meaning is that part of the overall meaning of an expression which consists of stereotypical *expectations* rightly or wrongly *associated with the referent* of the expression.

The word 'nurse' is a good example. Most people automatically associate 'nurse' with the idea of female gender, as if the word were synonymous with 'female who looks after the sick'. This unconscious association is so stereotypical and automatic that the term 'male nurse' has had to be coined in order to counteract its effect. Even so, the female connotations of 'nurse' continue to persist, witness the fact that 'he is a nurse' still feels semantically odd, as does also the phrase 'female nurse'.

Any area of reference where prejudices and stereotypes, however innocuous, operate is likely to give examples of associative meaning. Even something as banal as a date may trigger an associative meaning, for example 24 June, 14 July or 5

November. Similarly, in Spain and England – though not in Scotland – 'golf' will automatically trigger associations of an upper- or middle-class milieu.

The appreciation of associative meanings requires cultural knowledge, and the translator must constantly be on the look-out for them. Take, for instance, the function of the notion of 'romería' in García Lorca's play *Yerma* (1934). The cultural associations of 'romería' intrinsically involve both religious pilgrimage and sexual activity. To translate 'romería' in this text as 'pilgrimage' loses the connotations of illicit sexual activity which are culturally associated with the event and which are necessary to the characterization of Yerma and to the development of the plot. On the other hand, to translate it as 'fair' or 'carnival' loses the more fundamental meaning of pilgrimage as a religious observance. Thus 'romería' poses a particularly intractable problem of translation hinging on associative meaning. (Perhaps 'carnival' might, through its associations with Lent, offer the best solution; but this solution will require some compensation if the religious connotations are not to be lost in the TT.)

AFFECTIVE MEANING

Affective meaning is that part of the overall meaning of an expression which consists in an *emotive effect worked on the addressee* by the choice of that expression. The expression does not merely denote its referent, but also hints at some attitude of the speaker/writer to the addressee.

Features of linguistic politeness, flattery, rudeness or insult are typical examples of expressions carrying affective meanings. Compare, for instance, 'Hagan el favor de bajar la voz' with '¡Callaos!' These expressions share their literal meaning with English 'lower your voice', but their impact in terms of affective meaning is quite different: polite and deferential in one case, brusque and peremptory in the other. That is, the speaker's tacit or implied attitude to the listener produces a different emotive effect in each case.

Not only imperative forms, but also statements and questions, can have alternative forms identical in basic literal meaning yet totally different in affective meaning, as in 'Excuse me, Madam, I think that's my seat' versus 'Oy, Ducky, I was sitting there'; or, in Spanish, 'Perdone señora, ¿podría usted sentarse en otro asiento?' versus '¡Oye, tú! ¡Quítate de allí!'

Clearly, translators must be able to recognize affective meanings in the ST. But they must also be sure not to introduce unwanted affective meanings into the TT. Take, for example, 'Mañana me lo devolverá usted' translated as 'You will give it back to me tomorrow'. Whereas the Spanish is formal and polite, the English sounds rude and peremptory. A better TT would cushion what sounds to English ears as excessively assertive: 'Could you give it back to me tomorrow?'

REFLECTED MEANING

Reflected meaning is the meaning given to an expression over and above its literal meaning by the fact that its *form* is reminiscent of the completely different meaning of a *homonymic or near-homonymic expression* (that is, one that sounds or is spelled the same, or nearly the same).

An often-cited example of reflected meaning compares the connotative difference between the two synonyms 'Holy Spirit' and 'Holy Ghost' (see Leech, 1974, p. 19). Through homonymic association, the 'Ghost' part of 'Holy Ghost' is reminiscent of the reflected meaning of 'ghost' ('spook' or 'spectre'). Although such an association is not part of the literal meaning of 'Holy Ghost', it has a tendency to form part of the overall meaning of the expression, and therefore may actually interfere with its literal meaning. By another, near-homonymic, association, the 'Spirit' part of 'Holy Spirit' may call to mind the reflected meaning of 'spirits' ('alcoholic drinks'); here again, the association tends to interfere with the literal meaning. Clearly, then, while 'Holy Spirit' and 'Holy Ghost' are referential synonyms, their total semantic effects cannot be called identical, in so far as they evoke different images through different reflected meanings.

When a term is taken in isolation, its reflected meaning is usually merely latent – it is the *context* that triggers or reinforces latent reflected meanings. In the case of 'Holy Ghost' and 'Holy Spirit', if there is anything in the context that predisposes the hearer to think about 'spooks' or 'alcoholic drinks', reflected meaning may come across as a *double entendre*. If one were translating 'Espíritu Santo' (which, in writing, only shares the reflected meanings of its English synonyms when uncapitalized, 'espíritu santo'), one would have to take care that the TT context did not trigger the latent reflected meaning of whichever English expression was selected for the TT. Otherwise the TT could be marred by infelicitous innuendo, as for example if one wrote 'Holy Spirit' just after a reference to Communion wine.

Similarly, infelicitous reflected meanings might be doubly obtrusive in a TT rendering Gustavo Adolfo Bécquer's lines (from Rima XII):

> y verdes son las pupilas
> de las hurís del profeta.
>
> (Bécquer, 1961, p. 11)

as

> and green are the pupils
> of the Prophet's houris.

Conversely, a ST may deliberately trade on reflected meaning and innuendo, using an expression primarily for its literal meaning, yet expressly, if implicitly, expecting the addressee to perceive a connotation echoing the meaning of some homonymic expression. A good example is the *double entendre* in Lorca's use of

'¡Dale ya con el cuerno!' in Act III, scene 2 of his play *Yerma*, which refers to the actions of the archetypal dance of the *Macho* and *Hembra*, its symbolic referent, but which also has connotations reflected from the expression 'poner los cuernos', 'to cuckold'. (It is very common for an expression to combine more than one type of connotative meaning, as in this example.) In such cases, a fully successful TT would be one which deliberately traded on innuendo similar to that in the ST; but such a TT may be extremely difficult to construct.

COLLOCATIVE MEANING

Collocative meaning is given to an expression over and above its literal meaning by *the meaning of some other expression with which it collocates to form a commonly used phrase*. Thus, in the clichéd expression 'a flash of lightning', the word 'flash' collocates regularly with the word 'lightning', forming such a strong stereotyped association that 'flash' by itself is capable of evoking the meaning of its collocative partner. This no doubt is why a collocation like 'a flash of moonlight' feels a little unusual – there is nothing in the literal meaning of 'flash' to prevent its qualifying 'moonlight', but the connotation it has through collocative association with 'lightning' (sudden bright light) is carried over and clashes with the literal meaning of 'moonlight' (steady muted light). Similarly, the well-known gender-specific connotations of 'pretty' and 'handsome' can be seen as collocative meanings, deriving from the tendency of 'pretty' to collocate with words denoting females ('girl', 'woman' and so on) and the tendency of 'handsome' to collocate with words denoting males ('boy', 'man' and so on).

Some collocative meanings are so strong that they need very little triggering by context. For example, in modern colloquial English the word 'intercourse' (literally 'mutual dealings') can hardly be used at all without evoking its collocative partner 'sexual', and is well on the way to becoming a synonym of 'sexual intercourse'. Other collocative meanings need to be activated by the context, as with the humorous innuendo in 'I rode shotgun on the way to the wedding', based on activating the collocative echo of 'shotgun wedding'.

Collocative meanings are important for the translator, not only because they can contribute significantly to the overall meaning of a ST, but also because of the need to avoid unwanted collocative clashes in a TT. For example, translating '¿Tienes las vacaciones reservadas? /¿Ya ha reservado usted las vacaciones?' as 'Have you reserved your holiday yet?' produces a collocative clash or infelicity – according to English collocative idiom, seats or tables in restaurants are reserved, but holidays are *booked*. An unfortunate collocative clash is also produced – partly as a result of miscollocation, the correct collocation being 'to reserve a book', and partly as a result of an infelicitous play on words – by translating 'Quisiera/Me gustaría reservar este libro para mañana' as 'I'd like to book this book for tomorrow'.

Collocative clashes are always a threat to idiomaticity when the TL offers an expression closely resembling the ST one. Compare, for instance, 'floods of tears' with 'an ocean of tears' as translations of 'un mar de lágrimas'; or 'to sweeten / sugar the pill' with 'to gild the pill' as translations of 'dorar la píldora'. In fact, collocative clashes are often produced by failure to spot the need for a communicative translation, as in rendering 'más blanco que la nieve' by 'whiter than snow' instead of 'as white as snow'. Worse still, translating 'es un chaval hermoso' as 'he is a pretty boy' produces a collocative clash which totally distorts the meaning of the ST (better rendered as 'he's a nice-looking/good-looking lad/guy').

ALLUSIVE MEANING

Allusive meaning is present when an expression evokes, beyond its literal meaning, the meaning of some associated saying or quotation, in such a way that the meaning of that saying or quotation becomes part of the overall meaning of the expression.

Allusive meaning hinges on indirectly evoking sayings or quotations that an informed hearer can recognize, even though they are not fully spelt out. The evoked meaning of the quotation alluded to creates an added innuendo that modifies the literal meaning of what has explicitly been said. For example, saying that 'there are rather a lot of cooks involved' in organizing an event evokes the proverb 'too many cooks spoil the broth', and by this allusive meaning creates the innuendo that the event risks being spoilt by over-organization.

In the case of allusive meaning in STs, the translator's first problem is to recognize that the ST does contain an allusive suggestion. The second problem is to understand the allusive meaning by reference to the meaning of the saying or quotation evoked. The third problem is to convey the force of the allusion in the TT, ideally by using some appropriate allusive meaning based on a saying or quotation in the TL.

A simple example is from Pérez Galdós's *La de Bringas* (p. 143) in which the phrase 'y aquí paz' is an allusive echo of the proverb 'Aquí paz y después gloria', meaning 'and that's that'. Similarly, in the same text (p. 274), the sentence 'Y quién me había de decir que yo bebería de este [sic] agua' makes allusion to the proverb 'Nunca digas de esta agua no beberé' (literally 'Never say I shall not drink of this water'; implying 'Never say never'). Both these examples show how recognizing the proverbs alluded to is the key without which the meanings of the STs may remain obscure, even puzzling. Once these allusive meanings have been grasped, the translator's problem is whether they can be rendered by similarly allusive means in an English TT, or whether it is necessary to resort to compensation in kind. In the first example a communicative rendering, 'and that's that', with loss of a proverbial allusion, is probably the best option; in the second, a solution could perhaps be devised by some suitable use of a cliché such as 'Never say never' or 'There's no such word as "never" '.

Even these relatively simple examples, then, are potentially problematic, but really drastic difficulties can arise if an apparent allusive meaning in the ST is obscure. Considerable research may be necessary to track down the allusion; and even after it has been identified and understood, the translator faces another challenge if there is no parallel to it in the TL culture. The solution in such cases is usually to compensate by some other means for the absence of a suitable allusion.

A complex instance of allusion intricately woven into a text is found in Julio Cortázar's *Rayuela*:

> En setiembre del 80, pocos meses después del fallecimiento
> Y las cosas que lee, una novela, mal escrita, para colmo
> de mi padre, resolví apartarme de los negocios, cediéndolos
> una edición infecta, uno se pregunta cómo puede interesarle
> a otra casa extractora de Jerez tan acreditada como la mía;
> algo así.
>
> (Cortázar, 1984, p. 341)

This puzzling extract, and the entire section 34 of *Rayuela* from which it is drawn, is constructed as a confusing alternation between allusive segments (only some of which are textually marked by italics) quoted from Pérez Galdós's *Lo prohibido* – the novel which Oliveira, the protagonist of section 34, has been leafing through – and Cortázar's elaboration of his musings. Even once the translator has cracked the code whereby section 34 can be rendered intelligible to the reader, the problem of translating the ST as a mixture of allusions and musings remains a particularly difficult and challenging one.

A different sort of example of the same problem of allusive meaning is afforded by the title of Gustavo Adolfo Bécquer's poem 'Es sueño la vida' (Bécquer, 1961, p. 52). Here the allusion is, of course, to Calderón's classic *La vida es sueño* which forms the intertextual background to Bécquer's text. In order to build a recognizable literary allusion into the title of an English TT, a possible solution might be to base that title on an allusion to the Shakespearian lines 'We are such stuff as dreams are made on/And our little life is rounded with a sleep' (*The Tempest*), rendering it perhaps as 'Our little life'. This solution carries two main risks: the risk that, in the absence of an explicit mention of 'dream', the TT reader may miss the title's oblique allusion to dreams; and the risk that, embedded into the Shakespearian intertextual context, the resulting TT may come to connote a philosophy of life which distorts and falsifies the global impact of the ST. In either case the translator risks a form of translation loss which would vitiate the function of the allusion in the TT.

PRACTICAL 8

8.1 Connotative meaning

Assignment
Taking the expressions in bold type in the ST printed on p. 106:

(i) Categorize and discuss those in which connotative meaning plays a part and discuss the translation of them in the TT printed opposite the ST. Where appropriate, give an edited TT, rendering the ST connotations more successfully into English.

(ii) Identify and discuss expressions which have introduced unwanted connotative meanings into the published TT, give an edited TT in each case, and explain your decisions.

Contextual information
This extract is taken from Act III, scene 2 (the final scene) of Federico García Lorca's play *Yerma: un poema trágico en tres actos y seis cuadros* (written in the early 1930s). The ST and TT appear as parallel texts, edited and translated by Ian Macpherson and Jacqueline Minett, published in 1987. The extract appears at the beginning of the ritual fertility dance of the *Hembra* and the *Macho*. (NB Line numbers denote lines of *text*, not lines of verse.)

Source text

HEMBRA En el río de la sierra
la esposa triste se bañaba.
Por el cuerpo le subían
los caracoles del agua.
La arena de las orillas
y el aire de la mañana
le daban fuego a su risa
y temblor a sus espaldas
¡Ay qué **desnuda** estaba
la **doncella** en el agua!

NIÑO ¡Ay cómo **se quejaba**!

HOMBRE 1 ¡Ay **marchita de amores**!
¡Con el viento y el agua!

HOMBRE 2 ¡Que diga a quién espera!

HOMBRE 1 ¡Que diga a quién aguarda!

HOMBRE 2 ¡Ay con **el vientre seco**
y la color **quebrada**!

HEMBRA Cuando llegue la noche lo diré,
cuando llegue la noche clara.
Cuando llegue la noche de la **romería**
rasgaré los volantes de mi enagua.

NIÑO Y en seguida vino la noche.
¡Ay que la noche llegaba!
Mirad qué oscuro se pone
el **chorro** de la montaña.

(*Empiezan a sonar unas guitarras*)

MACHO (*Se levanta y agita el cuerno*)
¡Ay qué blanca
la triste casada!
¡Ay cómo se queja entre las ramas!
Amapola y clavel serás luego,
cuando **el macho despliegue su capa**. [...]
Si tú vienes a la romería
a pedir que **tu vientre se abra**,
no te pongas **un velo de luto**
sino **dulce camisa de holanda**.

Target text

FEMALE In the mountains, in the river,
the sad wife bathed.
Soft around her body
curled the water like a snail.
Sand from the banks by the river
and the morning breeze:
her bare arms shivered
and her laugh flowed free.
How naked was that maiden,
the maiden of the stream!

BOY O, how the maiden wept!

1st MAN Pity the loveless in the water!
Pity the barren in the wind!

2nd MAN Let her say for whom she wants!

1st MAN Let her say for whom she waits!

2nd MAN Pity the wife with the barren womb!
Pity her face with colour flown!

FEMALE When night-tide falls I'll tell,
in night-tide's lucid drift,
when pilgrims walk by night,
I'll tear my ruffled shift.

BOY Then quickly night-tide fell.
How fast that night did fall!
How dark, how dark as well,
the mountain waterfall.
(*Sound of guitars*)

MALE *(Gets up and brandishes his horn)*
Oh, how white,
the sorrowful wife!
Oh, how she sighs in the shade!
Carnation and poppy
you'll later be
when I unfold my cape. [...]
If you come as a pilgrim
to pray your womb flowers,
wear soft linen shift,
not sad widow's veil.

Reprinted by kind permission from Federico García Lorca, *Yerma,* edited and translated by Ian Macpherson and Jacqueline Minett (Warminster: Aris & Phillips, 1987, pp. 122–5), copyright © Macpherson, Minett & Lyon, 1987.

8.2 Connotative meaning

Assignment
Working in groups:

(i) Discuss the strategic problems confronting the translator of the following text, paying particular attention to connotation.
(ii) Translate a section of the text into English.
(iii) Explain the main decisions of detail you made in producing your TT.

Contextual information
The text is Rubén Darío's poem 'Sinfonía en gris mayor'. The Nicaraguan poet Rubén Darío (1867–1916) has been described as the chief representative of the 'modernista' (a term he himself is said to have coined) movement in Spanish poetry. His post-Romantic poetry, written at the turn of the century, is often characterized by an idealization of the sensual: in 'Sinfonía en gris mayor', this idealization takes the form of a highly pictorial 'mood poem', aptly termed a kind of 'word-etching'.

Text

SINFONÍA EN GRIS MAYOR

El mar como un vasto cristal azogado
refleja la lámina de un cielo de zinc;
lejanas bandadas de pájaros manchan
el fondo bruñido de pálido gris.

El sol como un vidrio redondo y opaco
con paso de enfermo camina al cenit;
el viento marino descansa en la sombra
teniendo de almohada su negro clarín.

Las ondas que mueven su vientre de plomo
debajo del muelle parecen gemir.
Sentado en un cable, fumando su pipa,
está un marinero pensando en las playas
de un vago, lejano, brumoso país.

Es viejo ese lobo. Tostaron su cara
los rayos de fuego del sol del Brasil;
los recios tifones del mar de la China
le han visto bebiendo su frasco de gin.

La espuma impregnada de yodo y salitre
ha tiempo conoce su roja nariz,
sus crespos cabellos, sus bíceps de atleta,
su gorra de lona, su blusa de dril.

En medio del humo que forma el tabaco
ve el viejo el lejano, brumoso país,
adonde una tarde caliente y dorada
tendidas las velas partió el bergantín...

La siesta del trópico. El lobo se aduerme.
Ya todo lo envuelve la gama del gris.
Parece que un suave y enorme esfumino
del curvo horizonte borrara el confín.

La siesta del trópico. La vieja cigarra
ensaya su ronca guitarra senil,
y el grillo preludia un solo monótono
en la única cuerda que está en su violín.

Reprinted from Rubén Darío, *Prosas profanas y otros poemas*, ed. Ignacio M. Zuleta (Madrid: Castalia, 1987, pp. 138–9),

9

Language variety in texts: dialect, sociolect, code-switching

In this chapter and Chapter 10, we discuss the question of language variety and translation. By way of introduction to the notion of language variety, here is a text from Luis Martín-Santos's *Tiempo de silencio*. It consists of a monologue in which Cartucho, a resident of the Madrid shanty-town, describes a knife-fight he has had with 'el Guapo' over a girl. This text can be used as a point of reference for both Practicals 9 and 10, and would repay some discussion in class.

> ¿Qué se habría creído? Que yo me iba a amolar y a cargar con el crío. Ella, "que es tuyo", "que es tuyo". Y yo ya sabía que había estao con otros. Aunque fuera mío. ¿Y qué? Como si no hubiera estao con otros. Ya sabía yo que había estao con otros. Y ella, que era para mí, que era mío. Se lo tenía creído desde que le pinché al Guapo. Estaba el Guapo como si tal. Todos le tenían miedo. Yo también sin la navaja. Sabía que ella andaba conmigo y allí delante empieza a tocarla los achucháis. Ella, la muy zorra, poniendo cara de susto y mirando para mí. Sabía que yo estaba sin el corte. Me cago en el corazón de su madre, la muy zorra. Y luego "que es tuyo", "que es tuyo". Ya sé yo que es mío. Pero a mí qué. No me voy a amolar y a cargar con el crío. Que hubiera tenido cuidao la muy zorra. ¿Qué se habrá creído? Todo porque le pinché al Guapo se lo tenía creído. ¿Para qué anduvo con otros la muy zorra? Y ella "que no", "que no", que sólo conmigo. Pero ya no estaba estrecha cuando estuve con ella y me dije "Tate, Cartucho, aquí ha habido tomate".

Discussing this text and the problems of translating it will immediately highlight certain features: the markers of sociolect, the colloquialisms, the grammar and vocabulary, and the slangy tone. It is, in fact, an excellent example of one of the most difficult aspects of textual 'meaning', namely the appreciation not of referential content, but of characteristics *in the way the message is expressed* that voluntarily or involuntarily reveal information about the speaker, the writer or the protagonist in a work of fiction. These stylistically conveyed meanings are connotations: they share with the types of connotation discussed in Chapter 8 the character of meanings 'read between the lines' on the basis of associations that are widespread, although not enshrined in the dictionary.

Sorting out significant information carried by such stylistic features can be a daunting practical problem: details have to be separated out as one comes to them. However, this is no reason for not trying to discuss the problem in general terms. There are two essential questions that arise. The first is: what are the objective textual characteristics from which stylistic information about the speaker or writer can be inferred? The simple answer must be: the way the message is expressed as compared with other possible ways it might have been expressed (whether by the same person or by somebody else). That is, the *manner in which the message is formulated* is the basic carrier of information about the person to whom that formulation is attributed. (In fiction this attribution is often a double one: the author of the fictional work, and the fictional protagonist whose 'voice' the author is evoking in the text.)

The second question that arises is: what *kind of information* can be carried through the particular manner in which the message is formulated? The answer is twofold: first, the manner, or style, reveals things about speakers/writers that they do not necessarily intend to reveal, notably social and/or regional affiliations, and the social stereotype to which they appear to belong; second, it reveals things that they do intend to reveal, notably the calculated effect they want their utterances to have on the listener/reader. Naturally, any or all of these features can and do occur together in overlap with one another. Social stereotype and effect on a listener/reader, in particular, are sometimes so closely associated that they cannot easily be distinguished; we shall discuss them, as different aspects of 'register', in the next chapter. In the present chapter, we look at translation issues raised by dialect, sociolect and code-switching.

DIALECT

To speak a particular **dialect**, with all its phonological, lexical, syntactic and sentential features, is to give away information about one's association with a particular region. A simple phonological example, drawn from a folk tale entitled 'Las tres preguntas' (Alvar, 1960, p. 510) is '¿En cuánto tiempo se le pué dá la güerta ar mundo?': an utterance heavily marked by phonic features characteristic of extreme Andalusian dialect speech (from Utrera). The same text offers a lexical example in the choice of the dialectal variant 'güerta' as opposed to Castilian 'vuelta'. It is sometimes also possible to infer the degree of speakers' regional affiliations from the proportion of dialectal features in their speech; for instance, whether they are natives of the region and have little experience of other regions, or whether they are originally from the region, but retain only traces of that origin overlaid by speech habits acquired elsewhere; or whether they are incomers who have merely acquired a veneer of local speech habits. Furthermore, some speakers are notable for having a repertoire including several dialects between which they can alternate (that is, they are capable of 'code-switching'), or on which they can draw to produce a mixture of dialects. All these aspects of dialectal usage are stylistic carriers of information about a speaker, and no sensitive translator can afford to ignore them. Four main problems arise from taking account of them.

The first problem is easily defined: it is that of recognizing the peculiarities from which dialectal affiliation can be inferred in a ST. Clearly, the more familiar the translator is with SL dialects, the better.

The second is that of deciding how important the dialectal features, and the information they convey, are to the overall effect of a ST. The translator always has the option of rendering the ST into a bland, standard version of the TL, with no notable dialectal traces. This may be appropriate if the dialectal style of the ST can be regarded as incidental, at least for the specific purposes of the TT. For example, in translating an eyewitness account of a murder for Interpol, one might be well advised to ignore all dialectal features and concentrate on getting the facts clear. However, if the dialectal nature of the ST cannot be regarded as incidental – for example, in a novel where plot or characterization actually depend to some extent on dialect – the translator has to find means for indicating that the ST contains dialectal features. This creates some difficult practical problems.

For instance, suppose the ST is so full of broad dialectal features as to be virtually incomprehensible to a SL speaker from another region. The translator's first strategic decision is whether to produce a TT that is only mildly dialectal, and totally comprehensible to any TL speaker. Arguments against this solution might be similar to those against 'improving' a ST that is badly written. However, there can be circumstances where this is the best alternative; depending, as any strategic decision does, on such factors as the nature and purpose of the ST, the purpose of the TT, its intended audience, the requirements of the person or organization paying for the translation, and so on. In some cases one may decide to inject a mere handful of TL dialectal features into the TT, just to remind the audience that it is based on a ST in dialect. On the other hand, the very obscurity of a piece of ST dialect may serve important textual purposes which would be vitiated in the TT if the piece were not rendered in an equally obscure TL dialect. In such a case – and probably *only* in such a case – it may be necessary for the translator to go all the way in the use of a TL dialect.

The third problem arises if the translator does opt for a broad TL dialect: just what dialect should the TT be in? Supposing that the ST is in Andalusian dialect, is there any dialect of English that in some way corresponds to it, having similar status and cultural associations among English dialects to those held by Andalusian among Spanish dialects? There is no obvious objective answer to this question – after all, what exactly *is* the position of Andalusian dialect among Spanish dialects?

Of course, there may be certain stereotypical assumptions associated with given ST dialects which might be helpful in choosing a TT dialect (for instance, 'Andalusians have the reputation of being lazy', or 'Cockneys are cheeky and cheerful'). When a dialect is used in the ST specifically in order to tap into such stereotypes, it could conceivably be appropriate to select a TL dialect with similar popular connotations. In other cases, the choice of TL dialect may be influenced by geographical considerations. For instance, a northern dialect of Spanish (say, Asturian), in a ST containing references to 'northerners', might be plausibly rendered in a northern dialect of English. Even more plausibly, a Spanish ST with a plot situated in an industrial setting, say Bilbao, might be rendered in a TL dialect from an industrial city in the Midlands or the North of England, perhaps Birmingham or Manchester.

A final difficulty, if one decides to adopt a specific TL dialect, is of course the problem of familiarity with its characteristics. If the translator does not have an accurate knowledge of the salient features of the TL dialect chosen, the TT will become as ludicrous as all the texts which, through ignorance, have Scots running around saying 'hoots mon' and 'och aye the noo'.

It will be clear by now that rendering ST dialect with TL dialect is a form of cultural transplantation. Like all cultural transplantations, it runs the risk of incongruity in the TT. For instance, having broad Norfolk on the lips of country folk from Valencia could have disastrous effects on the plausibility of the whole TT. The surest way of avoiding this would be to transplant the entire work – setting, plot, characters and all – into Norfolk; but, of course, this might be quite inappropriate in the light of the contents of the ST. Short of this extreme solution, the safest decision may after all be to make relatively sparing use of TL features that are recognizably dialectal without being clearly recognizable as belonging to a specific dialect. Fortunately, there are many features of non-standard accent, vocabulary and grammar that are widespread in a number of British dialects. Nevertheless it would be even safer, with a ST containing direct speech, to translate dialogue into fairly neutral English, and, if necessary, to add after an appropriate piece of direct speech some such phrase as 'she said, in a broad Andalusian accent', rather than have a woman from Andalusia speaking Scouse or Glaswegian.

SOCIOLECT

In modern sociolinguistics, a distinction is made between regional dialects (dialects proper) and language varieties that are, as it were, 'class dialects'. The latter are referred to by the term **sociolect**. Sociolects are language varieties typical of the broad groupings that together constitute the 'class structure' of a given society. Examples of the major sociolects in British culture are those designated as 'lower class', 'urban working class', 'white collar', 'public school' and so on. It is noticeable, and typical, that these designations are relatively vague in reference. This vagueness is due partly to the fact that sociolects are intended as broad, sociologically convenient labels, and partly to the lack of rigid class structure in British society. In more rigidly stratified societies, where there is a strict division into formally recognized 'castes', the concept of sociolect is more rigorously applicable.

A further possible reservation as to the usefulness of purely sociolectal labels is that, very often, a social classification is virtually meaningless without mention of regional affiliations. For example, the term 'urban working-class sociolect' cannot designate a particular language variety of English unless it is qualified by geographical reference. While 'upper-class' and 'public-school' sociolects are characteristically neutral to regional variations, the further down one goes on the social scale, the more necessary it is to take social and regional considerations together, thus creating concepts of mixed regional and sociolectal language varieties such as 'Norwich urban working class', 'Edinburgh "Morningside" urban middle class' and so on. Such mixed socio-dialectal designations are generally more meaningful labels for recognizable language variants than purely sociological ones. The situation in a Spanish context is somewhat different from the situation in Britain: regional variations tend to cut across the social scale, with each regional dialect having sociolectally higher and lower forms. Nevertheless, as in Britain, regional dialects are stigmatized and variations within the range of 'upper-class' and 'upper-middle-class' sociolects of Spanish (often identified as 'castellano culto') are limited. The situation is, of course, further complicated by Latin-American varieties of Spanish, whose status is by no means matched by non-British varieties of English (American, Canadian, Australian and so on). Unlike these sociolinguistically autonomous varieties of English, Latin-American varieties of Spanish have, in terms of prestige, remained to date somewhat in the shadow of Castilian. They are often perceived as though they were 'sub-standard' varieties of Spanish in a way that parallels the popular view of Canadian French as a 'sub-standard' variety of 'Parisian' French.

Whatever one's reservations about the notion of sociolect, it remains true that sociolectal features can convey important information about a speaker or writer. If they are obtrusive in the ST (in the form of non-standard, or non-prestigious, features of accent, grammar, vocabulary or sentential marking), the translator cannot afford to ignore them. Characteristic features of 'lower-class' sociolect in Spanish include the use of the infinitive instead of forms of the imperative, as in '¡Sentaros!' instead of '¡Sentaos!'; lexical peculiarities such as the use of 'camelar' instead of 'coquetear'; and phonic peculiarities such as 'cuidao' instead of 'cuidado' or 'pa' instead of 'para'. Even in these examples, the question arises of regional differences between various 'lower-class' non-standard versions.

There are, clearly, literary texts (the passage from *Tiempo de silencio* on p. 110 is a case in point) in which sociolect is a central feature and requires attention from the translator. However, the mere fact that the ST contains marked sociolectal features does not necessarily mean that the TT should be just as heavily sociolectally marked. As with translating dialects, there may be considerations militating against this, such as whether the sociolect has a definite textual role in the ST, or the purposes for which the ST is being translated. In many cases it is sufficient for the translator to include just enough devices in the TT to remind the audience of the sociolectal character of the ST. Alternatively, there may be good reasons for producing a TT that is in a bland 'educated middle-class' sociolect of the TL – this also is a sociolect, but, for texts intended for general consumption, it is the least obtrusive one.

Once the translator has decided on a TT containing marked sociolectal features, the problems that arise parallel those created by dialect. The class structures of different societies, countries and nations never replicate one another. Consequently, there can be no exact matching between sociolectal varieties of one language and those of another. At best, something of the prestige or the stigma attached to the ST sociolect can be conveyed in the TT by a judicious choice of TL sociolect. The translator may therefore decide that a valid strategy would be to render, say, an 'urban working-class' SL sociolect by an 'urban working-class' TL sociolect. But this does not solve the question of *which* 'urban working-class' sociolect. The decision remains difficult, especially as the wrong choice of TL sociolect could make the TT narrative implausible for sociological reasons. This question of the socio-cultural plausibility of the TT is one of the translator's major considerations (assuming, of course, that the ST is not itself deliberately implausible). Finally, as with dialect, it goes without saying that the translator must actually be familiar enough with features of the chosen TL sociolect(s) to be able to use them accurately and convincingly (in general, it is also safest to use them sparingly).

CODE-SWITCHING

Passing mention was made above of **code-switching**. This well-known phenomenon occurs in the language use of speakers whose active repertoire includes several language varieties – dialects, sociolects, even distinct languages. It consists of a rapid alternation from one moment to another between using different language varieties. Code-switching is used, by ordinary speakers and writers, for two main strategic reasons: first, to fit style of speech to the changing social circumstances of the speech situation; and second, to impose a certain definition on the speech situation by the choice of a style of speech. Examples of both are provided by the trilingual code-switching in the *Señas de identidad* extract used in Practical 3.

Since code-switching is a definite strategic device, and since its social-interactional function in a text cannot be denied, the translator of a ST containing code-switching should convey in the TT the effects it has in the ST. For written dialogue, the possibility of explaining the code-switch without reproducing it in the TT does exist, as in 'he said, suddenly relapsing into the local vernacular'. There is, of course, no such option for the text of a play or a film, except as an instruction in a stage direction. At all events, it would be more effective, if possible, to reproduce ST code-switching by code-switching in the TT. Such cases place even greater demands on the translator's mastery of the TL, two or more noticeably different varieties of the TL needing to be used in the TT.

There is no code-switching in the *Tiempo de silencio* passage, but it is clearly illustrated in the following extract from José María de Pereda's *Sotileza*. This should be prepared for discussion and translation in class. (Note that the code-switching in this text is, of course, not on the part of the characters but of the author: it is used as a means of portraying protagonists as social stereotypes.) (*Contextual information*. José María de Pereda (1833–1906) wrote novels which created vigorous portrayals of rural Spain. He was known for his *cuadros de costumbres*. In the extract below, Cole, Muergo and Sula are local lads: Asturian fishermen's sons. Their direct speech is markedly dialectal. The *fraile* speaks a more standard version of *castellano*.)

–¿A qué vienen esas risotadas, bestias, y esas palabrotas sucias, puercos?–dijo el fraile, mientras largaba los coscorrones.

–Es la callealtera..., ¡ju, ju, ju!–respondió Muergo, rascándose el cogote, machacado por los nudillos de fray Apolinar.

–La conocemos nosotros–expuso Cole, palpándose la greña.

–Que de poco se ajuega, si no es por Muergo–añadió Sula.

Muergo volvió a reírse estúpidamente, y la muchacha tornó a hacerle burla.

–¿Y por eso te ríes, ganso?–dijo el fraile, largándole otro coquetazo–. ¡ Pues el lance es de reír!

–Es callealtera...–replicó Cole–, estaba haciendo barquín-barcón en una percha que anadaba en la Maruca... Yo y Sula estábamos allí tirándole piedras desde la orilla. Dimpués, allegó Muergo..., la acertó con un troncho y se fue al agua de cabeza.

–¿Quién?–preguntó el fraile.

–Ella–respondió Cole–. Yo pensé que se ajuegaba, porque se iba diendo a pique... Y Muergo se reía.

–Y yo–saltó Sula–le dije: '¡Chapla, Mergo, tú que anadas bien, y sácala porque se está ajuegando!' Y entonces se echó al agua y la sacó. Dimpués la ponimos quilla arriba; y a golpes en la espalda, largó por la boca el agua que había embarcao.

–¿Y eso es verdad, muchacha?–preguntó a esta el exclaustrado.

–Sí, señor–respondió la interpelada, sin dejar de remedar a Muergo, que volvió a reír como un idiota.

–Corriente–dijo el exclaustrado–. Pero ¿a qué vienes aquí y a qué vienes tú, Andresillo, y por qué la traes de la mano? ¿En qué bodegón habéis comido juntos y qué pito voy a tocar yo en estas aventuras?

Reprinted from José María de Pereda, *Sotileza*, in *Obras completas, Tomo II* (Madrid: Aguilar, 1965, p. 197).

PRACTICAL 9

9.1 Language variety: dialect and sociolect

Assignment

You will be played a sound recording that should be treated, for the purposes of the assignment, as an extract from the sound-track of a television interview. The interviewee is talking about his seafaring experiences, and the dangers of the sea. After brief discussion of the salient features of the text, you will be given a transcript of it. Working in groups on sections of the text:

(i) Identify and discuss the dialectal and sociolectal features in the text.
(ii) Reconstruct a standard Spanish (Castilian) version of the text.
(iii) Discuss the strategic problems involved in translating the text (a) for voice-over in a television documentary and (b) for a speech in a play.
(iv) Produce a translation for voice-over for discussion in class.

9.2 Language variety: sociolect and code-switching

Assignment

Working in groups, take the extract from *Sotileza* given on p. 116 and:

(i) Discuss the strategic problems it poses for the translator. Outline your strategy for translating it, particularly with reference to code-switching, bearing in mind that it is a dialogue in a novel.
(ii) Translate the text into English.
(iii) Explain the main decisions of detail you made in producing your TT.

10

Language variety in texts: social register and tonal register

From dialect and sociolect, we move on to conclude our survey of language variety by looking at two other sorts of information about speakers/writers that can often be inferred from the way the message is formulated. Both are often referred to as 'register', and they do often occur together, but they are different in kind. We shall distinguish them as 'social register' and 'tonal register'.

SOCIAL REGISTER

A **social register** is a particular style from which the listener reasonably confidently infers what kind of person is speaking, in the sense of the social stereotype to which he or she belongs. To explain this concept, we can start by taking two extremes between which social register falls.

It is possible to imagine, at one extreme, a way of formulating messages that is so individual that it instantly identifies the author, narrowing down the possibilities to just one particular speaker and writer. Writers with very clearly recognizable individual styles, such as Lorca, Brecht or James Joyce, and singers for whom a characteristic voice quality acts as an additional identifying mark, such as Mercedes Sosa, Edith Piaf or Joan Baez, come to mind as obvious examples. At the other extreme, a message can be formulated in such a bland, neutral and ordinary way as to give away virtually no personal information about its author: the speaker/writer could be almost any member of the SL speech community.

Usually, however, a style will be recognized as characteristic of a certain *kind* of person, seen as representing some previously encountered social stereotype. This information is, obviously, distinct from information carried specifically by dialectal features. Perhaps less obviously, it is also distinct from information carried specifically by sociolect: though dialect and sociolect may be ingredients of a given social register, dialect only conveys regional affiliations, and sociolect corresponds to very broad conceptions of social grouping (limited to sociological notions of 'class structure'), whereas social register designates fairly narrow stereotypes of the sorts of people one expects to meet in a given society. (For example, the textual features in the extract from *Tiempo de silencio* on p. 110 indicate a social register more immediately than they do a sociolect.) Since, in general, we organize our interactions with other people (especially those we do not know intimately) on the basis of social stereotypes to which we attach particular expectations, likes and dislikes, it is easy to give examples of social register.

For instance, encountering a man given to using four-letter expletives, one may perhaps infer that he is the vulgar, macho type. (Terms like 'vulgar' and 'macho' are typical stereotyping terms.) Difficulties of precisely pinpointing the appropriate stereotype are similar to those of precisely pinpointing attitudinal meaning (see p. 99). Nevertheless, what is significant is that a whole section of the population is eliminated from conforming to this type – one's genteel maiden aunt is unlikely to speak like this – while other types (such as young, unskilled urban manual worker) remain likely candidates. Similarly, a style full of 'thank you' and 'please' is not indicative of just any speaker. A middle-class, well-bred, well-mannered person (note again the typical stereotyping terms) may be implied by such a style.

As these examples suggest, whatever information is conveyed by linguistic style about the kind of person the speaker/writer is will often be tentative, and will require support from circumstantial and contextual evidence before it adds up to anything like the 'characterization' of an individual. For example, in the *Tiempo de silencio* text on p. 110, while the slang elements of grammar and lexis suggest that the speaker is a stereotypical 'habitante de chabola', it is circumstantial details like references to knifings that allow one to be reasonably confident in this inference. (In any case, that example also shows that, as we have suggested, sociolect is subordinate to social register as an indication of what 'kind of person' is speaking.)

Despite reservations, the fact remains that the mere observing of linguistic style invites unconscious social stereotyping, both of people and of the situations in which they find themselves. Linguistic style is understood as an unconscious reflex of a speaker's perception of 'self', of situations and of other people present. All the time that one is unconsciously stereotyping oneself and others, and situations, into various social categories, one is also unconsciously correlating the various stereotypes with appropriate styles of language use. Inferences from social stereotype to linguistic stereotype and vice versa are virtually inevitable.

As soon as a particular stylistic indication places a speaker and/or a social situation into one of the relatively narrowly circumscribed social categories used in stereotyping personalities and social interactions in a given society, the amount of stylistic information is seen to be relatively rich. In such cases, that information is likely to include fairly clear pointers to a combination of specific characteristics of speaker and/or situation. Among these characteristics may figure the speaker's educational background and upbringing; the social experience of the speaker (for example, social roles the speaker is used to fulfilling); the speaker's occupation and professional standing; the speaker's peer-group status, and so on – the list is in principle inexhaustible.

This, then, is the sort of information carried by what we are calling 'social register'. In other words, when speakers provide linguistic clues about their social personae and specific social milieux (as distinct from broad class affiliations), we say that they are using particular social registers, each one held in common with other speakers answering a similar stereotypical description. Equally, if the style reveals details of the way participants perceive the social implications of the situation they are speaking in, we refer to this style as the social register appropriate both to a type of person and to a type of situation.

When authors' social credentials are of some importance (perhaps because of the need to establish authority for speaking on a particular subject), they will select and maintain the appropriate social register for projecting a suitable social persona. This use of social register accounts for much of the use of jargon, not only the jargon in technical texts (which is at least partly used to maintain the author's self-stereotyping as a technical expert), but also jargon consisting of clichés, catch-phrases and in-words that build up other social stereotypes.

Use of jargon frequently springs from expectations, and the fulfilling of expectations, with respect to social register. In moderation, this does work as a successful means of signalling social stereotype. However, when taken to excess, jargon may become ridiculous, putting its users into stereotypes they do not welcome. The parodying of social stereotypes by pastiche that uses jargon to excess is illustrated in Benito Pérez Galdós's *La de Bringas*. It is worth analysing this extract in Practical 10, to identify the social register the pastiche is caricaturing, to determine how the caricature is done and how successful it is, and to attempt a TT:

> PEZ – Al punto a que han llegado las cosas, amigo don Francisco, es imposible, es muy difícil, es arriesgadísimo aventurar juicio alguno. La revolución de que tanto nos hemos reído, de que tanto nos hemos burlado, de que tanto nos hemos mofado, va avanzando, va minando, va labrando su camino, y lo único que debemos desear, lo único que debemos pedir, es que no se declare verdadera incompatibilidad, verdadera lucha, verdadera guerra a muerte entre esa misma revolución y las instituciones, entre las nuevas ideas y el Trono, entre las reformas indispensables y la persona de Su Majestad.
>
> (Pérez Galdós, 1991, p. 108)

This example clearly shows the potential of exaggeration in social register as a comic device, and also the attendant problem of finding an appropriate social register, as well as getting the degree of exaggeration right, when translating a ST parodying some SL social register. The example also shows a different, but related, problem in translating *serious* STs: while it may be important to choose an appropriate social register, it is just as important not to over-mark it, otherwise the TT may become unintentionally comic.

In a narrative or play, an essential part of making sure the characters stay plausibly true to type is to ensure that they express themselves consistently in an appropriate social register. (The extract from *Sotileza* on p. 116 shows this need for consistency with respect to social register.) It would indeed be very odd for simple country folk suddenly to assume the social register of a contemplative intellectual or an aristocrat, unless, of course, there were special textual/narrative reasons for doing this deliberately. (Still more interesting in the *Sotileza* extract is the mixing of slang and dialect features with standard Spanish: to what extent do the speaking characters share a common repertoire consisting of both non-standard and standard Spanish?) Good characterization demands two things: insight into the way in which people belonging to identifiable social stereotypes tend to express themselves, and the ability to use consistently the stylistic quirks and constraints of these social registers. (By *quirks* we mean the kind of thing representatives of a given stereotype would say; by *constraints*, the kind of thing they would never say.)

It is important to remember that, in literature and real life, social register can be marked on any or every level of textual variable, including accent and delivery. Practical 10 may include discussion of two taped extracts, both from recordings of interviews, given here in transcript:

Text 1

La tasa mayor de desempleo sigue siendo la feminina; ese es el problema, ¿eh?, que puede ser quizá porque ha sido cuando más las mujeres han... han acudido... hemos acudido a las oficinas de desempleo, pues quizá, pero sigue... sigo insistiéndote que efectivamente la mujer todavía se la antepone al hombre, o sea, se la deja en segundo plano, entonces, eh, sí que es verdad que el paro es muy grande, pero dentro de ese paro todavía la... la selección de personal en un puesto de trabajo se prefiere al hombre a la mujer.

Reprinted by kind permission from *Voces de España*; BBC Radio for Schools and Colleges, Modern Languages Student's Workbook (Falmer: Brighton Polytechnic, The Language Centre, p. 38), copyright © BBC 1990.

Text 2

¡Ay sí! El ruido de trópico. Porque es muy distinto, hay muchas diferencias en cuanto al trópico y a... a los países europeos, obviamente, pero sobre todo en relación a Inglaterra. O sea, bajarte del avión en Maiquetía, que es el aeropuerto de Caracas, es como si te lanzaran a un mundo totalmente distinto cuando sales por esa puerta: primero te invade el calor, te invade la luz (o sea, hasta el punto que los ojos te duelen cuando bajas de la escalerilla del avión), y... y sobre todo es eso, es la sensación de ruido.

Adapted from *Voces Hispánicas; Spoken Documents for Advanced Learners of Spanish*, compiled by María Fernández Toro (London: Birkbeck College, p. 8), copyright © Department of Spanish, Birkbeck College, 1992.

It will be clear by now that in translating a ST which has speaking characters in it, or in which the author uses a social register for self-projection, the construction of social register in the TT is a major concern. Equally clearly, in translating, say, P. G. Wodehouse into Spanish, one would have to do something about the fact that Jeeves speaks in the social register of the 'gentleman's gentleman', and Bertie Wooster in that of the aristocratic nitwit. The fundamental problem is this: how can essentially English stereotypes like Jeeves and Bertie be transplanted into a Spanish-speaking context, produce plausible dialogue in Spanish, and still remain linguistically stereotyped so as to hint at the caricatures of gentleman's gentleman and inane aristocrat? There are no obvious global answers to such questions.

A choice of appropriate TL registers can, however, sometimes seem relatively easy when the translator is operating between similar cultures, where certain social stereotypes (such as the plain-clothes detective) and stereotype situations (such as an Embassy ball) do show some degree of cross-cultural similarity. It may well be that some social stereotypes can be fairly successfully matched from one culture to another. The translator is then left with a two-stage task. First, a ST stereotype must be converted into an appropriate target-culture stereotype; and second, a plausible social register must be selected and consistently applied for each of the target-culture stereotypes chosen.

However, 'parallels' in social stereotyping are in fact far from exact. There are obvious discrepancies between, for example, the stereotypes of British aristocrat and Spanish aristocrat, or British policeman and Spanish policeman. In any case, is it desirable for Bertie Wooster to become every inch the Spanish aristocrat in a Spanish TT? Is the translation not vitiated if the translator fails to convey to the Spanish reader a sense of Wooster's essential Britishness (or even Englishness)?

Even greater difficulties arise when it comes to matching stereotypes that have no likely parallels in the target culture. For instance, there seem to be no close target-culture parallels for the British *gentleman farmer* from the shires, the first-generation Italian immigrant from Brooklyn, the Spanish *torero* or the Central American *cacique*. Given any of these types in a ST, what social register would be appropriate for the corresponding character in the TT? Or should their speech be rendered in a fairly neutral style, with very few marked features of social register? For that matter, should these characters be rendered as culturally 'exotic'? After all, for the characters portrayed in a *novela costumbrista,* such as Pereda's *Sotileza*, to lose all trace of Spanishness in an English translation would surely be as disappointing as for Bertie Wooster to come across as completely Spanish. Even once the strategic decisions have been taken, there remains the eternal double challenge to the translator's linguistic skill: to be familiar with the quirks and constraints of TL varieties, and to be able to produce a consistently plausible TL social register.

TONAL REGISTER

A fourth type of speaker-related information that can be inferred from the way a message is formulated is what we shall call **tonal register**. Tonal register is what is often called 'register' in dictionaries and textbooks on style. It often combines with any or all of dialect, sociolect and social register in an overall stylistic effect, but it is qualitatively different from them. Tonal register is *the tone that the speaker/writer takes* – perhaps vulgar, or familiar, or polite, or formal, or pompous and so on. That is, the effect of tonal register on listeners is something for which speakers can be held responsible, in so far as they *are being* familiar, pompous, and so on. Dialect, sociolect and social register are different from tonal register in that they are not matters of an attitude that speakers intentionally adopt, but the symptomatic result of regional, class and social-stereotype characteristics that they cannot help. So a listener might reasonably respond to tonal register by saying 'don't take that tone with me', but this would not be a reasonable response to dialect, sociolect or social register. If, in a given situation, Bertie Wooster *is being* polite, that is a matter of tonal register; but it would be odd to suggest that he *is being* an upper-class nitwit – he *is* an upper-class nitwit, as one infers from his sociolect, social register and general behaviour. (Of course, it is a different matter when someone *puts on* an accent, sociolect or social register as a form of mimicry or play-acting at 'being', say, Glaswegian or Sloane; in 'playing the Sloane', the speaker is not taking a tone with the listener, but is consciously or unconsciously projecting herself as having a particular social persona.)

Many of the labels dictionaries attach to certain expressions, such as 'familiar', 'colloquial', 'formal' and so on, are, in fact, reflections of the tone a speaker using these expressions can be said to be taking towards the listener or listeners. It is, therefore, helpful to assess levels of tonal register on a 'politeness scale', a scale of stylistic options for being more or less polite, more or less formal, more or less offensive, and so on.

Looked at in this way, tonal register is relatively easy to distinguish from social register. As we have suggested, being polite on a particular occasion is different from being stereotyped as a well-brought-up kind of person. Nevertheless, tonal register often overlaps with social register, in two ways.

First, there are ambiguous cases where it is not clear whether a style of expression is a reflection of social stereotyping or of the speaker's intentions towards the listener. For example, it may be impossible to tell whether a speaker 'is being' deliberately pompous in order to convey a patronizing attitude (tonal register), or whether the pomposity is just a symptom of the fact that the speaker fits the stereotype of, for example, the self-important academic (social register). Thus, the difference in register between 'this essay isn't bad' and 'this essay is not without merit' might equally well be classified as social or as tonal (in fact it consists in elements of both).

Second, the characteristics of particular social registers are very often built up out of features of tonal register – and of dialect and sociolect, for that matter. This is especially true of social stereotypes characterized by 'downward social mobility'. For instance, a middle-class, educated person who is adept at the jargon of criminals and down-and-outs will have an active repertoire of vulgarisms and slang expressions. As we have seen, 'vulgarism' and 'slang' mark points on the politeness scale of tonal register; but, at the same time, they go towards building up the complex of features that define a particular social register. Similarly, the girl pretending to be a Sloane is thereby also using the amalgam of tonal registers that helps to constitute the Sloane social register.

The notions of 'social register', 'tonal register', 'dialect' and 'sociolect' do therefore overlap to some extent, and all four are likely to occur intermingled in a text. Their separation is consequently something of a methodological abstraction, but, practically speaking, it is still very useful to keep them as clearly distinct as possible in analysing style, because this helps the translator to recognize what is going on in the ST, and therefore to make correspondingly important strategic decisions. Where it does remain unclear whether a particular case is an instance of tonal or of social register, it is legitimate to use the cover-term 'register'. (Similarly, where dialect, sociolect and social register overlap indistinguishably, the cover-term 'language variety' can be used.)

The implications of tonal register for the translator are essentially no different from those of dialect, sociolect and social register. Since tonal register is linked to intended effects on the listener/hearer, interpreting the impact of a ST depends very greatly on identifying its tonal register. Once this has been done, care must be taken to match the tonal register of the TT to intended audience effect. Inappropriateness or inconsistency in register can all too easily spoil a translation. For example, there would be unacceptable translation loss in rendering '¿Pero qué e' lo que ha' hecho con la ropa?' as 'Gosh, I say, wotcher bin an' gone an' done to your garments?', or 'Me cago en el corazón de su madre, la muy zorra' as 'I shit on her mother's grave, the whore'. In the first of these cases, translation loss results from an unfortunate mixing of mutually incompatible tonal registers; in the second case, from the use of an excessively vulgar, and in itself implausibly un-English, tonal register.

As with the other language varieties, looking for suitable renderings of tonal register puts translators on their mettle, giving ample scope for displaying knowledge of the SL and its culture, knowledge of the target culture, and, above all, flair and resourcefulness in the TL.

PRACTICAL 10

10.1 Language variety: social register and tonal register

Assignment

(i) Identify and discuss the salient features of register in the following text. Pay special attention to social register and tonal register, but do not ignore other important instances of language variety. In the case of features of social register, explain what sort of social stereotype they signal.

(ii) Translate the ST with particular attention to using appropriate social and tonal registers in your TT. Explain your decisions in each case.

Contextual information

Pedro Calderón de la Barca's *La vida es sueño* was written in 1635 and first published in 1636. One of the principal themes of the play is the opposition between free will and predestination. Segismundo, son of King Basilio of Poland, has been shut in a tower since birth and has consequently been cut off from the civilizing influence of society. This extract is from the 'Jornada segunda'. (NB Line numbers denote lines of *text*, not lines of *verse*.)

Text

ESTRELLA Séd más galán, cortesano.
ASTOLFO (*Ap.*) ¡Soy perdido!
CRIADO 2º (*Ap.*) El pensar sé
de Astolfo, y le estorbaré.
Advierte, señor, que no
es justo atreverse así,
y estando Astolfo...
SEGISMUNDO ¿No digo
que vos no os metáis conmigo?
CRIADO 2º Digo lo que es justo.
SEGISMUNDO A mí
todo eso me causa enfado.
Nada me parece justo
en siendo contra mi gusto.
CRIADO 2º Pues yo, señor, he escuchado
de ti que en lo justo es bien
obedecer y servir.
SEGISMUNDO También oíste decir
que por un balcón, a quien
me canse, sabré arrojar.
CRIADO 2º Con los hombres como yo
no puede hacerse eso.
SEGISMUNDO ¿No?
¡Por Dios que lo he de probar!
(*Cógele en los brazos y éntrase, y todos tras él; vuelve a salir inmediatamente*)
ASTOLFO ¿Qué es esto que llego a ver?
ESTRELLA Idle todos a estorbar. (*Vase*)
SEGISMUNDO Cayó del balcón al mar.
(*Volviendo*) ¡vive Dios que pudo ser!
ASTOLFO Pues medid con más espacio
vuestras acciones severas,
que lo que hay de hombres a fieras
hay desde un monte a palacio.

SEGISMUNDO Pues en dando tan severo
en hablar con entereza,
quizá no hallaréis cabeza
en que se os tenga el sombrero.
(*Vase Astolfo*)

10.2 Language variety: dialect, social register and tonal register

Assignment

(i) Listen to the recording played to you by your tutor and identify the salient features of language variety in the text. (Your tutor may give you a transcript of the spoken text.)

(ii) Discuss the strategic problems of translating the text as (a) part of a dramatized text and (b) a voice-over spoken by actors in a television documentary on Latin America.

(iii) Working in groups, translate the interview into English, paying appropriate attention to language variety. The TT should be suitable as a text for voice-over.

(iv) Explain the decisions of detail you made in producing your TT.

11

Textual genre as a factor in translation: oral and written genres

At various points in this course we have spoken of the ST both as a starting-point for translation and as a point of reference in evaluating TTs. However, before it is ever thought of as a ST requiring translation, any text is already an object in its own right, something that belongs to a particular genre of the source culture. Any given ST will share some of its properties with other texts of the same genre, and will be perceived by a SL audience as being what it is on account of such genre-typical properties. Therefore, the translator must, in order to appreciate the nature of the ST, be familiar with the broad characteristics of the appropriate source-culture genre. Furthermore, since any source culture presents a whole array of different textual genres, the translator must have some sort of overview of genre types in that culture. This does not imply an exhaustive theory of genres – even if such a theory were available, it would be too elaborate for a methodology of translation. All that is needed is a rough framework of genre types to help a translator to concentrate on characteristics that make the ST a representative specimen of a particular source-culture genre.

The most elementary subdivision in textual genres is into *oral* text types and *written* ones. Both these major categories, of course, break down into more narrowly circumscribed minor categories, and ultimately into specific genres.

ORAL GENRES

In the case of oral genres, we suggest the following breakdown into sub-genres:

conversation
oral narrative
oral address
oral reading
dramatization
sung performance

Conversation

As a sub-genre, conversation is characterized by its genuinely unscripted nature, and by the fact that its guiding structural principle is 'turn-taking', that is, the rule-governed alternation between participant speakers.

Oral narrative

The sub-genre of oral narrative includes the continuous (though not necessarily uninterrupted) telling, by one speaker, of tales, stories, anecdotes, jokes and the like, and the recounting of events (whether true or apocryphal). Characteristic of such texts is the fact that they are organized by a narrative structure, which may be idiosyncratic to specific genres (for example, 'There was an Englishman, a Scotsman and an Irishman').

Oral address

In this sub-category are placed all forms of public speaking (lectures, talks, seminars, political speeches, verbal pleadings in a court of law, and so on). The defining feature of this genre type is that, nominally at least, a single speaker holds the floor, and elaborates on an essentially non-narrative theme. There is a clearly felt intuitive distinction between oral narratives and oral addresses: while stories are 'told', addresses are said to be 'delivered'. (Though an address may be interspersed with items of oral narrative, for instance anecdotes or jokes, its structural guiding principle is clearly not narrative, being geared to information, instruction or persuasion rather than to entertainment.)

Oral reading

Oral reading is introduced as a separate genre type in order to distinguish, not only 'reading aloud' from 'silent reading', but also the 'flat' reading-out of written texts from 'dramatized reading'. In other words, what is typical of oral reading is that readers do not attempt to act out the script by assuming the characters of imaginary unscripted speakers. (This, incidentally, is distinct from the habitual manner of poetry recitation, where the reader normally assumes and interprets the part of the poet.) Where dramatized reading tries to give the impression of unscripted oral performance, oral reading is simply the vocalized delivery of a written text. Oral reading is also distinct from oral address: witness the clear intuitive difference between a lively lecturing style (oral address) and the technique of 'reading a paper' at a seminar or conference.

Dramatization

By this category we mean the entire gamut of plays, sketches, dramatized readings, films and the like, manifested in actual spoken performance (whether on stage, screen, radio or television). Such texts are characterized by the necessary role of an actor or actors in their performance, and by the fact that their effectiveness depends on a dramatic illusion entered into by both actors and audience.

Sung performance

The sub-category of sung performance includes all oral texts set to music, whether figuring as songs performed in isolation, or as part of a longer work (for instance, an oratorio, or an opera). It is important to remember that, where these are written down, the printed text of a song or a libretto may be denoted by the cover-term 'lyrics'. However, what we are concerned with here is not the written lyrics as such, but the verbal content of actual oral renderings of songs, musicals, operas, operettas and the like. Consequently, it is important for translators in this genre not to deal with the lyrics in the abstract, but to consider verbal texts as forming part of a live musical performance.

This list, while it does not claim to be exhaustive, gives a good general coverage of oral genres in western cultures. Each genre type can, of course, be further subdivided (for example, oral narrative into folk tales, ghost stories, anecdotes, autobiographical accounts, jokes and so forth). However, even as it stands, the list enables us to pick out the basic features that concern translators of oral texts.

The defining property all these genres have in common is the fact that they are realized in a vocal medium. Though a truism, this fact has important implications. First, an oral text is in essence a fleeting and unrepeatable event that strikes the ear and 'then is heard no more'. Second, vocal utterance may be accompanied by visual cues (such as gestures or facial expressions) that are secondary to it, and equally transitory, but which do form a part of the overall text and play a role in colouring its meaning. This all means that, on every level of textual variable, oral texts must obey the 'rules' of a spoken language first and foremost. It also means that an effective oral text avoids problems of comprehension arising from informational overloading, elaborate cross-reference, excessive speed and so forth. Of course, in all these respects, what is true for oral STs is also true for oral TTs – an obvious fact, but one that is all too often overlooked.

Another important implication is the appearance of spontaneity that characterizes the majority of oral genres (with the exception of oral reading). This goes not only for impromptu conversation or unrehearsed narrative, but for prepared texts as well: stories told and retold in a carefully formulated version; memorized lines in a play or film; even such texts as speeches or lectures, where the speaker may stick closely to a script but the delivery is imitative of unscripted oral texts. To a lesser degree, dramatized reading, recited verse, song lyrics and libretti, if well performed, all give the audience a chance to enter into the illusion of spontaneous vocal utterance.

As these remarks suggest, an oral text is always quite different in nature and impact from even its most closely representative written version. For instance, a recited poem is quite distinct from its printed counterpart, and so is a performed song from the bare text set down on paper. Even the most blatant oral reading has certain nuances of oral delivery, such as intonation and stress, that make its reception quite different from the experience of silent reading.

An awareness of these properties of oral texts and genres is a necessary starting-point for discussing the particular types of problem that confront anyone wanting to translate an oral ST into an oral TT. The most specialized branch of oral-to-oral translating is on-the-spot interpreting. (In fact, terminologically, interpreting is usually distinguished from other kinds of translating.) There are three major types of interpreting.

The first is *bilateral interpreting* of conversation, where the interpreter acts as a two-way intermediary in unrehearsed dialogue. Bilateral interpreting can be the most relaxed of the three types; as part of the multi-lingual social situation, the interpreter can even clarify obscure points with the speakers. What this kind of interpreting involves mainly is a broad facility in understanding and speaking the languages involved, familiarity with the relevant cultures, and sensitivity to the conversational nuances of both languages (including awareness of tonal registers and of visual cues of gesture and facial expression).

The second type is *consecutive interpreting*. This requires all the same skills as bilateral interpreting, and more besides. The interpreter listens to an oral text, makes detailed shorthand notes and, from these, ad libs an oral TT that relays the content and some of the nuances of the ST. The training for consecutive interpreting is intensive, and takes several months at least.

The third type is *simultaneous interpreting*. Here, the interpreter relays an oral TT at the same time as listening to the oral ST. This is the most specialized form of interpreting, and requires the longest training. Grasping the content and nuances of a continuous oral ST, while at the same time producing a fluent oral TT that does justice to the content and nuances of the ST, can be very taxing. Trainees do not usually start learning simultaneous interpreting until they have acquired considerable skill in consecutive interpreting.

Since it is a specialized skill, interpreting is not part of this course, and we shall not dwell on it. It is very useful, however, to try a session of bilateral interpreting and one of consecutive interpreting, partly as an exercise in gist translation (as defined on p. 9), but mostly because it sharpens awareness of specifically oral textual variables, which may require special attention in translating any kind of text, spoken or written.

An exercise in interpreting will also confirm that spoken communication has stylistic quirks and constraints that are very much language-specific. The eternal problem of translating jokes is a good example of this. It is not merely that some jokes are hard to translate because they depend on word-play, but that both humour itself and techniques of joke- and story-telling are to a great extent culture-specific. Translating oral jokes is an especially clear illustration of the fact that oral translation is not simply a matter of verbal transposition from one spoken language to another: the genre-related norms and expectations of the target culture must be respected as well, including gestures, facial expressions, mimicry and so on. Texts in most oral genres are not only utterances, but also dramatic performances. This will have been vividly seen by anyone who tried putting 'El susto más grande' (Practical 9.1) into colloquial English. To do so, one is almost bound to produce a written TT, but this will only be an interim approximation to the combination of phonic and prosodic features essential to a successful, performed, oral TT.

Another oral genre dealt with in Practical 11, the genre of the song lyric, highlights a second set of difficulties peculiar to oral translation. Assuming that the TT is to be sung to the same tune as the ST, overriding strategic priority will have to be given to the prosodic and phonic levels of textual variables. It is therefore hardly surprising that translators of songs, and even libretti, sometimes take considerable liberties with the literal meanings of STs. Popular songs may, of course, have completely new TL lyrics made up for them; and if they are translated, it is very freely. Libretti cannot enjoy the same degree of freedom, since the TT still has to make sense within the framework of a plot that does not depart significantly from that of the original ST. Libretto translators have an extremely demanding task, because they have to do three things: respect the dramatic needs of the ST (with its linguistic and stylistic implications); produce a dramatic TT matching the expectations that a TL audience has of the genre; and work under the very strict prosodic constraints imposed by the music. As we have seen (pp. 52–6), different languages have differently organized prosodic properties. Consequently, when translating from Spanish to English, one needs to understand the prosodic features not only of the SL, but also of the TL, so that the TT can actually be sung without sounding ridiculous.

In addition, the translator of lyrics must be alert on the phonic level, and pay attention to the quality of syllabic vowels as they correspond with notes in the score. For example, in Spanish lyrics it is feasible to sing a long note on an unstressed syllabic vowel, as in Mercedes Sosa's rendering of 'vid**a**'; but a schwa sung on a long musical note in English is incongruous if it falls on a syllable that is unstressed in ordinary speech – compare 'ret**ur**n', which is acceptable, and 'etern**a**lly', which is not. Consonant clusters must also be attended to, so that the performer is not given a tongue-twister to sing.

In Chapter 12, where we look at the issues that arise in translating written STs for oral delivery and oral STs into written TTs, this brief survey of the main requirements of oral-to-oral translation will need to be borne in mind. First, however, we need to survey – equally briefly – the field of written genres.

WRITTEN GENRES

There are, in Western cultures, so many different varieties of written text that any typology of practical use for translation is bound to be even more approximate than the one suggested for oral genres. We shall approach the categorization of written genres by looking back to a time immediately predating the literary explosion that has continued to escalate since the sixteenth and seventeenth centuries. The approach implies that innovation in written textual genres, for at least the past four centuries, has been limited to the invention of new subdivisions of five already existing genres, the seeds of which were probably sown in classical antiquity. On this assumption, the fundamental and most general categories of written genres are:

literary/fictional
religious/devotional
theoretical/philosophical
empirical/descriptive
persuasive/prescriptive

This classification is primarily based on a global view of textual subject matter, or, more precisely, on *the author's implicit attitude to the treatment of subject matter*.

Literary/fictional genres

The essence of texts in this category is that they are about a 'fictive', imaginary world of events and characters created autonomously in and through the texts themselves, and not controlled by the physical world outside. However close a text of this type may be to autobiography, it still approaches its subject matter by recreating experience in terms of a subjective, internal world, which is fundamentally perceived as fictive, for all its similarities to real life. In texts in this category, the author is understood to be ultimately in control of events and characters.

Literary genres have, of course, subdivided and diversified very greatly. Even poetry, which is just one genre in this category, has split up over the last two centuries into innumerable sub-genres, each with different characteristic styles. (One need only compare the poems used in this course to begin to appreciate this proliferation.) As for prose fiction, there are not just the genres of novel and short story, but a wide variety of minor genres such as detective stories, thrillers, historical romances and science fiction.

Religious/devotional genres

The subject matter of devotional and religious works implies belief in the existence of a 'spiritual world'. Seen from the outside (that is, by an atheist or agnostic), there may seem to be little difference between this and the fictive and imaginary subject matter of literary/fictional genres. However, and this is the point, seen in terms of the author's attitude to the treatment of the subject matter, there is nothing fictive about the spiritual world dealt with in religious/devotional texts: it has its own extratextual realities and unshakeable truths. That is, this category has more in common with 'empirical/descriptive' than with 'literary/fictional' genres. The author is understood not to be free to create the world that animates the subject matter, but to be merely instrumental in exploring it.

Of all five categories of genre, this one seems to have changed and diversified least of all. Even the Good News Bible represents only a minor diversion from the Authorized Version, and Thomas Aquinas or Julian of Norwich have only to be brought modestly up to date to feel remarkably modern.

Theoretical/philosophical genres

These genres have as their subject matter a 'world' of *ideas*, which are understood to exist independently of the individual minds that think them. So-called pure mathematics is the best example of the kind of subject matter and approach to subject matter that define theoretical/philosophical genres. The vehicle used by authors is not fictional imagination or spiritual faith, but reasoning. (In Western cultures, the primary form of abstract, rational thinking is deductive logic.) The author of a theoretical/philosophical text, however original it may be, is understood not to be free to develop theoretical structures at will, but to be constrained by standards of rationality.

The proliferation of genres in this category has been less spectacular than that of literary genres, but it is strikingly diverse nonetheless – compare, for instance, Spinoza's *Tractatus theologico-politicus*, Kierkegaard's *Lidelsernes evangelium* and Kant's Kritik *der reinen Vernunft*.

Empirical/descriptive genres

Genres in this category purport to treat of the real objective world as it is experienced by specialist observers. An empirical/descriptive text is one with a necessarily 'factual' reference (though, again, sceptics may refuse to accept that factuality); it is a text that sets out to give an objective account of phenomena.

This category has diversified in direct proportion to the creation and diversification of specialized scientific and technical disciplines. Each discipline and each school of thought tends to develop its own technical vocabulary and its own style. In this way, a virtually endless list of minor genres is being constantly generated.

Persuasive/prescriptive genres

The essence of these genres is that they aim at influencing readers to act and think in textually prescribed ways. This aim can be pursued through various means: explicit and helpful instructions; statutory orders, rules and regulations; oblique suggestions. Thus, we are uniting in a single category the entire gamut of texts from instruction manuals, through documents stating laws, rules and regulations, to propaganda leaflets, advertisements and so forth. Like the other four genre categories, this one can be broken down into an indefinite number of sub-categories. Nevertheless, it is held together by a common purpose, the purpose of getting readers to take a certain course of action, and perhaps explaining how to take it.

The category of persuasive/prescriptive genres has also undergone immense proliferation, thanks not only to the growth of bureaucracy, technology and education, but also to the modern escalation in advertising.

The reason why this classification is useful for translation methodology is that *differences in approach to subject matter* entail fundamental *differences in the way a text is formally constructed*. In other words, differences in genre tend to correspond to characteristic differences in the use of textual variables. So – to take a simple example – sound-symbolism and the deliberate use of connotative meanings are inappropriate in English empirical/descriptive texts. Apart from the interesting case of 'hybrid' texts that cut across categories, linguistic and stylistic expectations are in general distinct from one genre category to another.

The importance of genre distinctions for the practice of translation is actually very clearly illustrated by the phenomenon of 'hybrid genres'. There are three main ways in which a particular text can cut across basic genre distinctions. Either it can belong by subject matter to one category, but borrow the stylistic form of another (as in Norman Mailer's *The Armies of the Night*, or Goethe's scientific treatises in verse): hybrids of this type have a double purpose, such as providing literary enjoyment along with empirical description. Or a text may be compounded of sections allocated to subject matters falling into different genres (as in *Time* magazine, *The Observer*, *Cambio 16* or *El País*): the Bible is a good example of such a 'hybrid' text in which different books represent different genre categories (for instance, the Song of Songs represents a literary genre, Paul's Epistle to the Romans a religious/devotional genre, the Acts of the Apostles a historical/descriptive genre, and Leviticus a prescriptive one). Alternatively, a text can use genre-imitative subsections as a conscious stylistic device. A good example is this descriptive passage from Juan Goytisolo's *Señas de identidad* parodying the style of a certain type of travel guide:

> Situada a 2 grados 9 minutos de longitud Este del meridiano de Greenwich y a 41 grados 21 minutos de latitud Norte, Barcelona se extiende en el llano que, entre los ríos Besós y Llobregat, baja en suave pendiente desde el anfiteatro de montañas que la limitan y protegen por septentrión hasta el viejo Mare Nostrum. Nuestra Ciudad goza de un clima templado cuyas temperaturas extremas rara vez alcanzan los 30 grados ni descienden bajo cero, lo cual da una temperatura media ideal que para estos últimos cinco años ha resultado ser de 16,12 grados centígrados. En el mismo período de tiempo la presión atmosférica ha oscilado entre 769,5 mm. y 730 mm. La humedad, quizá el

factor más acusado de nuestro clima, ha dado un promedio para los mismos años del 70 por ciento. [...]

El anfiteatro de montañas que rodea a Barcelona por el Norte se está repoblando totalmente como parque forestal. El punto más alto, la cumbre del Tibidabo (532 metros sobre el nivel del mar) es el mirador ideal de la Ciudad, punto turístico de fácil acceso, en el que se erige la basílica, aún sin terminar, dedicada al Sagrado Corazón, cuya fundación inició San Juan Bosco. Otro mirador de la ciudad es la cumbre y ladera de Montjuich, el monte en que se inició su historia, coronado por la fortaleza que, perdido hoy su carácter militar, vuelve a la ciudad como museo.

This passage repays discussion in class. It is also very instructive to compare it with real tourist guides such as the following:

COLOMBIA: PAÍS DE ELDORADO

Cuando el territorio que hoy ocupa Colombia comenzó a ser conquistado por los españoles en el siglo XVI nació una leyenda: Eldorado... fabuloso tesoro que se suponía escondido en el fondo de todas las aguas, enterrado en todos los socavones, tropezado en cada mina...

Sin embargo, los conquistadores no pudieron localizar aquella inmensa riqueza cuya sola descripción exaltaba los ánimos e infundía valor aún en los cobardes... Los conquistadores no sabían que no todo lo que brilla es oro y que no todos los tesoros pueden ser sometidos a acuñación: el tesoro saltaba a la vista, estaba a flor de tierra:... eran los climas el tesoro, los frutos generosos, los cielos abiertos, las llanuras, y montañas: Colombia, era Eldorado...

(from a brochure by Avianca)

'Hybrid' texts, especially literary ones, illustrate why translators need to have a clear view of available genres and of their linguistic and stylistic characteristics. For instance, the point of the text from *Señas de identidad* would be lost if the typical style of TL tourist guides were not used (with appropriate adaptation) in the TT. A sense of genre characteristics enables translators to set themselves clearly formulated targets before they start producing TTs. It also forewarns them about any special needs in translating a particular text, such as finding the necessary dictionaries and source materials, doing the necessary background reading, and so on. No translation can be undertaken without due preparation, and identifying the genre of the ST is the first step towards adequate preparation.

As the example from *Señas de identidad* shows, awareness of genre is vital in that translators have to be familiar with the styles of presentation and language use expected from particular genres in particular cultures. It is often genre that makes a communicative rendering preferable to literal translation. For instance, if a

Spanish tourist brochure talks of a place as a 'punto turístico de fácil acceso', genre practically demands that this be rendered by 'a beauty-spot easily accessible by road/rail/public transport', the familiar cliché of countless English-language tourist brochures. This particularizing translation could easily be avoided by translating literally – 'a touristic location with easy access' – but, as very often happens, the demands of the genre outweigh those of literal accuracy. These considerations are equally valid for written and oral genres, and will be of central importance in Practicals 11–14.

Between textbook and poetry

There is another parameter on which genres can be compared in a way relevant to translation. This parameter can be visualized as a scale or continuum defined by the relative textual importance of explicit literal meaning at one extreme, and of implicitly conveyed connotative and/or stylistic meaning at the other. At one end of the scale are texts like scientific or legal documents, or textbooks, that require maximum attention to precision in literal meaning and minimum attention to 'aesthetic' effects. What connotative nuances or overtones do exist in these texts can be virtually ignored by the translator – indeed, care must be taken not to let such effects creep into the TT inadvertently, as they could be a distraction from the literal meaning.

At the opposite end of the scale are texts that depend maximally on subtle nuances of non-literal meaning and aesthetic effect, and minimally on the explicit, literal meaning. Poetry tends towards this extreme. In poetry, understanding the literal content of sentences is often no more than perceiving the vehicles of a more subtle textual meaning. A lyric poem may have relatively slight content in literal meaning and yet be both a serious poem and a very rich one (Rubén Darío's 'Sinfonía en gris mayor' is a case in point). It is inherent in poetry that a given poem's precise combination of literal meaning, connotative (or 'emotive') meanings, syntactic articulation, prosody and phonic patterning produces a text which works largely through *suggestion*. Experienced commentators will usually agree broadly – but never in all details – on the 'import' of the poem. Poetry may, simply because it has words, tempt the inexperienced translator to identify its meaning with its literal content – whereas, in fact, to reproduce the total import of a poem in a TT would require recreating the whole unique bundle of meanings and sounds presented in the ST. That is the prime reason why poetry is often said to be untranslatable. In our view, however, if one accepts that translation loss is *inevitable*, and that the translator's role is to reduce it as much as possible, then it is feasible to envisage at least highly honourable failure in translating poetry – witness the many well-known translations of Spanish poetry by Roy Campbell, or Gilbert Cunningham's excellent translations of Góngora (1964).

Translators can usefully gauge the genre of a ST, and also of their own TT, by rating its position on this scale between textbook and poetry. Obviously, this cannot be done objectively or precisely, but it is possible to assess roughly the *proportions* in which literal meanings and connotative 'resonances' contribute to the overall meaning of a given text. So, for example, poetry is to be taken as increasingly 'poetic' the less important literal meaning is in proportion to connotative resonances; and it will be taken as increasingly 'prosaic' the more important literal meaning is relative to connotative resonances. Certain examples of poetry disguised as prose (such as the Cortázar passage studied in Practical 4) would seem to occupy the middle ground in the continuum; but, in principle, connotative meaning has a slight edge over literal meaning in even the most prosaic forms of poetry. (It is, incidentally, important not to be misled by textual layout: verse is not necessarily poetry, and prose may well be.) Conversely, even the most poetic prose will not be classified as poetry if literal meaning has overall precedence over connotative meaning.

At the other end of the scale, scientific texts represent the extreme point of meaning in directly expressed and logically structured form. But the translator must be on the alert for the pseudo-scientific text, in which apparent 'objectivity' is a consciously adopted register, and therefore constitutes a stylistic device requiring attention in translating.

In conclusion, then, we can say that even a rough-and-ready typology of oral and written genres pays dividends by concentrating the translator's mind on four vital strategic questions.

First, what genre is represented by the ST and what problems are expected in connection with this genre? Second, given the genre of the ST, what ST features should be given priority in translation? Does the ST have recognizable, perhaps clichéd, genre-specific characteristics that require special attention? Third, what genre(s) in the TL provide a match for the ST genre? What can a scrutiny of available specimens of these TL genres suggest about the manner in which the TT should be formulated? Finally, what genre should the TT be couched in, and what genre-specific linguistic and stylistic features should it have?

PRACTICAL 11

11.1 Genre

Assignment
Working in groups:

(i) Listen to the song, without following the printed text. *Treating it as an oral text*, discuss its genre, content and impact.
(ii) Examine the printed lyrics of the song (on pp. 138–9) and discuss its salient features *as a written text*.
(iii) Listen to the song again, following it in the text, and discuss the relation between the words and the music. (Note the points where there are discrepancies between the sung text and the written lyrics.)

(iv) Discuss the strategic problems of translating the song into a TT intended to be sung in English at a folk-festival.

(v) Each group taking one stanza, produce a TT suitable for musical performance on stage.

Contextual information

'Gracias a la vida' by the Chilean Violeta Parra (1917–67) was first released on the album *Las últimas composiciones de Violeta Parra* (1966). Parra began collecting folk songs in the early 1950s and in 1954 won a prize as folklorist of the year. Her own compositions grew out of her interest in popular song and often described her feeling of identification with the pueblo. Whilst Parra was not actively involved in politics, Pring-Mill (1990) categorizes 'Gracias a la vida' as a 'canción de lucha y esperanza' and records that Joan Baez described it as 'the underground anthem of all those people who are living under dictatorships in Latin America'. The printed text below is taken from Pring-Mill (c. 1990); the singer most closely associated with the song is the Argentinian Mercedes Sosa.

Text

Gracias a la vida que me ha dado tanto.
Me dio dos luceros que, cuando los abro,
perfecto distingo lo negro del blanco,
y en el alto cielo su fondo estrellado
y en las multitudes el hombre que yo amo.

Gracias a la vida que me ha dado tanto.
Me ha dado el oído que, en todo su ancho,
graba noche y día grillos y canarios,
martillos, turbinas, ladridos, chubascos,
y la voz tan tierna de mi bien amado.

Gracias a la vida que me ha dado tanto.
Me ha dado el sonido y el abecedario,
con él las palabras que pienso y declaro:
madre, amigo, hermano, y luz alumbrando
la ruta del alma del que estoy amando.

Gracias a la vida que me ha dado tanto.
Me ha dado la marcha de mis pies cansados;
con ellos anduve ciudades y charcos,
playas y desiertos, montañas y llanos,
y la casa tuya, tu calle y tu patio.

Gracias a la vida que me ha dado tanto.
Me dio el corazón que agita su marco
cuando miro el fruto del cerebro humano;
cuando miro el bueno tan lejos del malo,
cuando miro el fondo de tus ojos claros.

Gracias a la vida que me ha dado tanto.
Me ha dado la risa y me ha dado el llanto.
Así yo distingo dicha de quebranto,
los dos materiales que forman mi canto,
y el canto de ustedes que es el mismo canto
y el canto de todos, que es mi propio canto.

Gracias a la vida que me ha dado tanto.

11.2 Genre

Assignment
Working in groups:

(i) Discuss the strategic problems confronting the translator of the following text, paying careful attention to considerations of genre.
(ii) Translate a section of the text allocated to your group. (For the purposes of the exercise, assume that the TT will be published in the review section of *The Observer* or some other quality newspaper specified by your tutor.)
(iii) Explain the main decisions of detail you made in producing your TT.

Contextual information
The text is taken from the 'Gaceta' column of *Babelia*, a regular weekend supplement to the quality paper *El País*. The reviews below are from the issue dated 23 May 1992.

Text

GACETA

Más diarios de Thomas Mann

Acaba de aparecer el octavo volumen. Empezó en 1977 con la publicación de los *Tagebücher* (*Diarios*) del bienio 1933–34, los primeros años del exilio. Siguieron todos los *Diarios* no destruidos por Thomas Mann, a partir precisamente de 1933, pero con la excepción de los *Tagebücher 1918–1921*, que el autor salvó de la hoguera porque los necesitaba para documentarse sobre el *Doktor Faustus*. El quinto volumen (1940–43) fue el último editado por Peter de Mendelssohn. Con su muerte (1982) el proyecto entró en crisis. ¿Cómo sustituir a un tal conocedor de Thomas Mann? Hasta que apareció Inge Jens, que consiguió que no se echara en falta a su predecesor. Tuvo a su cargo los dos volúmenes siguientes, y ahora aparece el tercero *Tagebücher 1949–50* (S. Fischer Verlag), un grueso tomo de 780 páginas, con 379 páginas de prosa manniana y el resto, compuesto por las notas y los índices.

'Signos'. Nueva colección de poesías

Editada por la Agencia Española de la Propriedad Intelectual y bajo la dirección de Leopoldo Alas y Ángel Luis Vicaray, responsables a su vez de una revista del mismo nombre, acaba de aparecer una nueva colección de poesía, *Signos*, con una triple voluntad: la publicación de contemporáneos, el rescate y la traducción. Sus tres primeros títulos son emblemáticos de estas direcciones. Así, por una parte, bajo el título *Poemas* de Theodore Roethke se publica una antología, traducida por Alberto Girri, con prólogo de Luis Antonio de Villena, de este poeta nacido en 1908 y fallecido en 1963. El segundo libro es la recuperación de un poemario publicado en 1914, *Reliquias*, de Fernando Fortún, a quien Luis Antonio de Villena sitúa dentro de la corriente del *crepuscularismo*, también conocida como *segunda generación modernista*. La tercera entrega, *La condición y el tiempo*, recoge la poesía de Leopoldo Alas entre 1988 y 1991.

La letra de la ópera

El resurgimiento de la afición operística en nuestro país ha provocado el interés por la bibliografía relacionada con el tema así como por los libretos, que constituyen el complemento indisociable a la partitura musical. Fruto de este interés es la iniciativa de Ediciones Cátedra de publicar una colección de *Libretos de ópera Expo '92* que constituye, una vez desaparecida la colección Diamond y dejando aparte la excelente colección Ópera, de la editorial catalana L'Avenç, muy vinculada a la programación del teatro del Liceo de Barcelona, una novedad absoluta en la bibliografía española. Las ediciones, que constan de estudio introductorio, apéndices y, en algunos casos, la traducción de los libretos, han sido encargados a reconocidos especialistas del mundo musical como Arturo Reverter, José Luis Téllez, Rafael Banús o Juan Ángel Vela, entre otros. Los títulos de la serie se corresponden con los programados para la temporada de ópera de la Maestranza de Sevilla en el año en curso. Los primeros volúmenes aparecidos son *Carmen*, de Georges Bizet, y *María Estuardo*, de Donizetti.

12

Genre marking and the crossover between oral and written genres

In Chapter 11 we concentrated mainly on the ST as an object belonging to a given genre. We outlined certain major categories of oral and of written genres, and suggested that translators should be familiar with the characteristics of SL and TL genres and have the ability to couch a TT in a form appropriate to the chosen TL genre. We also suggested that demands of genre often outweigh those of literal accuracy in a TT. In this chapter, we shall explore two related themes, one of which follows on from the other. The first of these themes concerns the use of features that mark a TT as being a plausible text in a particular TL genre. The second concerns the problems attendant on the fact that, in the course of translation, there is very frequently a **crossover** between oral and written texts and their corresponding genres. As we shall see, a careful view of such a crossover is of vital importance for minimizing translation loss. At the same time, such a view invites direct comparison between oral and written texts, providing the clearest and most economical way of bringing out features specific to each. The theme of 'crossover' also builds on lessons drawn from Practical 11, linking these to Practical 12.

GENRE MARKING

A TT must stand, independently of any support from the ST, as a plausible text in terms of the expectations of a TL audience. While this holds for any genre, it is probably most immediately obvious in the case of certain oral genres, since the audience can publicly applaud, or boo, or walk out.

Making a TT fit a particular genre means not only tailoring it to the standard grammar of the TL genre, but also giving it features that conform to typical stylistic properties of that genre. Some of these features may be simply formulaic; certainly, formulaic features give the most tangible examples of what we mean. For instance, in translating a traditional folk tale told by a Spanish story-teller, it would be reasonable to open the TT with the phrase 'Once upon a time there was ...'. This is a genuine choice, since one could translate the formulaic Spanish beginning 'Érase una vez ...' more literally as 'There was once ...'. Choosing 'Once upon a time' is an autonomous TL-biased decision motivated by the fact that English folk tales typically begin with this standard formula and that this opening therefore instantly signals the genre of the TT. Formulaic expressions such as 'Once upon a time ...', '... they lived happily ever after', 'Érase una vez ...' and '... y vivieron felices y comieron perdices' are simple genre-marking features, and good examples of genre-marking as a significant option for the translator. Similarly, TL linguistic etiquette suggests that the Spanish expression '¡Diputados!' should, in the genre of a parliamentary address, be rendered by the English formula 'Honourable Members'. Ordinary conversation, too, has its share of genre-marking formulas, such as ritualized greetings, to which interpreters need to be sensitive and where the choice of a given formula is a matter of TL etiquette. So, for example, whether to render 'Buenos días' by 'How do you do', 'Good morning' or 'Hello', and, conversely, whether to render 'Hello. How are you?' as 'Buenos días. ¿Cómo está?' or '¡Hola! ¿Qué hay?', has in each case to be an autonomous decision made in the light of target-culture etiquette, with ST tonal register acting as a guideline. Note also that differences in linguistic etiquette lead native speakers of English to over-use the expression 'por favor'; even though the influence of Anglo-American culture is leading to its increased usage among native Spanish speakers. Among other things, students of Spanish forget that when the response 'gracias' is given to an offer a Spanish speaker is indicating acceptance.

As these simple examples show, genre-marking a TT influences the process of translation in the direction of TL orientation. This may affect small details or general translation strategy; both types of effect are illustrated in the following extract from Alfonso Sastre's play *Escuadra hacia la muerte*. (*Contextual information*. The play was written in 1953 and is set in a military context. Here the 'Cabo' is addressing a motley company of raw recruits who have been assigned to him for training.)

> Este es mi verdadero traje. Y vuestro 'verdadero traje' ya para siempre. El traje con el que vais a morir.[...] Este es el traje de los hombres: un uniforme de soldado. Los hombres hemos vestido siempre así, ásperas camisas y ropas que dan frío en el invierno y calor en el verano... Correajes... El fusil al hombro... Lo demás son ropas afeminadas..., la vergüenza de la especie.[...] Pero no basta con vestir este traje..., hay que merecerlo... Esto es lo que yo voy a conseguir de vosotros..., que alcancéis el grado de soldados, para que seáis capaces de morir como hombres. Un soldado no es más que un hombre que sabe morir, y vosotros vais a aprenderlo conmigo. Es lo único que os queda, morir como hombres. Y a eso enseñamos en el Ejército.
>
> (Sastre, 1969, pp. 13–14)

This text is clearly intended for oral delivery in the social register of the stereotypical 'drill sergeant' and in a bullying, contemptuous tonal register. Sastre's text is not, of course, a **transcript** – that is, it does not represent and record a pre-existing oral text. Nevertheless, Sastre has included enough features drawn from an appropriate genre of oral address to act as genre-marking cues. Whatever other components there are in the genre to which this monologue belongs (theatre; military setting; social and political critique), an essential feature is use of a genre of oral address. In the following literal TT, there is no allowance made for these genre-marking features of the ST; this translation strategy yields a poor text for stage performance:

> This is my true garb. And your 'true garb' henceforth. The garb in which you are going to die. This is the garb of men: a soldier's uniform. Men have always dressed like this: rough shirts and clothes that let you freeze in the winter and swelter in the summer ... leather straps ... a gun over the shoulder ... Anything else is effeminate clothing ..., a disgrace to mankind. But it is not sufficient to put on this garb ... you have to earn it ... And that is what I am going to make sure you do ... that you attain the rank of soldiers, so you become capable of dying like men. A soldier is nothing more than a man who knows how to die, and you are going to learn this with me. That is the only thing which remains to you, to die like men. And that is what we teach in the Army.

Compare this TT with one that, in strategic approach, resembles the ST in being a **script** – that is, a written text designed for oral performance. In detail, this TT makes plausible use of communicative translation, clichés, illocutionary particles, contracted forms and vulgarisms, all as genre-marking features:

> *This* is my proper suit. And that goes for you lot too from now on. Your togs until yer six feet under, get it? An Army uniform: that's what real men wear, I tell you. Real men 'ave always worn kit like this: rough shirt, gear that freezes you in winter and makes you sweat in summer ... boots you can see yer face in ... rifle over your shoulder ... Anything else is for pansies ..., the scum of the earth. But it's no good you just putting this uniform on ... you've got to earn it ... and I'll bloody make sure that's what you do ... I'm going to make soldiers of you lot ... teach you how to die like men, right? 'Cos that's all a soldier is, a man that knows how to die, and that's what you're going to learn, got it? It's all about dying like men ... right ...? and you can forget the rest. That's what we teach you in the Army.

As we saw in Chapter 3, communicative translation is a form of cultural transposition. It is usually a crucial factor in genre-marking a TT. In the case of the

Sastre extract, the translator might decide to go still further by introducing an element of cultural transplant, in order to increase the TL bias of the TT: 'Sergeant' as a rendering of 'Cabo' might then give way, say, to 'Sergeant-major', 'you lot' to 'you 'orrible shower', and 'Army' to 'Regiment'. (Whether to go this far would, of course, depend on an initial strategic decision about whether to keep Spanish militarism as the target of social criticism, or to transfer the attack to British militarism, or militarism in a more universal sense.)

TL genre-marking characteristics can be over-used, of course. Compare, for example, these five lines from Violeta Parra's 'Gracias a la vida' (used in Practical 11) with the student TT that follows:

[...]
perfecto distingo lo negro del blanco,
y en el alto cielo su fondo estrellado
y en las multitudes el hombre que yo amo.

[...]
As my eyes I open
I can see so clearly
The distant from the nearly
In the heav'ns above
Among shimmering stars awaits the man I love.

Unlike the ST, the TT is heavily marked for some kind of sentimental or lyrical 'poetic' genre. This is done through lexical items ('distant', 'heav'ns', 'shimmering', 'awaits'); contrived syntax ('my eyes I open'); hackneyed rhymes (one of which is achieved at the cost of the ungrammatical 'from the nearly'); clichéd pseudo-poetic collocations ('heav'ns above', 'shimmering stars'); and the line filler 'so' in line 2.

The lesson to be learnt from these examples is simple but important: there is a middle course to be steered between under-marking genre features, as in the literal translation of the Sastre extract, and over-marking them, as in the song TT.

A particular genre-marking translation problem occurs in the case of STs heavily marked by slang. Sociolect and register are crucial here, but so is the fact that languages differ from one another in respect of the referential domains covered by slang, and in the kinds of slang available. The example given below comes from the dialogue of the film *El pico* (1983). (*Contextual information*. The plot of the film is set in Bilbao; the speakers are two urban youths.)

– Si es que estoy hasta los huevos. Yo no tengo la culpa de que mi padre sea picolito.

– Cada uno tenemos el padre que nos ha tocado.

– Ya, pero seguro que si no estuviéramos en este rollo, tú tampoco serías amigo mío.

– Anda, déjate de chorradas, nos metimos juntos, ¿no?
– Sí, pero...
– Si tú no me hubieras caído bien, no me habría enrollado contigo, ni con esto, ni para nada. Que te comes mucho el coco, chabal.
– Venga, vamos a casa de Bety, tengo ganas de meterme un tirito.
– ¡No te jode, y yo!
– Ponte un momento junto a la foto de tu padre.
– Anda, déjate de chorradas.
– Déjame ver, coño.

(*El pico*, 1983; transcription by José Barroso Castro)

CROSSOVER BETWEEN ORAL AND WRITTEN GENRES

Except in some forms of (bilateral or simultaneous) interpreting, translators actually do a great deal of their work in a written medium. This means that when their ST is in an oral medium, or in a written medium whose basis lies in an oral genre, or when the eventual TT is meant for oral performance, the translation process crosses over the important boundary between oral and written texts. This is easily overlooked, but merits serious attention by translators. Given that both ST and TT are, ideally, carefully genre-marked, one should not lose sight of the inevitable metamorphoses resulting from the conversion of an oral text into a written one, and conversely, of a written text into an oral one. These metamorphoses are due partly to the lack of precise correspondence between speech and writing (see Chapter 6, pp. 72–4), which makes writing a pale copy of speech in terms of expressive force, and partly to the different genre-marking expectations associated with oral and written genres. The point is that in crossing over from oral to written versions of a ST important genre-marking features may be lost in transcription (for example, the oral register features of the Sastre extract on p. 142); while, in producing a written TT that is ultimately to be converted into an orally performed one, the translator may fail to indicate, or even allow for, the inclusion of suitable oral genre-marking features in the TT script (as in the first version of the Sastre TT on p. 143). There is also the analogous problem of transposing or implanting into written texts genre-marking features with oral origins, like the slang in the extract from *El pico* given above.

Crossover in the process of translation may take a number of forms. Four in particular deserve mention here. In the first, the translator starts with a live or recorded ST in an oral medium, transfers to the use of a written transcript, and then composes a TT which is a script suitable for oral performance: *song lyrics* are typically translated in this way. In the second form of crossover, the translator starts with a written script, transfers to considerations of how the ST might be performed orally and then composes a TT which is a script suitable for eventual oral performance: this is the usual process by which *plays* are translated. In a third type of case, the translator starts with an oral ST and its transcript, but produces a TT suitable for silent reading (though perhaps with some suggestion of the oral origins of the ST): *film subtitles* are typically produced in this way. In the fourth type, the translator starts with a written script, has recourse to oral performance of the ST, but produces a TT suitable for silent reading (though, again, perhaps with a hint of the oral properties of the ST): *poetry* will usually be translated in this way.

In discussing crossover between oral and written genres, drama texts deserve special mention. Dramatic traditions in different cultures are usually markedly different, despite various degrees of cross-fertilization. This implies that the translation of stage-plays will often involve an element of genre transposition, in deference to the different expectations and tastes of TL audiences. (In any case, as the Sastre example shows, the appearance of spontaneity essential to a stage performance often implies that a faithful ST-oriented translation is inappropriate, since it would not sound plausible.) On the other hand, complete transposition of the TT into some traditional TL genre may mean that the point is lost, and with it the merits of the ST. Thus, a translation of Calderón de la Barca's *La vida es sueño* as an imitation of the genre of Jacobean comedy would fail on at least two counts: the TT would convey none of the technical merits of the genre of Calderón's play, and retain little or nothing of the merits of the genre of Jacobean comedy. The translations of stage drama that are most successful from the performing point of view are usually based on compromises between reflecting some of the features that confer merit on the ST and adopting or adapting features of an existing TL dramatic genre.

(There are, of course, plays that deliberately trade on incongruity for the creation of absurd effects resulting from the clash between the improbability of the plot or dialogue and the apparent spontaneity of performance. Antonio Buero Vallejo's *El tragaluz* (1967) is a case in point. In this play 'una pareja de investigadores', named as Él and Ella in the dramatis personae, present twentieth-century Madrid life from the perspective of a distant future and comment upon the action. In such instances, one of the translator's main tasks is to preserve the absurdity of this clash, otherwise the TT could lose its satirical impact.)

Related to theatre is film, but film dialogue presents special problems for translators. Putting aside the alternatives of subtitling and voice-over (which is normally only used in certain kinds of documentary), actual oral translation of film dialogue requires *dubbing* – that is, creating the impression that the TT heard by the audience is actually the text spoken by the characters on screen. This impression depends largely on the skill of the dubbing specialist in synchronizing the oral TT with the gestures, facial expressions and lip movements of the screen actors.

Dubbing is difficult to do successfully, and a more feasible alternative is subtitling. (Note, however, that under Franco the dubbing of foreign films into Spanish was obligatory by law.) A subtitle is not an oral TT, but an excellent example of crossover between an oral ST and a written TT. It has special requirements, however. First, it is essentially a form of gist translation. Second, while working in a written medium, under very tight constraints of time and space, the translator will usually want to produce a TT that, within reason, hints at some of the characteristics of the oral style of the ST. These may include features of social register, tonal register, dialect, sociolect, and so on. While it would be difficult, unnecessary and undesirable to pay attention to every little quirk of the oral delivery of the ST, it could also be unfortunate to produce an over-polished TT suggesting that the ST speaker 'talks like a book'. Here, as ever, compromise seems to be indicated, between making the subtitles easily digestible as a written text and injecting into them features reminiscent of an appropriate oral style.

The special requirements of subtitling make it into a very useful exercise for students, because it forces them to focus especially clearly on many of the issues raised in this chapter and the previous one. Even without the equipment for subtitling film or videotape, a useful practical can still be done simply using an audiocassette. An exercise of this type figures in Practical 12. To assist in preparation for it, we end this chapter with some general notes on subtitling as practised by professionals (for which we are indebted to John Minchinton), followed by a sample of the amateur version using an audiocassette.

NOTES ON SUBTITLING

The subtitler-translator usually has a dialogue list, that is, a transcript of all the verbal contents of the film. The dialogue list does not include details of cuts. The subtitler runs the film on a viewing/editing table, measuring the time of each phrase, sentence and shot to determine when titles should start and stop. This process is called 'spotting'. The technicalities of spotting vary, depending on whether one is working with 35mm film or videotape, but the essential rules are the same:

- A single-line subtitle requires at least two seconds' viewing time.
- A double-line subtitle requires at least four seconds.
- Never show a title for less than two seconds or more than six seconds.
- Avoid carrying a title over a cut (except, for example in newsreel with many cuts).
- Voices off, such as telephone voices or narrations, are in italics (unless the speaker is present but simply not in camera view).

- Observe the basic rules of punctuation, but, where the end of a subtitle coincides with the end of a sentence, omit the full stop.
- In double-line titles, try to make the second line shorter than the first, but do not be inflexible: it is most important that the first line should read well and not end clumsily.
- Make every title a clear statement. Avoid ambiguity (unless the ST is deliberately or significantly ambiguous): viewers have only a limited time to take in the message, and cannot turn back as they can with a book or a newspaper.

- When a sentence is split over more than one title, end the first one with three suspension points, and begin the next one with three suspension points.
- Do not use telegraphese: viewers do not have the time to work it out.

When timings are short, it is sometimes helpful to have two speakers' dialogue as a double-line subtitle (ideally for question and answer). In such cases, use a dash to introduce each line, and justify left, so that the titles are not centred on the screen. For example:

> – Where have they gone today?
> – To the country

Here is an example of how to split a sentence over two or more titles. The text itself conveys the point we are making: 'In such cases, it is especially important to make each title sensible in itself, unless the speaker is rambling, delirious, or similar, so that viewers maintain a steady understanding of the dialogue.' This sentence might be effectively subtitled as follows:

Title 1	In such cases...
Title 2	...it is especially important to make each title sensible in itself...
Title 3	...unless the speaker is rambling, delirious, or similar...
Title 4	...so that viewers maintain a steady understanding of the dialogue

Here is an example of how *not* to do it:

Title 1	In such cases, it is especially...
Title 2	...important to make each title sensible...
Title 3	...in itself, unless the speaker is rambling, delirious, or similar...
Title 4	...so that viewers maintain a steady understanding of the dialogue

Apart from other errors, the weakness of this version is that breaks between titles correspond to neither the structure nor the oral phrasing of the sentence. Despite the suspension points, Title 2 looks like the end of a sentence or clause, and Title 3 like the start of one. The result is that the 'unless ...' clause looks like a clause parenthetically inserted in mid-sentence. The text might seem to be saying 'In itself, unless the speaker is rambling in such a way that viewers maintain a steady understanding [...]'. But the anticipated resolution of this apparent sentence does not materialize, so that the viewer is (at best) momentarily puzzled.

NB The maximum number of spaces allowed for a line of title varies, depending on the equipment used. We shall take as an example a maximum of 36, which is not untypical. This includes letters, spaces between words, and punctuation marks. So, for instance, the following line of title is exactly 36 spaces long:

... so that viewers maintain a steady

Sample subtitling exercise using audiocassette

Dialogue list

(*Contextual information*. The dialogue is between an Argentinian student, Aurora, and her male tutor. The use of Argentinian Spanish is not wholly consistent throughout the extract.)

– ¿Puedo hablar contigo un momento?

– Claro, cómo no. Pero siéntate, déjame acabar un segundo.

– No, no. Tengo prisa. Sólo quiero saber por qué me has puesto un seis en el examen. No estoy de acuerdo con esta calificación. Es el mejor examen que he hecho y en el que he tenido la peor nota. Y tú sabes mejor que nadie que esto es algo que, en estos momentos, me importa por encima de todo.

– Mira, Aurora, yo no puedo establecer excepciones y..., y mucho menos hacer favores a nadie. Creo que es la nota que te merecías.

– No. Sabés muy bien que no.

Reproduced from *En español; materiales video; guía didáctica*, 4 (Madrid: Ministerio de Cultura, 1988, p. 26).

Spotting

Following the taped text on the dialogue list, mark off convenient sections coinciding, if possible, with pauses and intonational cues in the spoken delivery. Each of these sections will subsequently form the basis of a subtitle. At the end of spotting, the dialogue list should look something like this:

– ¿Puedo hablar contigo un momento? /

– Claro, cómo no. Pero siéntate, déjame acabar un segundo.

– No, no. Tengo prisa. / Sólo quiero saber por qué me has puesto un seis en el examen. / No estoy de acuerdo con esta calificación. / Es el mejor examen que he hecho y en el que he tenido la peor nota. / Y tú sabes mejor que nadie que esto es algo que, en estos momentos, me importa por encima de todo. /

– Mira, Aurora, yo no puedo establecer excepciones / y..., y mucho menos hacer favores a nadie. / Creo que es la nota que te merecías. /

– No. Sabés muy bien que no. /

Timing

The sections marked off in spotting are numbered, and the time between the start of one section and the start of the next is measured (with a stopwatch if possible, but the second hand of a watch will do very well for our purposes). The timing of the subtitles is based on these measurements. (*Remember that any pauses in and between sentences are part of the overall time the text lasts*. They are invaluable allies for the subtitler, because they give extra time for viewers to read and digest the titles.) The timed list should look like this:

Title 1	3.0 sec	Puedo ... momento?
Title 2	4.0	Claro ... prisa.
Title 3	4.0	Sólo ... examen.
Title 4	3.0	No estoy ... calificación.
Title 5	4.0	Es el mejor ... nota.
Title 6	5.0	Y tú ... de todo.
Title 7	3.5	Mira ... excepciones.
Title 8	3.0	y..., y mucho ... nadie.
Title 9	4.0	Creo ... merecías.
Title 10	3.0	No. Sabés muy bien que no.

Creating subtitles

Each of the spottings into which the dialogue list has been divided is translated into English, observing the following constraints:

(i) *Not more than two lines* can be shown on the screen at once.
(ii) *Lines cannot be longer than 36 spaces*, as explained on p. 148.
(iii) The maximum time available for displaying each subtitle is given by the timing measurements above; allow at least *two seconds for a single-line title*, and at least *four seconds for a double-line title* (but not more than six seconds for any title).

Here is a possible TT:

Title 1	3.0 sec	Can I speak to you?
Title 2	4.0	– Sure. Sit down while I finish – I can't. I'm in a hurry
Title 3	4.0	Can you just tell me why I only got a six in my exam?
Title 4	3.0	It's the best exam I've ever done...
Title 5	4.0	...and I got my worst mark ever. I should've got a better mark
Title 6	4.0 (+1)	I don't need to tell you how vital this is for me right now
Title 7	3.5	I can't make any exceptions, Aurora
Title 8	3.0	I can't show any favouritism
Title 9	3.0 (+1)	I think it was a fair mark
Title 10	3.0	No! You *know* it wasn't

(The times given in brackets are moments during which no title is shown.)

Note that the order of the speaker's sentences has been changed, for the express purpose of subtitling. The TT follows a more transparent order of the speaker's grievances, not the order in which she mentions them. To see why this was done, compare our TT with the following one, which keeps the ST order:

Title 1	3.0 sec	Can I speak to you?
Title 2	4.0	– Sure. Sit down while I finish. – I can't. I'm in a hurry
Title 3	4.0	Can you just tell me why I only got a six in my exam?
Title 4	3.0	I should've got a better mark
Title 5	4.0	It's the best exam I've ever done and I got my worst mark ever...
Title 6	4.0 (+1)	...and I don't need to tell you what this means to me right now
Title 7	3.5	I can't make any exceptions, Aurora
Title 8	3.0	I can't show any favouritism
Title 9	3.0 (+1)	I think it was a fair mark
Title 10	3.0	No! You *know* it wasn't

As with any subtitled text, the message is given in a series of short bursts, each of which disappears for good after a few seconds. Therefore, as we have seen, viewers need to concentrate harder than readers (who can see the whole text on a page and go at their own pace) or even listeners (who have phonic and prosodic cues to help them assimilate important information). These factors may create a minor problem in our second TT where information is fed in slightly 'out of turn'. That is, the speaker is complaining about the injustice of 'getting a six' in her exam, but the explanation for her sense of injustice is not given until later. Furthermore, while the referent of the anaphoric 'this' (in 'how vital *this* is for me') must be the phrase 'a better mark', in the second TT 'this' is not in close enough proximity to its logical antecedent. For the reader of a printed page these slight hitches in transparent continuity would present no problems. However, when reading on screen while watching a film, it is more difficult to realize that the antecedent of 'this' is not in the immediately preceding title, but in the earlier 'I should've got a better mark'. Keeping the ST order in the subtitles may well put viewers on the wrong track, or puzzle them momentarily by making them ask 'Why does the speaker think she should have got a better mark?', 'What is it that she thinks is vital for her?'. While they are sorting these out, they will not register the next subtitle properly, and could end up losing the thread altogether. (Students should be on the look-out for similar problems in Practical 12.)

Improving transparent cogency is why we changed the ST order in our first TT. Normally, 'improving' a ST in this or any other way is not necessary or desirable, but, for reasons of 'user-friendliness', it is sometimes a serious option in oral-to-oral translating (especially interpreting), in cases of crossover between oral and written texts (in either direction, but especially in subtitling), and, as we shall see in Chapter 13 and Practical 13, in empirical/descriptive or persuasive/prescriptive texts where the paramount concern is clarity.

PRACTICAL 12

12.1 Subtitling

Assignment
Working in groups:

(i) Listen to the recording of the following ST (from Luis Buñuel's film *Viridiana*) and discuss the strategic decisions that have to be made before translating it into film subtitles; outline your own strategy for doing so.
(ii) Taking the dialogue list, use a stopwatch or wristwatch to convert it into a list with timed spottings.
(iii) Translate the text into English subtitles; lay your TT out as shown on p. 150. (Remember to indicate any 'gaps' during which there is no title shown.)
(iv) Explain the main decisions of detail you made in producing your TT.

Contextual information
The main protagonist of the film, Viridiana, has recently given up the novitiate and moved into the large country mansion she has inherited from her uncle. In an excess of piety, she has filled her house with a motley group of homeless misfits. Lines 2, 4, 6, 13, 18, 23 and 26 are spoken by Viridiana; lines 3, 9, 19, 21–2 and 24 by Poca; lines 1, 5, 7–8, 10 and 14 by the pregnant woman, Refugio; lines 11–12 and 20 by don Amalio. Line 25 is spoken by another man who is painting a picture (off screen). Lines 15 and 16 are spoken by two members of the group about to set off for the village, and line 17 by another woman.

Text

– Buenos días, señorita. * ¿Ha dormido usted bien?

– Bien, Refugio.

– Buenos días nos dé Dios.

– Necesito saber cuánto te falta para dar a luz.

– ¿Pa qué?

– Mujer, para tener prevenido al médico...

– No lo sé, yo creo que unos cuatro meses, pero no se lo puedo asegurar a usted.

– Tampoco sabe quién es el padre. Dicen que era de noche y ni la cara le vio.

– ¡Cállate!, que no te lo he contao pa' que vayas publicándolo.

– ¡A callar! No se debe hablar así y menos delante de nuestra santa protectora, que es persona decente.

– De veras que me das compasión,** ¿has tenido más hijos?

– No señorita, éste es el primero. Con su permiso.

– Señorita, nos vamos al pueblo.

– Con permiso de Dios y de usted.

– Tienen que traer patatas, tocino y arroz.

– Tomen y no tarden tanto como ayer.

– ¿Podrían traer un poquito de tabaco?

– No señorita, que le siente mal fumar y escupe mucho.

– ¡Mal fumar! Colillas. ¡A ti te sientan mal otras cosas y no te las digo por respeto a la señorita, que si no!

– ¡Basta!, traigan tabaco; yo lo administraré.

– Gracias, señorita.

– Señorita, acérquese a ver el cuadro.

– Ande, vayan.

* cut to Viridiana

** cut to two members of the group about to set off for the village

12.2 Speed translation

Assignment

You will be asked to translate a text given to you in class by your tutor, who will tell you how long you have for the exercise.

13

Technical translation

In so far as all texts can be categorized in terms of genre, there is no reason why one particular genre should be singled out for special attention rather than any other. However, since technical translation is a far more 'marketable' skill than literary translation, and since most language students are, owing to their lack of training in science or technology, in awe of 'technical' texts, we feel the need to devote a separate chapter to problems confronting the translator of texts in this genre. By 'technical' translation we mean especially the translation of empirical/descriptive texts written in the context of scientific or technological disciplines. As a matter of fact, any specialist field, from anthropology to zymurgy via banking, history, numismatics and yachting, has its own technical register, its own jargon, its own genre-marking characteristics, with which translators should be familiar if they are to produce convincing TTs in the appropriate field. It is also worth emphasizing that the problems met in translating technical texts are to a great extent no different from those met in translating in any genre, specialized or not. Textual variables are textual variables, particularizations are particularizations, whatever the genre and whatever the subject matter; and the relative merits of literal and communicative translation need to be considered in translating any text. Nevertheless, the very fact that technical texts are at the far extreme of unfamiliarity for many language students makes them especially valuable illustrations of all these points. There are three reasons, then, for devoting a chapter to technical translation: first, because it probably offers the widest field of employment for translators; second, because it is often so unnerving for language students; and third, because it is so exemplary of issues crucial to translation methodology.

A notable generic property of technical texts is that they are seldom aimed at complete non-specialists. Thus, in subject matter and comprehension, the typical technical ST is not easily accessible to most native SL speakers, let alone to those who have learnt the SL as a foreign language. There are three main reasons for this relative inaccessibility. One is lexical and the other two are conceptual. All three can be illustrated from the following text, the abstract of an archaeological paper by Duccio Bonavia, to which we shall refer in our discussion:

LA IMPORTANCIA DE LOS RESTOS DE PAPAS Y CAMOTES DE ÉPOCA PRECERÁMICA HALLADOS EN EL VALLE DE CASMA

Se hace una revisión crítica de los datos existentes sobre el hallazgo de papa (Solanum tuberosum) y camote (Ipomoea batatas) en contexto precerámico del Área Andina Central. Se concluye que las únicas evidencias a las que se puede dar validez científica, corresponden a los especímenes excavados en el yacimiento de Huaynuma del valle de Casma (costa Nor-central peruana), con una antigüedad aproximada de 2,000 años a. d. C.

(Bonavia, 1984, p. 20)

LEXICAL PROBLEMS IN TECHNICAL TRANSLATION

There are three sorts of problem arising from the specialized use of technical terms. First, there is the obvious problem of terms not used in everyday, ordinary language, which are, therefore, unfamiliar to the lay translator. The text given above contains an example of this problem. A term such as 'precerámico' is instantly recognizable as belonging only to a specialized scientific context. Without specialist knowledge, therefore, translators cannot guess the exact meaning of the term or make a *reliable* guess at its correct TL rendering. Of course, 'preceramic' (or 'pre-ceramic') is a likely candidate, but its appropriateness, as well as whether the word should be written with or without a hyphen, can only be established by dictionary research, or by consultation with an archaeologist.

The second problem is that of terms which have ordinary uses familiar to the translator, but which in the ST are manifestly used in some other, technically specialized, way. That is, the familiar senses of the terms do not help, and may even hinder, the translator in finding an appropriate rendering of their technical senses. The ST above contains a simple example of this in the phrase 'revisión crítica'. In its ordinary usage, Spanish 'revisión' could easily be taken to mean simply English 'revision' (in the sense of 'modification'); however, in context within 'revisión crítica', this rendering is inappropriate and misleading. What is at issue is a critical reviewing of a certain body of evidence. Thus, 'revisión crítica' is more accurately rendered as 'critical review'.

Almost any science or technology has such lexical pitfalls. Medicine, for example, is rich in these. Anyone familiar with medical terminology will instantly gloss 'soplo cardíaco' as 'heart murmur', but the translator not used to medical texts may find the phrase puzzling at first sight. Similarly puzzling in a medical context is 'estenosis' (which has nothing whatever to do with shorthand typing) used as a technical term referring to 'narrowing of the arteries'.

Third, a term may have an ordinary, everyday sense that is not obviously wrong in the context. This is the most dangerous sort of case, because the translator may not even recognize the term as a technical one, and carelessly render it in its ordinary sense. For example, 'hallazgo', in the archaeological text above, is glossed in a standard 1988 dictionary as 'finding, discovery; find, thing found'. The right technical translation in the archaeological context (where reference is to vestiges indicating the former presence of potatoes and yams) certainly lies well within the range of meanings implied by the dictionary glosses; but the translator needs experience or advice in order to have the confidence to select 'traces', and in the present context this is clearly preferable to the available alternatives such as 'finding' or 'discovery'. Likewise, a translator in a hurry might (especially if arts-trained) translate 'las únicas evidencias' (in the same text) either as 'the only evidence' or as 'the only proofs', where an archaeologist might expect 'the only findings'.

As these examples show, access to technical dictionaries and up-to-date databanks is indispensable for translators of technical texts. However, not even these source materials can be guaranteed to keep the translator out of difficulties. For one thing, technical texts are liable to be innovative – why publish them unless they make some new contribution? This means that dictionaries and databanks must always lag slightly behind the most up-to-date use of technical terms. Second, even the best source materials do not necessarily give a single, unambiguous synonym for a particular technical term, so that the translator may still have to make an informed choice between alternatives. Finally, even established technical terms are sometimes used loosely or informally in technical texts, in which case it may be misleading to render them by their technical TL synonyms. All of this suggests that the normal limitations on the use of dictionaries apply also to technical translation, but in a particularly acute form. That is, translators can only select the appropriate TL terminology from a range of alternatives offered by the dictionary if they have a firm grasp of the immediate textual context and of the wider technical context. The problem is not lessened, of course, by the awkward fact that some of the context may remain obscure until the correct sense of the ST terms has been identified. This brings us to the two conceptual reasons why technical texts may be difficult to translate.

CONCEPTUAL PROBLEMS IN TECHNICAL TRANSLATION

The first type of conceptual problem is caused by failure to understand the background assumptions and knowledge taken for granted by experts in a science, but not shared by non-specialists and not explicit in the ST. This is a point that can be illustrated from the following: 'el ozono que en los cielos antárticos protege la vida de las letales radiaciones ultravioleta' (*Enciclopedia Universal Ilustrada*, p. 45).

The phrase 'protege la vida de las letales radiaciones ultravioleta' is potentially ambiguous. Purely syntactically, it may be construed either as meaning 'protects the life of lethal ultraviolet rays' or as 'protects life from lethal ultraviolet rays'. This ambiguity is almost certainly not present for the author or for the informed SL reader who is aware of the function of the ozone layer. It is this awareness, that is to say a piece of technical knowledge, which effectively neutralizes the syntactic ambiguity in question. Yet the translator still has to choose between 'protects the life of' and 'protects life from'; the wrong choice would seriously mislead the TL reader, and would damage the translator's reputation (and possibly the author's too) in the eyes of an informed readership. In this instance, of course, few translators are likely to be so ill-informed as to make the wrong choice. In short, translation problems like this are generally easily resolved by any TL speaker with a basic grasp of the technical discipline in question. In more difficult cases of a similar kind, however, non-specialist translators may reach a conceptual impasse from which no amount of attention to syntax or vocabulary can rescue them. In that case they have only two options: study the technical field in which they are translating, or work in close consultation with experts.

The most intractable problems in technical translation arise in translating the development of new ideas. In such an instance, even basic grasp of background knowledge may be insufficient to save the translator from a conceptual impasse. This is the second conceptual reason for inaccessibility in technical texts. What one might call the 'logic' of a discipline – methods of argumentation, the development of relations between concepts – is normally specific to that discipline. There may therefore be translation problems that hinge crucially on that logic. It may transpire that the translator is quite unable to solve a conceptual problem of this nature, and that the only alternative is to consult either an expert or, if necessary (and if possible), the author of the ST.

Even in less advanced texts, the translator may face serious conceptual difficulties in grasping the 'logic' of a discipline, in particular the relationship between concepts. This is illustrated in the following extract drawn from a later section of the 'Congelación' article used in Practical 13: 'Uno de los mayores problemas que se plantean en este sistema de conversión reside en la separación de los cristales de hielo y la salmuera'.

Without a grasp of desalination processes in general, and of the particular refrigeration technique discussed in the text, student translators cannot be absolutely sure whether, in the above sentence, the problem is how to *prevent* the separation of ice crystals, or whether the problem is how to *achieve* this separation. What is more, the use of 'y' in the ST creates another uncertainty: do both the ice crystals and the brine (salmuera) need to be separately extracted from some third substance, or is the important thing to extract the crystals from the saline solution? According to different understandings of these issues, student translations vary between:

> One of the main problems posed by this conversion system resides in the fact of the separation of the ice crystals and the brine.

> One of the main problems requiring solution in this conversion system resides in the separation of the ice crystals from the brine.

> One of the main problems for this conversion system resides in separating off the ice crystals and the brine.

The decision as to which of these alternatives is the appropriate one hinges, of course, on one's understanding of how desalination systems work: the technical expert will know without hesitation that the problem referred to is how to find a way of extracting the ice crystals from the surrounding saline solution. (Indeed, a further reading of the article makes this relatively clear in context.)

Experience in Spanish will tell the translator two things: first, there is in general a strong chance that 'reside en la separación de' should not be literally rendered as 'resides in the separation of', but will require some form of particularization, while ST 'y' may need to be particularized as 'from'; second, the essential evidence for the appropriate particularizations must be sought in the wider context, more precisely in terms of the internal 'logic' of the ST and of its subject matter. (The only real internal evidence, a subsequent description in the ST of how the problem referred to has been solved, merely underlines the importance of context.) But, while the context strongly hints at a particular interpretation, the 'logic' of the ST is so dependent on technical knowledge that even the closest and most sensitive linguistic analysis is bound to be less reliable (and less cost-effective) than a brief consultation with a technical adviser. Trying to 'crack' a technical text on the basis of linguistic experience alone is valuable for honing one's translation skills, and fun as a challenge; but delivering a *dependable* technical TT usually requires consultation.

To summarize thus far: the non-specialist is not sufficiently equipped to produce reliable technical TTs guaranteed to be useful to technical experts in the target culture. Prospective technical translators must acquire as soon as possible some degree of technical competence in the field in which they intend to work. Training technical translators usually has this as its main target. Such training cannot be general, however: technical translators can only train by specializing in particular fields. Naturally, a combination of an academic degree in a science and a qualification in a foreign language is an ideal background for a technical translator. However, not even people with this kind of qualification can expect to keep abreast of research while at the same time earning their living as translators, and they will sooner or later come up against problems that can only be solved by consulting technical experts.

These remarks about the need for consultation are not to be taken lightly. They raise the important question of the responsibility – and perhaps the legal liability – of the translator. There is a difference here between literary translation and technical translation. It is not that literary translators are not held responsible for their published TTs, but that the practical implications of mistranslation are seldom as serious for them as for technical translators, whose mistakes could cause financial damage or loss of life and limb. This is another respect in which technical translation is exemplary, bringing out extremely clearly a golden rule which is in fact essential to all translation: *never be too proud or embarrassed to ask for help or advice.*

The spectre of legal liability is a reminder that even the minutest error of detail on any level of textual variables is typically magnified in a technical text. This is not surprising, given that matters of factual correctness rank maximally high in empirical/descriptive genres. Some such errors are in the category of *faux amis* – banal, but no less potentially embarrassing. For example, in a financial text, translating 'acción' as 'lawsuit' or 'legal action', as opposed to 'share' or 'stock(s)', could at the very least cause confusion.

Much more dangerous (and more likely, if the translator is not a specialist) is confusion between closely similar technical names. Consider, for example, the many minutely differentiated prefixes and suffixes that can be attached to the root 'sulph':

per-		
bi-		-ate
de-	sulph	-ite
hypo-		-ide
hydro-		-onate

Obviously, the slightest error in affixation here will constitute a major factual error, whereas, in non-technical language, slight differences in affixation may often go unnoticed. For example, in Spanish, there is a fine but clear distinction of meaning between the verbs 'colorar' and 'colorir'. 'Colorar' might well be used in the specific sense of 'to dye', whereas 'colorir' could mean 'to take on a colour/colour up'. In translating technical texts, the difference between the two terms would have to be scrupulously observed. In non-technical texts, however, the translator *may* choose to render either term as (among other options) 'to colour', prompted more by considerations of idiomaticity, genre and register than by those of literal accuracy. Similarly, there is only a relatively subtle difference in English between 'defrock' and 'unfrock', between 'levitating' and 'levitation', or, in popular usage (increasingly, if confusingly), between 'disinterested' and 'uninterested'. In literary texts one can, to some extent, base such choices on questions of euphony or style. But that temptation must be resisted absolutely in translating technical terms.

Again, in a literary text, choosing the wrong synonym is, at worst, a stylistic infelicity; but in a technical text it might create a serious misnomer showing ignorance, thus undermining the reader's confidence in the text. For example, it is not immaterial, in a given chemical context, whether vanilla is referred to by its trivial name 'vanilla', its technical name 'vanillin', its old systematic name '4-hydroxy-3-methoxybenzaldehyde', or its empirical formula $C_8H_8O_3$. Similarly, 'heat' and 'thermal energy' are, to all intents and purposes, referentially synonymous: yet the choice of one or the other in technical contexts is not a matter of indifference to a physicist.

Some parts of technical texts may be expressed with mathematical precision. (Indeed, they may actually be formulated in mathematical symbols, in which case they only need a modicum of effort in translation. Mathematical formulae cannot always be literally transcribed, however; one of the elementary things to note in this respect is the mathematical use of the comma on the Continent, where British conventions require the use of a decimal point.) In these cases, the important thing is for the TT to achieve, relative to the conventions of the TL, the same standard of mathematical precision as the ST.

Having said this, we should not forget that even the driest technical text is bound to have more informal passages – perhaps introductory, parenthetical or concluding remarks in ordinary, even colloquial, prose. Such passages pose another kind of problem for the technical translator, for it is here that the technical author may let personality intrude, or even deliberately cultivate a persona. Thus, although technical translators are chiefly accountable for the literal and factual content of the ST, they cannot always remain insensitive to such stylistic ploys as register, connotation, humour, polemic and so on. The TT should at least not spoil, cancel or contradict what is to be read between the lines in the ST. The overall register of the text – if only the question of pompous versus casual style – is also a matter of concern. To this extent at least, no text can avoid being the result of stylistic choices. In short, as we suggested at the beginning of this chapter, technical translators should not see themselves as having nothing in common with, for example, literary translators. On the contrary, because problems of style affect all texts, all translators have problems and methods in common. To this we must add that, while 'factuality' in a text may on the face of it appear antithetical to 'style', the cult of factuality is in itself a kind of style, and may on occasion even be a carefully cultivated pose manifested in excessive use of technical jargon.

Returning finally to the question of error and accuracy, there is – as with any text – the problem of what to do if the ST is badly written, ungrammatical, or even factually deficient. Should the deficiencies of the ST be reflected in the TT or should they be ironed out? This is a general and controversial issue. In our view, translators are not in principle responsible for 'improving' defective STs. However, we saw in the last chapter that this may sometimes be advisable in dealing with oral texts. It is more strongly advisable, perhaps even necessary, in the case of technical texts – or indeed any empirical/descriptive or prescriptive text – because the paramount concern is factual accuracy. If there is any ambiguity, obscurity or error in the ST, and it is potentially misleading or dangerous, there is every reason to keep it out of the TT – if necessary (as ever) after consultation with the author or an expert. Failing that, the translator may feel the need to append a translator's note to the TT calling attention to the deficiency in the ST.

Some of our examples in this chapter were drawn from the text on p. 155. As part of Practical 13, the problems in this text should be analysed, and a translation attempted. The work on Practical 13 will show that, apart from the lexical and conceptual problems outlined above, technical translation is not essentially different from most other sorts of prose translation: as long as specialist help can be called on (and students should be strongly encouraged to enlist the aid of their own technical advisers), there is no reason why technical translation in most fields should be more daunting than translation in any other genre.

PRACTICAL 13

13.1 Technical translation

Assignment

(i) Discuss the strategic problems confronting the translator of the text given on p. 155 and outline your own strategy for translating it.
(ii) Translate the text into English.
(iii) Explain the main decisions of detail you made in producing your TT.

NB We give no contextual information for this text (apart from the points made in Chapter 13). This is so that you can distinguish clearly between the problems requiring specialist knowledge and those raised by the usual characteristic differences between Spanish and English.

13.2 Technical translation

Assignment

Working in groups:

(i) Discuss the strategic problems confronting the translator of the following text, and outline your own strategy for translating it.
(ii) Translate the text into English.
(iii) Explain the main decisions of detail you made in producing your TT.

Contextual information

The passage is an extract of about 235 words from an article by Felipe Cantera Palacios entitled 'Tecnología de los principales procesos de potabilización de las aguas de mar' from the Spanish scientific journal *Dyna*. (The article was reprinted in Leo Hickey's *Usos y estilos de español moderno*, 1977, pp. 127–8.)

Text

CONGELACIÓN

Cuando el agua salada se congela, el agua pura forma cristales de hielo, mientras las sales permanecen en solución en el agua que no se ha congelado. La destilación por congelación es una operación de dos etapas que requiere un enfriamiento y un calentamiento. En cualquier proceso de congelación el agua salada es enfriada hasta la formación de hielo. Posteriormente el hielo es separado de la salmuera y fundido para producir el agua potable del proceso.

Vamos a ver algunos de los principios generales y factores de operación en los que se basa el proceso de congelación.

El agua es enfriada por transferencia de calor desde agua a menor temperatura con la que se halla ésta en contacto. Cuando el agua es enfriada, su temperatura desciende hasta alcanzar el punto de fusión. Después de llegar al punto de fusión, la temperatura permanece constante mientras continúa en enfriamiento hasta que la congelación se completa. La cantidad de energía térmica que debe ser extraída del agua a la temperatura de fusión para convertirla en hielo, se denomina calor latente de fusión del agua o, simplemente, calor de fusión. Una de las principales razones del interés que suscita el proceso de congelación para conversión de agua salada es que el calor de fusión del agua es menor de 1/6 parte del calor de evaporación y, además, los problemas de corrosión e incrustaciones desaparecen casi por completo.

Reprinted by kind permission of Thomas Nelson & Sons Ltd, from Leo Hickey, *Usos y estilos del español moderno* (London: Harrap, 1977, pp. 127–8); originally from Felipe Cantera Palacios, 'Tecnología de los principales procesos de potabilización de las aguas de mar', in *Dyna*, junio 1971, pp. 267–8.

13.3 Technical translation

Assignment

Working in groups:

(i) Discuss the strategic problems confronting the translator of the following text, and outline your own strategy for translating it.
(ii) Translate the text into English.
(iii) Explain the main decisions of detail you made in producing your TT.
(iv) Discuss the published TT, which will be given to you by your tutor.

Contextual information

The passage is the Spanish abstract at the beginning of an article, 'La Espectroscopía de Resonancia de Spin Electrónico (RSE) en España', by Carlos Sieiro del Nido, published in the journal *Política Científica*, 37, 1993, Madrid: Comisión Interministerial de Ciencia y Tecnología. The journal contains reports on a variety of economic, scientific and technological projects.

Text

LA ESPECTROSCOPÍA DE RESONANCIA DE SPIN ELECTRÓNICO (RSE) EN ESPAÑA

Desde que el físico ruso Zavoitski realizó en 1945 la primera experiencia de Resonancia de Spin Electrónico (RSE), esta técnica ha alcanzado cotas de desarrollo importantes, comparables hoy a las que ha experimentado la espectroscopía de Resonancia Magnética Nuclear (RMN). Este artículo trata de los grupos que trabajan en este área y las líneas de investigación que se siguen en España en RSE. Para la mayoría ha sido o sigue siendo una técnica complementaria a sus investigaciones y, aunque la incorporación de ésta ha sido tardía, en la actualidad se está consolidando con fuerza, tanto por el equipamiento como por la masa crítica existente.

Reproduced by kind permission from Carlos Sieiro del Nido, 'La Espectroscopía de Resonancia de Spin Electrónico (RSE) en España', in *Política Científica*, 37, Madrid: Comisión Interministerial de Ciencia y Tecnología, 1993, p. 45.

14

Translation of consumer-oriented texts

A real translation, as distinct from a translation done as an academic exercise, is always produced in response to the specific demands of an audience, a publisher or some other paymaster. This puts a particular kind of pressure on the translator. We have tried to simulate such demands and pressures in some of the practicals in this course, for example by asking for a TT that can be sung to a particular tune, or a TT suitable for subtitles. These exercises are necessarily artificial, but they should make it clear that TTs are purpose-made texts, their manner of formulation heavily influenced, both strategically and in detail, by who and what they are intended for. It is to emphasize this vital point that we are giving an entire chapter to consumer-oriented texts, for the decisive influence of 'translation-for-a-purpose' is nowhere more strongly felt than in translating such texts.

Of course, all texts are in a certain sense consumer-oriented. One may assume that every type of text appeals to the tastes of a particular audience. In that sense, short stories are consumer-oriented to satisfy readers who enjoy short stories, television soap operas are consumer-oriented to satisfy viewers who like watching soaps, and so forth. The first thing a publisher asks when offered a manuscript is what potential readership there is for the text. The whole question of marketability turns primarily on this kind of consumer orientation.

However, consumer orientation takes a much more acute form in texts that do not merely promote themselves, but have other things to promote. These are texts that fall into the persuasive/prescriptive genre, texts whose main purpose is to recommend commodities, attitudes or courses of action.

The most transparently consumer-oriented sub-category of this genre is advertising. Indeed, one may initially think of this genre as epitomized by advertising copy. The self-evident consumer-oriented purpose of advertising is to boost sales of particular commodities. However, many advertising campaigns show that sales-promotion techniques shade into the promotion of opinions, beliefs, attitudes and courses of action. Examples are government health warnings about driving under the influence of alcohol, drug abuse and AIDS. Along with party-political election campaigns, these examples point to a flourishing genre of texts directly aimed at instructing and persuading audiences to do or not to do (as well as to think or not to think) a wide gamut of things. Consumer-oriented texts consequently share common imperatives: they must capture attention and hold it, they must in some sense speak directly to their public, and they must convey their message with neatly calculated effect.

That much is clear. What is perhaps less immediately clear is that the range of texts suitably grouped under the heading of 'publicity' is wider than one would think at first sight. It includes, for instance, things like tourist brochures and information leaflets, public notices, posters and even instructions for the use of appliances, recipe books and so on.

It is therefore necessary to bear in mind that the title or explicit description of a text (for example, 'Instructions for Use') does not always clearly indicate that the text belongs to the same persuasive genre as those that are explicitly labelled as advertisements. It could be argued, in fact, that some of the most successful advertisements are those that appear to belong to some other genre, masking their consumer-oriented purposes under the guise of being informative or educational, or even literary. The upshot of this is that translators may sometimes have to look carefully at STs in order to recognize and identify their covert consumer-oriented persuasive/prescriptive features.

Take the average recipe book, for instance. On the face of things, it may seem to belong to the category of empirical/descriptive genres, for it appears to classify different cooking techniques in a descriptively systematic manner, to offer factual and objective accounts of the contents and appearance of dishes, as well as of their preparation. In itself, this almost makes recipe books sound like scientific texts. But it does not account for a number of manifest textual features of recipe books: even the most apparently factual recipe books are rarely written in a technical and scientifically neutral style; their use of tonal register is often calculated to draw the reader into a comfortable, possibly flattering, relationship; they have a transparently helpful organization, beyond what could be expected of the most indulgent scientific textbook; and they are often lavishly furnished with glossy pictures. (Some of these features are illustrated in the three extracts from recipe books on pp. 169–70.) Such features indicate a consumer-oriented purpose in these recipe books, and are well worth looking out for when translating certain kinds of 'commercial' ST. Even if not directly consumer-oriented to the sale of particular foodstuffs or the promotion of fashionable cuisine, most recipe books are, at the very least, specimens of a hybrid genre characterized by the dual purpose of description and persuasion.

One must, then, be alert to covertly persuasive STs, in order to be able to translate them into appropriately persuasive TTs. But this is only the tip of the iceberg. The more methodologically interesting aspects of consumer orientation in STs and TTs are revealed when it is realized that literal translation of persuasive STs is likely to produce TTs that are far from persuasive for TL audiences.

This point, too, shows up most transparently of all in the case of advertising copy. To find examples hinging on cultural difference one need only observe differences of style and impact in different English-speaking cultures. For instance, hectoring and hard-sell styles appear in general to be more acceptable in American than in British advertising, where overpraising a product is seen as unpleasantly boastful, and any kind of overkill can only be used for humorous purposes. Much of British television advertising is based on comic effects of some kind or another, whereas American-style advertisements may strike British customers as bombastic and unsubtle. For the rest, the tendency in British advertising is to stereotype the customer as a discerning equal, not someone to be browbeaten or patronized; consequently, the tonal register of some American advertisements might be considered offensive by some British customers. In cultures where they are in favour, hard-sell techniques may spread over the entire range of persuasive genres – not just commercial, but also ethical and political publicity, as well as many of the less obviously consumer-oriented textual types. To the extent that this is so, importing, for example, an American-style consumer-oriented text without modification from an American to a British context runs the risk of producing adverse effects on British consumers.

This intercultural comparison holds a lesson for translators. The fact that different cultures (even those nominally speaking the same language) have different expectations with regard to style in consumer-oriented genres explains why literal translations of persuasive STs are likely to prove less than persuasive in the TL. In other words, persuasiveness in consumer-oriented texts is culture-specific.

The advice to the translator of persuasive/prescriptive texts is therefore the same as for translating any other genre of text. Look not only at the style of the ST, but also at the style(s) of other SL texts in the same or similar genres. Look not only at the surface literal meaning of the ST, but also at the details of the stylistic choices made in the ST. From detailed observation of stylistic choices in a number of texts in a given genre it is possible to build up a general picture of the stylistic tendencies or expectations associated with particular types of text in a given culture. Naturally, only a specialist will have the requisite time and experience to develop a clear and detailed sense of stylistic appropriateness in a given genre. (Practical 14 may be seen as a first step towards becoming a specialist translator of recipe books, by considering some general tendencies in the style of Spanish recipes as compared with English ones.)

Further recommendations to the translator of consumer-oriented texts concern the nature of TTs. Here again, the same principles apply as to any other text: do not be afraid to break away from literal translation where the needs of persuasive effect indicate such a break; do not produce TTs without having first built up a knowledge of the style of specimen TL texts in the appropriate genre. First-hand analysis of such TL specimens means building up, through careful observation, a kind of 'genre grammar' consisting of generalizations concerning the stylistic norms, tendencies and expectations typical of the genre of the eventual TT. This does not mean that the TL specimens are models for slavish copying; but comparing the stylistic tendencies of the ST genre with those of the TT genre is the best starting-point for tackling decisions about departures from literal translation.

Conducting the kind of investigation we are talking about may typically involve contrasting texts relating to the same product in the SL and TL. An example is given here from the English and Spanish versions of the pamphlet packaged with Kodachrome 40 Movie Film cartridges. This should be prepared for discussion in Practical 14. Corresponding passages are given in the order in which they appear in the original texts, and are, as far as possible, arranged opposite one another.

KODACHROME 40 Movie Film (Type A) In super 8 cartridge	Película KODACHROME 40 de Cine (Tipo A) En cargador Súper 8
This film can be used only in super 8 cameras and projected only in projectors that accept super 8 film. Do not move film in slot on cartridge front, or turn core by hand.	Para uso en cámaras súper 8. Solo puede utilizarse en los proyectores que aceptan película súper 8.
DAYLIGHT MOVIES: Use daylight filter. With automatic cameras, simply expose whenever the camera indicates there is enough light.	PARA FILMAR CON LUZ DIURNA: Use el filtro* No. 85 para luz diurna. Con **cámaras automáticas**, exponga la película si la cámara indica que hay suficiente luz.
With non-automatic cameras, set your exposure meter at ASA 25 (15 DIN) and use the lens opening nearest 1/40-second shutter speed, or follow the exposure table on your camera.	Con **cámaras no automáticas**, ajuste el exposímetro en **25 ASA (15 DIN)** y use la abertura de diafragma más próxima a la velocidad de obturación de 1/40 segundo, o guíese por la tabla de su cámara.
INDOOR MOVIES: Use movie lights (3400 K) and remove the daylight filter. With automatic cameras expose whenever the camera indicates there is enough light.	PARA FILMAR EN INTERIORES: Use lámparas de cine (de 3400 K) y retire el filtro para luz diurna (consulte el manual de la cámara). Con **cámaras automáticas**, exponga la película cuando la cámara indica que hay suficiente luz.
With non-automatic cameras, set your exposure meter at ASA 40 (17 DIN) and use the lens opening nearest 1/40-second shutter speed, or use the settings indicated on the movie light or lamp package.	Con **cámaras no automáticas**, ajuste el exposímetro en **40 ASA (17 DIN)** y use la abertura de diafragma más proxima a la velocidad de obturación de 1/40 segundo, o use los ajustes sugeridos en la lámpara de cine o en el envase de las bombillas.

PROCESSING: Film price includes processing by Kodak. The film itself is so identified.
To mail film for processing, put the cartridge in the mailing envelope and address it to one of the processing labs listed.

PROCESADO: El precio de la película incluye el procesado por KODAK. Coloque el cargador de película expuesta en el sobre postal y envíelo a uno de los laboratorios de procesado en esta hoja. El remitente paga los derechos y gastos especiales de transporte para el envío internacional de esta película.

*Este filtro viene incorporado en las Cinecámaras KODAK INSTAMATIC, KODAK XL y KODAK EKTA-SOUND.

These parallel texts are not actually a ST and a TT; rather, they are two different presentations of the same subject matter. The contrasts between them are informative in that they may suggest possible culture-specific differences between British and Spanish instructions for use.

We have recommended departures from literal translation in translating consumer-oriented STs, and have just illustrated substantial divergences in literal meaning between two parallel texts in Spanish and English. However, this does not mean licence for indiscriminate distortion. The example of translating 'Instructions for Use' (or instruction manuals in general) aptly illustrates what we mean. The translator's prime responsibility to the manufacturer is to give a correct, unambiguous and comprehensible account of how the product is to be used. This places limits on possible departures from the substance of the ST. It does not, however, imply that the TT should be a carbon copy of the ST. First, as the Kodachrome example illustrates, textual cogency and the conventions by which information is presented are to some extent culture-specific. Consequently, readers from one culture might find the logic of presentation of a given text patronizingly over-explicit, whereas readers from another culture might find it over-economical and unclear. The literal exactitude of such corresponding texts is more a matter of neither text falsifying the technical details described than of a TT faithfully matching the form of the ST.

Second, it is not unusual to find that, in certain fields, different pieces of background knowledge will be expected from SL consumers and TL consumers. Thus the text in one of the languages may take for granted details which it is considered necessary to include in the text in the other language. For example, in the Kodachrome instance, English consumers are expected to know how to remove the daylight filter, whereas Spanish consumers are reminded that, for information about the filter, they should consult the instruction manual for their camera. Conversely, Spanish consumers do not, it seems, require a warning not to tamper with the cartridge by winding the film by hand, whereas such a warning is felt to be necessary in the English text. In other words, there are points on which a Spanish text spells out more details than a corresponding English one, as well as, conversely, points on which a Spanish text needs to be less explicit than an English one.

All this implies that when, for cultural reasons, a higher degree of sophistication is to be expected from either SL or TL consumers, that difference in sophistication needs to be reflected by formulating TTs in either more technical or less technical ways than the corresponding STs.

Closely related to these considerations is the question of register. The social and tonal registers of ST and TT may need to differ in ways reflecting different consumer expectations. Features of register in consumer-oriented texts tend to stereotype three things: first, the purveyor of the commodity; second, the targeted consumer; and third, the relationship between purveyor and consumer. One feature that plays a major role in this stereotyping is the choice of alternative imperative forms: compare 'use daylight filter' with 'you should use a daylight filter', 'a daylight filter should be used', 'you must use a daylight filter', 'the use of a daylight filter is recommended', 'we recommend use of a daylight filter', and so on. The choice between different command formulations used in instruction pamphlets is far more restricted, and therefore less richly nuanced in tonal register, in Spanish: lexical alternatives apart, plausible grammatical forms in this genre are limited to 'utilice un filtro para luz diurna', 'se utiliza un filtro para luz diurna', 'utiliza un filtro para luz diurna' and 'utilizar un filtro para luz diurna'. The issue of giving orders would repay discussion in Practical 14; it is also linked to the subject matter of Chapter 19.

It may be that in the ST the relationship between purveyor and consumer is stereotyped as being, for example, one of the expert addressing poorly informed non-experts, while, for cultural reasons, the relationship in the TT is more aptly stereotyped as one of expert to other experts, or of non-expert to non-experts. Recipe books are a case in point: it is probably a fair assumption that a British reader of a recipe book is less likely to feel insulted by being 'talked down to', but more likely to react adversely to curt directives, than most Spanish readers. (There will be a chance to test this assumption in Practical 14.)

Where the need arises for differences in stereotyping, it follows that the register of the TT will differ from that of the ST in terms of a number of features: vocabulary; grammatical/syntactic structure (for example, active and personal constructions may be preferable to passive and impersonal ones); sentential structure (for example, the presence or absence of parenthetical clauses; use or non-use of 'telegraphese'; colloquial or formal use of sentential markers, illocutionary particles and connectives); discourse structure (for example, marked or less marked use of devices signalling textual cohesion, more or less transparent textual layout); and so on. In principle, every level of textual variable may be drawn on to signal register.

In particular, features of tonal register may need to be altered between ST and TT in order to establish and maintain a certain desired relationship between TT and consumer which is different from that between ST and consumer. The genre-specific tendencies of the ST may, for instance, lead one to expect a text that addresses the SL consumer in a formal tonal register, whereas the chosen genre of the TT may lead one to expect a text that addresses the TL consumer in an informal tonal register. In a situation like this, the knock-on effects of a change of register may imply quite drastic departures from the framework of the ST, on any or all levels of textual variables discussed in Chapters 4–6.

Considerations of this sort will arise in Practical 14. It is important to remember, however, that changes in structure, vocabulary and register are as much subject to standard differences between languages as to genre-specific cross-cultural differences. For instance, compare these corresponding clauses from the section on daylight movies in the Spanish and English Kodachrome blurbs:

use the lens opening nearest 1/40-second shutter speed

use la abertura de diafragma más próxima a la velocidad de obturación de 1/40 segundo

Whatever the genre, if the Spanish text were translated over-literally into English, the resulting grammatical structure ('use the opening of the lens nearest to the shutter speed of 1/40 second') would sound stilted in register, and unidiomatic, since English has a clear preference for attributive noun-on-noun constructions ('lens opening', '1/40-second shutter speed') over nouns modified by prepositional complements (of the 'abertura de diafragma', 'velocidad de obturación de 1/40 segundo' type) favoured by Spanish.

All other considerations apart, choosing a register for a consumer-oriented TT can be problematic for the simple reason that there may be little in common between the groups of consumers targeted by the ST and the TT. In any case, any TL genre selected as a prototype for the TT will probably provide specimens in widely divergent styles and registers, leaving the translator with a number of possible models. We end this chapter with extracts from three different recipe books in English that amply illustrate these potential problems of choice. Thanks to their manifest consumer orientation, the extracts are also clear concluding reminders that every text – and therefore also every TT – is made for a specific *purpose* and a specific *audience*:

BOUILLABAISSE

NOTE: This, the most famous of all fish soups, is made chiefly in the South of France, different districts having particular recipes. It is a kind of thick stew of fish which should include a very wide mixture of different kinds of fish. The original French recipes use many fish not available in Great Britain. The following recipe is adapted to use the available fish. In order to get a wide enough variety a large quantity must be made.

[Ingredients listed]

Clean the fish, cut them into thick slices and sort them into 2 groups, the firm-fleshed kind and the soft kind. Chop the onion; slice the leek, crush the garlic; scald, skin and slice the tomatoes. In a deep pan make a bed of the sliced vegetables and the herbs, season this layer. Arrange on top the pieces of firm-fleshed fish; season them and pour over them the oil. [...]

(Beeton, 1962, p. 119)

ZUPPA DA PESCE

It doesn't matter whether you call it bouillabaisse, cippolini, zuppa da pesce, or just fish stew; whether it has lots of liquid, or, like this, is simmered in its own richly aromatic juices. It's not just good, it's wonderful. To put it in the oven is somewhat illegitimate, but you are less apt to overcook it. Serve with Spanish rice (for the hearty ones), tossed green salad, French bread to sop up the juices.

[Ingredients listed]

Put the olive oil and garlic in a warm, deep casserole and heat. Place the large fish on the bottom, then the mussels and shrimp. Season, and sprinkle the parsley over all. [...] Baste from time to time with the juices, using an oversized eyedropper called a baster. Serve in deep hot plates. Serves 6 generously. Time: 45 minutes.

(Tracy, 1965, n. p.)

FISH CAKES

[Ingredients listed]

1. Chop the parsley with both hands, one on the knife handle and one on the top of the knife blade. This chops the parsley smaller and keeps your fingers safely out of the way of the knife.
2. Put the potatoes on one plate and mash them up with the fork. Add the fish and mash it up too. Add the butter, parsley, salt and pepper. Mix them all together.
3. Turn the mixture out on to the board and make it into a roll with your hands like a big sausage. Cut off rounds with the knife.

[...]

(Anderson, 1972, p. 26)

PRACTICAL 14

14.1 Consumer-oriented texts

Assignment

(i) Compare and contrast the texts from the English and Spanish versions of the Kodachrome pamphlet, given on pp. 166–7.
(ii) Determine what general conclusions can be drawn from the comparison.

14.2 Consumer-oriented texts

Assignment

(i) Compare and contrast the texts from different English recipe books given on pp.169–70.
(ii) Compare and contrast the Spanish and English recipes given below.
(iii) Discuss what general conclusions can be drawn from these contrasts.

Contextual information

The texts below are taken, respectively, from a Spanish and an English recipe book chosen at random. The Spanish text is from Simone Ortega's *Mil ochenta recetas de cocina* (1972).

Text 1

RODAJAS DE MERLUZA EN SALSA VERDE

(6 personas)

6 rodajas gruesas de merluza cerrada (unos 200 gr. cada una),
4 cucharadas soperas de aceite,
1 cucharada sopera de harina,
1 cebolla mediana (80gr.),
1 diente de ajo,
unas ramitas de perejil,
1 cucharada sopera de perejil picado muy menudo,
1½ vasos (de los de agua) de agua fría,
1 lata pequeña (125 gr.) de guisantes (facultativo)
1 ó 2 huevos duros (facultativo),
sal y pimienta.

En una sartén se pone el aceite a calentar; cuando está, se echa la cebolla a freír. Mientras tanto, en el mortero se machaca el diente de ajo y las ramitas de perejil con un poco de sal. Cuando la cebolla se va poniendo transparente (unos 5 minutos más o menos), se añade la harina, se dan unas vueltas con una cuchara de madera y se agrega poco a poco el agua fría, se cuece un poco esta salsa y se coge un par de cucharadas, que se añaden a lo machacado en el mortero, revolviendo muy bien. Se incorpora el contenido del mortero a la salsa de la sartén y se revuelve todo junto.

En una cacerola de barro o porcelana (resistente al fuego) se cuela la salsa por un chino o un colador de agujeros grandes. Se colocan las rodajas de merluza ligeramente saladas y holgadas de sitio. La salsa las debe cubrir justo; si es necesario, se puede añadir algo más de agua (teniendo en cuenta que la merluza soltará agua también al cocerse). Se espolvorea un poco de pimienta molida, el perejil picado y los guisantes (si se quiere). Se agarra la cacerola por un costado y se sacude suavemente durante unos 15 minutos. Esto es fundamental para que se trabe bien la salsa. Se prueba entonces la salsa y se rectifica si fuese necesario. Se pican los huevos duros y se espolvorean por encima del pescado (esto es facultativo).

Se sirve en seguida en su misma cacerola de barro.

Text 2

POLLOCK IN GREEN SAUCE

To serve 6

3 lb. pollock steaks, each cut ½ inch thick, or substitute halibut, fresh cod or other firm white fish steaks cut ½ inch thick
2 ¾ oz. flour
4 tablespoons olive oil
1½ oz. finely chopped onions
¾ pint water
4 tablespoons dry white wine
1 scant teaspoon finely chopped parsley
1½ teaspoons salt
1½ tablespoons cooked fresh green peas or thoroughly defrosted frozen peas (optional)

Remove the skin from each steak with a small, sharp knife, and pat the steaks dry with kitchen paper. Sprinkle them with salt, then dip the steaks in 2 oz. of the flour, and shake them vigorously to remove any excess.

Heat the olive oil over a moderate heat in a large, heavy frying pan until a light haze forms above it. Add the fish and cook for about 4 minutes on each side, turning the steaks and regulating the heat so that they brown evenly without burning. Remove the pan from the heat and with a bulb baster transfer the oil remaining in the pan to a heavy, medium-sized frying pan. Cover the fish steaks in the larger pan to keep them warm while you prepare the sauce.

Heat the oil again until a light haze forms above it. Add the onions and, stirring constantly, cook for about 5 minutes, until they are soft and transparent but not brown. Stir in the rest of the flour, mix thoroughly and pour in the water and wine. Cook over a high heat, stirring constantly with a whisk until the sauce comes to the boil and thickens slightly. Reduce the heat to low and simmer for about 3 minutes.

Meanwhile, mash the garlic, parsley and salt to a smooth paste, using a pestle and mortar or the back of a wooden spoon. Thin it with about 3 tablespoons of the simmering sauce, then whisk it into the rest of the sauce. Cook, stirring constantly, for a minute or so. Taste for seasoning.

Scatter the peas, if you are using them, on top of the fish steaks, pour the sauce over them and cook uncovered over a low heat for about 3 minutes, basting occasionally until the fish and peas are just heated through. Serve at once on a large heated dish.

14.3 Consumer-oriented texts

Assignment

(i) Discuss the strategic decisions confronting the translator of the following text, and define your own strategy for translating it.
(ii) Translate the text into English.
(iii) Explain the main decisions of detail you made in producing your TT.

Contextual information

The text is from Simone Ortega's *Mil ochenta recetas de cocina* (1972).

Text

BRAZO DE GITANO

(8 personas)
2 cucharadas soperas de fécula de patata,
4 cucharadas soperas de harina,
5 cucharadas soperas de azúcar,
3 huevos,
1 clara,
un pellizco de vainilla en polvo,
1 cucharada (de las de café) de levadura Royal,
un pellizco de sal,
1 paño limpio,
mantequilla para untar la chapa,
azúcar glass.

Se montan a punto de nieve muy firmes las cuatro claras, con un pellizquito de sal. Se les añaden las yemas, después el azúcar y por último, cucharada a cucharada, la mezcla de la harina, la fécula y la levadura (estos tres elementos se mezclarán en un plato sopero antes de usarlos).

Se unta muy bien con mantequilla una chapa de horno bastante grande (37 x 26 cm. más o menos) y poco alta; en el fondo se coloca un papel blanco también untado con mantequilla. Se mete a horno más bien suave unos 35 minutos. Tiene que estar la masa cocida (al pincharla con un alambre, éste tiene que salir limpio), pero no muy dorada.

Se moja el paño de cocina en agua templada y se retuerce muy bien para que esté húmedo pero sin agua. Se extiende en una mesa y en seguida se vuelca el bizcocho. Se quita el papel pegado, se extiende el relleno con mucha rapidez y se enrolla el brazo de gitano ayudándose con el paño. Una vez bien formado, se pone en una fuente cubierto con un papel, hasta que se enfríe, y al ir a servir se cortan las extremidades y se espolvorea con azúcar glass.

Rellenos:

1º.) Crema pastelera:

½ litro de leche,
3 yemas de huevo,
5 cucharadas soperas de azúcar,

1½ cucharadas soperas de maizena,
½ cucharada sopera de harina,
un pellizco de vainilla.

2º.) Mermelada de frambuesa o grosella y nata montada:

Una vez el bizcocho en el paño de cocina, se extiende una capa muy fina de mermelada con un cuchillo. Encima de ésta se extiende nata montada dulce y se enrolla rápidamente.

Hará falta más o menos ½ kg. de nata.

14.4 Consumer-oriented texts

Assignment

(i) Discuss the strategic decisions confronting the translator of the following text, and define your own strategy for translating it.
(ii) Translate the text into English.
(iii) Explain the main decisions of detail you made in producing your TT.

Contextual information

The text is an extract from a tourist brochure entitled *Santo Domingo Tours* produced by the Santo Domingo Sheraton Hotel.

Text

TOUR EN LA CIUDAD

Salida: *9:00 a. m.*
Duración: *3 horas*

Esta excursión, de aproximadamente 3 horas, visita la más vieja ciudad de América, saliendo de su hotel en la mañana.

La primera parada se efectuará en la Primera Catedral del Nuevo Mundo (1540), Santa María La Menor. Este imponente monumento tiene el honor de albergar los restos de Cristóbal Colón, el descubridor de nuestra isla. Durante el recorrido por la zona colonial, usted podrá admirar impresionantes edificaciones, como son: La Torre del Homenaje, Casa de Tostado, Museo de Las Casas Reales, Casa del Cordón y la primera calle del Nuevo Mundo, Calle Las Damas.

Nuestra segunda parada, será en el Alcázar de Colón, casa de Diego Colón, hijo del descubridor. Aquí se podrá observar el modo suntuoso de vida de la época de la colonia. Caminando unos pasos hacia La Atarazana, con sus bellas casas al estilo colonial, usted encontrará una gran variedad de tiendas de joyas y 'souvenirs'.

Luego de finalizar el recorrido por la Zona Colonial, usted será llevado a la ciudad moderna, pasando por el Palacio Nacional y La Plaza de la Cultura, donde podrá ver el Museo del Hombre Dominicano, el Teatro Nacional, el Museo de Arte Moderno, y la Biblioteca Nacional, toda esta área rodeada por hermosos jardines, en el centro de los cuales está la fuente 'Rosa de los Vientos', un trabajo de arte hecho por Crismar. También, usted podrá dar un vistazo a los centros de diversión nocturnos, los sectores residenciales de Santo Domingo, cuyas avenidas están plantadas con árboles como la Palma Real, Caoba y Laurel; y finalmente, usted será llevado de vuelta a su hotel.

Reprinted from a leaflet distributed by the Santo Domingo Sheraton Hotel.

15

Stylistic editing

Throughout the course, we have considered translation sometimes as a process, and sometimes as a product (a TT). The assessment of existing TTs has been an important feature in practicals, even before we started discussing the question of genre. In this chapter, we turn our attention to the final stage of translation as a process, where the proposed TT is actually examined as a product. This stage is known as **editing**. A TT is only really complete after careful stylistic editing.

Any form of textual editing is intrinsically an operation carried out in writing on a pre-existent written text. (Even editing spoken dialogue is normally performed on a written transcript.) That is, the editor already has at least a tentative draft form of a text. Basic editing, of course, is concerned with eliminating outright errors – anything from incorrect spelling or punctuation, through ungrammatical constructions to obscure, ambiguous or misleading sentential configurations; all the linguistic levels of textual variables require checking for mistakes. When the object of editing is a TT, this process has to include checking back to the ST to make sure that its basic literal meaning has not been misrepresented in the TT. Nevertheless, much of this stage of textual editing is done on the TT as a TL text in its own right, without reference to the ST. In a sense, therefore, the transitional process of editing is a post-translational operation used for tidying up an almost complete TT, and is done with as little reference as possible to the ST.

In principle, no TT is ever finished and polished to the point where it could not be edited further. It is a practical question whether further editing will actually improve it. In practice there must, sooner or later (and for busy professional translators it is likely to be sooner), come a point where one has to stop tinkering with a TT. However, there is plenty of work to be done before that point is reached.

Just as basic editing presupposes at least a draft written text, so stylistic editing presupposes a text that is reasonably finished in such respects as literal meaning, grammar and spelling. This may turn out in practice to have been an unwarranted assumption, but it has to be the methodological starting-point. (A text might be rejected as unsuitable for stylistic editing if it were clearly not substantially correct.)

In the stylistic editing of a TT the translator considers only the alternative ways of expressing the literal meanings of parts of the text, rather than the possibility of altering the substance of what is expressed. This is admittedly a thin dividing line (as will be seen in Practical 15), because the way something is expressed is, to a great extent, part of what is expressed. Nevertheless, methodologically speaking, stylistic editing is purely a process of tinkering with stylistic effects in a TT. Thus it is not, in essence, a bilingual operation. It is perfectly possible for someone with no knowledge of, for example, Arabic to be called in to help with the stylistic editing of a TT translated from Arabic. As this observation suggests, the primary concern in editing is to enhance the quality of the TT, less as a translation than as a text produced in the TL for the use of a monolingual audience. Indeed, it is not uncommon for translations to be done by collaboration between one translator whose contribution is knowledge of the SL and another translator whose contribution is knowledge of the TL. With any luck, such collaboration would help in avoiding blunders like these classic captions:

OUR MILK COMES FROM BRUCELLOSIS ACCREDITED HERDS

WHY KILL YOUR WIFE WITH HOUSEWORK?
LET ELECTRICITY DO IT FOR YOU!

Stylistic editing is most effective if the editor lays the ST aside and concentrates on assessing the probable effects of the TT on a putative TL audience. One of the biggest problems in translating is that it is hard to put oneself in the shoes of a TL reader looking at the TT with a fresh eye. This is why translations from Spanish often have a Hispanic flavour which immediately signals that the text is a translation. Even the translator who manages to avoid outright translationese is not best placed to judge how well the TT would convey particular meanings or nuances for a reader who did not know the ST. There is therefore a lot to be said for asking an independent TL-speaking observer, who does not know the ST, to help with the editing.

Perhaps the most central features for stylistic editing are connotative meanings, because they require to be triggered by the context of the TT alone. The translator, who is inevitably immersed in the ST context, is unlikely to be able to assess confidently whether a connotation that is crystal-clear in the context of the ST and the SL is equally clear to someone who only looks at the TT from the viewpoint of the TL culture. It is vital that this be checked. It is just as vital to check the converse – that there are no obtrusive unwanted connotations evoked by the TT. At best, such unwanted connotations show that the translator has failed to anticipate the stylistic effects the TT is liable to produce on its TL audience, and is not fully in control of its style. At worst, they may distort and subvert the overall content and impact of the TT, or they may create textual anomalies, contradictory connotations clashing either with one another or with the literal meaning.

Of course, it is easier for the independent editor to help with the second of these constraints than with the first. For instance, whatever the ST expression may be, the phrase 'a world authority in French letters' risks unfortunate innuendo and the editor may suggest that the translator think again. (Going back to the ST, the translator may then decide that the TT is an unfortunate rendering of 'una autoridad mundial en letras francesas', and opt for 'a world authority in French literary studies' instead.) But, without knowing the ST, how can editors tell when connotations are *missing* from a TT? The best thing is to give them the ST and hope that they do not get so deeply immersed in it that they, too, cannot see the TT objectively. Otherwise, if there is time, the translator can put the TT away for a month and then look at it with fresh eyes; even so, there is no guarantee that missing connotations will be spotted.

The twin constraint of spotting both missing connotations and unwanted ones is best illustrated in cases of connotative clash. The elimination of connotative clashes is one of the principal aims of stylistic editing. Thus, for instance, only an unbiased reading of the TT may reveal that juxtaposed literally exact expressions in the TT convey conflicting attitudinal meanings which make the text anomalous by virtue of the clash between contradictory attitudes ascribed to the author or speaker. Such textual anomalies leave the TT audience in doubt as to how to take the attitudes connoted in the text. Attitudinal anomalies are exemplified in the first of the Sastre TTs on p. 143:

Este es mi verdadero traje. Y vuestro 'verdadero traje' ya para siempre.	This is my true garb. And your 'true garb' henceforth.

The connotations of this TT extract are likely to convey an attitude of lofty idealism, the sentences reading as an expression of praise and appreciation, even flattery, for the men addressed, not a thinly veiled threat. This clashes with the attitudes of the speaker conveyed elsewhere in the TT, from which it is clear that the Cabo's attitude to soldiering is one of pride mixed with a hard-nosed determination, while his attitude to the recruits is contemptuous and threatening. Stylistic editing might produce a better suggestion: '*This* is my proper suit. And that goes for you lot too from now on.'

Lo demás son ropas afeminadas..., la vergüenza de la especie.	Anything else is effeminate clothing ..., a disgrace to mankind.

The phrase 'a disgrace to mankind' has inappropriate attitudinal connotations suggesting a situation of solidarity and equality between the speaker and the addressees, whereas the context demands a blustering expression of contempt in which any of the recruits who do not qualify as 'real men' are automatically included: 'Anything else is for pansies ..., the scum of the earth' conveys exactly the right nuances, given the bullying machismo implicit in the situation.

Clashes like these tend to reduce the connotative content of the TT to absurdity and paradox. Where the ST is not itself deliberately enigmatic and paradoxical, this constitutes a distortion of its overall meaning. However, even where no outright clashes occur, translators should be careful not to let gratuitous attitudinal meanings insinuate themselves into the TT. These should be picked up and eliminated, as far as possible, at the stylistic editing stage.

Similar considerations apply for all other types of connotation. Thus, for instance, the loss of an allusive meaning with a subtle but thematically important role in the ST is a significant translation loss. Here is an example from Gustavo Adolfo Bécquer's poem 'Es un sueño la vida' (Bécquer, 1961, p. 52), already mentioned in Chapter 8, p. 104. The title alludes, as we have noted earlier, to Calderón's famous play 'La vida es sueño' and creates irony by means of the contrasting moods of the poem and the play. A translation from which an appropriate allusion is missing would, therefore, be unsatisfying.

Reflected meanings in a ST are also notoriously difficult to render adequately in a TT; and, conversely, unforeseen and potentially embarrassing reflected meanings can create translation loss by jeopardizing the seriousness of a TT through unwanted comic effects or innuendo, as in the example of the French letters given above.

As regards collocative meanings, the most obvious flaws to look out for are miscollocations. These are a likely result of the translator's immersion in the ST and the SL at the earlier stages of translating. (Even where, strictly speaking, they do not trigger problems of collocative meaning as such, they are a common source of translation loss on the grammatical level. Our discussion here embraces miscollocations in general, as well as collocative meaning.) Some miscollocations may actually amount to outright grammatical errors, not merely stylistic ones. For example, the collocation of superlative 'más' and any adjective is grammatical and idiomatic in Spanish, but is ungrammatical with many adjectives in English; compare 'la más vieja ciudad' with 'the most old city'. This kind of grammatical mistake will presumably be eliminated at an early editing stage. However, there may be collocations that are not categorically ungrammatical in the TL, yet introduce a jarring note into the TT. It is sometimes hard to pin down just what makes a certain collocation seem ungainly. At best, one can suggest that speakers of a language have a sense of 'euphonic order' by which they judge certain collocations to be more acceptable than others. For example, Spanish 'ir y venir' is felicitous where 'venir y ir' is not; whereas, in English, 'come and go' is felicitous but 'go and come' is not. Similarly, Spanish 'de pies a cabeza' may, according to context, need to be rendered as 'from top to toe', 'from head to toe' or 'from top to bottom', but never as 'from toe to top' or 'from toe to head', and rarely as 'from bottom to top'.

When differences between felicitous collocations in one language and those in another are overlooked, a TT will often signal, by its clumsiness, the fact that it is a translation and not an indigenous text. Here are some examples of such translationese:

de acá para allá	from here to there (*edit to*: back and forth/up and down)

niños de 2 a 5 años	children from 2 to 5 years (*edit to*: children between 2 and 5)
un film en blanco y negro	a film in white and black (*edit to*: black and white film)
Ya lo sabía yo.	I knew it already (*edit to*: I thought as much)
Se pasa todo el tiempo estudiando.	He spends all the time studying (*edit to*: He spends all his time studying)

As seen in the last example, **deictic** and anaphoric elements often create collocational problems of a stylistic rather than a grammatical nature. Deictic elements like 'this', 'that', 'the' and 'a' are often involved in subtle and complex collocational euphonics. So, for example, 'my hand hurts' and 'this hand hurts' convey different messages and seem both to be felicitous; 'that hand hurts' is (depending on context) less so, while 'the hand hurts' and 'a hand hurts' are in most contexts unacceptable. (Note that Spanish avoids the use of a possessive pronoun where the verbal form makes possession unambiguous; for example, 'me duele la mano izquierda', 'my left hand hurts' or 'Jaime llevó la chaqueta verde', 'Jaime wore his green jacket'.) 'When I aim, I close an eye' is somewhat ungainly, while 'when I aim, I close one eye' is felicitous. Anaphorics, too, show clearly that there are collocational choices to be made on the basis of felicity or infelicity in a given language. For example, 'aquel libro lo leí en dos días' is usually better rendered as 'I read the book in two days' than as 'that book, I read it in two days'. The translation of deictics and anaphora is far from being a straightforward matter of literal translation. Here are some examples:

El agua es enfriada por transferencia de calor desde hielo con *el* que se halla *ésta* en contacto.	Water is chilled by heat transfer from *the* ice with which *it* is in contact.
y además ...	and for another *thing* ...
... me pareció que estaba más contenta	... *she* seemed happier to me
La segunda parte de *la* excursión es *la* visita *al* Jardín Botánico.	The second part of *the* tour is *a* visit to *the* Botanical Gardens.
[*in the directions for use of a product*] Aplicar *el* PREPARADOR mediante fibra tipo Scotch Brite.	Apply PREPARER with *a* ScotchBrite-type abrasive pad.

Más grave que *el* materialismo conceptual tan típico del siglo XIX es *este* materialismo activo que [...]	More serious than *the* conceptual materialism of the 19th century is *the* active materialism that [...]

Infelicity in the use of anaphora and deictics may in some cases originate from a factor of tedious repetition. That is, collocational possibilities may be stylistically affected by some kind of textual 'boredom factor'. If this is the case, however, it must be said that different textual genres in different languages have very different tolerances to repetition. In an English novel, for example, there may be countless repetitions of 'he said', without this repetition being thought obtrusive or tedious. If the dialogue is translated into Hungarian, however, the translator soon begins to feel the need to vary the formula through translating 'he said' by various verbs descriptive of the manner of utterance (the Hungarian counterparts of 'he replied', 'he queried', 'he whispered', 'he affirmed', and so on). Thus it would seem that, in certain genres at least, the English-speaking reader's tolerance to the 'boredom factor' caused by continual use of 'he said' is higher than the Hungarian reader's tolerance of repetitions of the corresponding formula in Hungarian.

In a similar vein, it is clear that Spanish has in general a lower tolerance than English for the repetition of adverbial suffixes when they are joined by a conjunction, as exemplified by the clear preference for 'ni rápida ni eficazmente' (as opposed to 'ni rápidamente ni eficazmente'), 'lenta y decididamente' (as opposed to 'lentamente y decididamente'), 'política y económicamente' (as opposed to 'políticamente y económicamente'), and so on. These differential tolerances and preferences have obvious implications for translating and for stylistic editing.

It is clear from these examples that stylistic editing is in part an exercise in taste. Even if it means taking liberties with the literal faithfulness of TT to ST, rooting out unidiomatic collocations is a recommended editing process, except, of course, where the ST deliberately exploits them. This last proviso, however, highlights a vital point concerning all stylistic editing: while it is highly desirable to test the TT on SL speakers who do not know the ST, and to take careful account of their suggestions, *the ultimate editing decisions must always be taken by the translator, with reference to the ST*.

Rooting out unidiomatic collocations is one thing, but there is, of course, also the converse case to consider, where the TT collocation is idiomatic to the point of being clichéd. Clichés can be obtrusive in their own way, and are therefore capable of creating their own unwanted stylistic effects. In particular, if the ST produces unusual twists by means of unexpected collocations, the use of clichés in the corresponding TT amounts to significant translation loss, trivializing the text or even falsifying it. This effect is illustrated in an example from the Lorca text in Practical 8:

Por el cuerpo le subían los caracoles del agua.	Soft around her body curled the water like a snail.

As we have suggested, it should not be forgotten that collocative clashes may be used deliberately. In such cases it will usually be appropriate for the TT to coin equally deliberate miscollocations. The main thing then is to make sure that the contrived miscollocations in the TT are stylistically plausible in the light of the TL, and are clearly recognizable as deliberate ploys, not stylistic hitches. Here is a good example from the Rubén Darío text in Practical 8:

El sol como un vidrio redondo y opaco	The sun like a sheet of glass opaque and round (*edit to*: The sun like an opaque globe of glass)

In this example, the ST presents an unusual simile of the sun likened to a globe made of glass. Since glass is normally thought of as two-dimensional (as in 'a sheet of glass'), it is the function of the contrived collocation of 'vidrio' with 'redondo' (rounded) to provide the image with its necessary three-dimensional quality. The innovative 'vidrio redondo' contrasts with such standard collocations as 'vidrio cilindrado' (plate glass), 'vidrio plano' (sheet glass), which convey two-dimensional images, or, for that matter, 'vidrio pintado', which evokes colour.

For affective meanings, and stylistic uses of language varieties of all sorts, the same considerations hold as for the types of connotative meaning we have been discussing. These considerations can be summed up by calling attention to four problems: the problem of losing from the TT important connotations contextually triggered in the ST; the problem of accidentally creating unwanted connotative effects in the TT; the problem of bringing about connotative clashes in the TT; and the problem of deliberately introducing gratuitous connotations into the TT. These are the main points to look for in stylistic editing.

One other thing that should be reviewed at the stylistic editing stage is the textual effects of language variety – alternatives associated with different social registers, dialects, sociolects and tonal registers. Even though conscious choices have been made about these things at the drafting stage, stylistic editing offers one more chance to weigh up how successful the outcome of these choices is over the TT as a whole. The four problems outlined above are all likely to arise here as well, *mutatis mutandis*. It is also particularly important, when using a marked language variety in a TT, to avoid the two extremes of 'too little' and 'too much'. Editing offers the chance to make sure that the TT contains enough features of language variety to prevent its coming across as a neutral, standard sample of the TL, but not so many that it seems caricatural. The 'boredom factor' we referred to earlier can also be invoked here, and so can an 'irritation factor': over-using stylistic features all signalling the same language variety can very easily lead to tedium, embarrassment or exasperation (as witness some of the dialectal features of D. H. Lawrence's writing).

There is always a threat of connotative clash in the stylistic use of language variety. There is only one genuine excuse for mixing features from different registers, dialects and sociolects in a TT, and this is when the ST itself deliberately uses code-switching for specific thematic purposes, as for instance in the text from *Sotileza* used in Chapter 9 (p. 116). (If the mixture is accidental, then the ST will probably not be worth translating anyway, unless it is a potboiler that has sold a million copies and been turned into a television series with an all-star cast – in which case, the last thing the likely readership is going to be interested in is accuracy of language variety.)

Finally, here are two passages manifestly in need of stylistic editing, and which are well worth discussion in class:

(i) The Ministry of Education and Science has granted, on its fifth edition, the Scientific Research National Awards 'Santiago Ramón y Cajal', Technical Research 'Leonardo Torres Quevedo', Humanistic and Social Research 'Ramón Menéndez Pidal' and for young scientists 'Rey Juan Carlos I'. The Jury for these awards was composed by specialized professors in each area. These awards will be handed over by Their Majesties the King and Queen at an act to be held at the Royal Palace.

(ii) The Offices for the Transfer of Research Results (OTRIs) came into being in 1988 for promoting the transfer of scientific and technical offerings to productive sectors, thereby enabling universities and public research centres (CPI) to interrelate with companies in a coherent, planned and activated way.

PRACTICAL 15

15.1 Stylistic editing

Assignment

Discuss the two passages given immediately above and edit them to read better where you think they are stylistically or idiomatically defective. Earmark points where you think editing may be necessary but cannot be done without reference to the ST.

15.2 Stylistic editing

Assignment

(i) Working in groups, each taking roughly equal amounts of the text, edit the following English TT to read better where you think it is stylistically or idiomatically defective.

(ii) Earmark points where you think further editing may be necessary but can only be done with reference to the ST.

(iii) After discussion of your provisional edited version, you will be given the ST and asked (a) to assess the accuracy of the TT and (b) to complete the editing of the TT.

Contextual information

The text is taken verbatim from a travel brochure entitled *Colombia: país de Eldorado; the Country of Eldorado* distributed by Avianca airlines in the late 1980s.

Target text

COLOMBIA
THE COUNTRY OF ELDORADO

When the Spanish Conquer started in the actual colombian territory during the XVI century a legend was born: Eldorado... a fabulous treasure supousedly hidden beneath every water, buried in every cave, hit an in every mine...

Nonethe less the conquerors could not find that immerse richness which if only described exalted the spirits and gave courage to the cowards...

The conquerors did not know that every shining thing is not always gold and that all treasures can not be minted: the treasure was evident, It was just on the surface... the treasure was the weather, the generous fruits, the open skies, the plains and mountains: Colombia was the Eldorado!!!

Thus, this country located at the extreme northern tip of South America was undescribable in the usual language of tourist booklets. In order to talk about it you have be possesed by passion, use the language habitual to legends weavers...

Very sure you have read One Hundred Years of Solitude, that famous novel by the colombian author Garcia Márquez, where girls fly and the deads keep on tied up to the trees or stroll throgh the old mansions...

Well then, you already have an aproximate idea about this misterious country... full of unatainable dreams... Believe every thing they tell you about Colombia... This is an excessive country... Our territory is already a surprising amount of fullness, coastal borders on two oceans, inviolable jungles (some of them with airports), three outstanding mountain systems and big rivers giving surviving to inaccountable towns...

Colombia has also been called a country of cities... We have to many... small... quiet... and traditional, full of historic relics... Some are modern... up to the XXth Century, thrown into progress... But all of them connected by a net of good roads, railroads and airways...

Contrastive topics and practicals: introduction

The following four chapters will deal with a selection of topics from the 'contrastive linguistics' of Spanish and English. Each of these chapters is self-contained, and can be used as the basis of a practical at whatever stage of the course it seems most useful. The aim of including these contrastive topics is to sharpen students' awareness of certain characteristic difficulties in translating particular types of construction from Spanish to English, and increase their awareness of the range of options open to them in translating these constructions.

A contrastive study of Spanish and English is especially valuable as a component in a course on translation for the insight it offers into those structural differences between the two languages which constitute stumbling-blocks to literal translation. In principle there are a vast number of such systematic discrepancies between Spanish and English usage. 'Compensation in kind', discussed in Chapter 3, is generally made necessary by one or more of these numerous differences between the two languages. Anaphora and deictics, which we looked at briefly in Chapter 15, offer good examples of such areas of interlingual contrast, to each of which a complete chapter could have been devoted. The common feature these contrasts display from the translator's point of view is the frequent need for **grammatical transposition**. By grammatical transposition we mean the replacement of a particular type of structure containing given parts of speech in the ST by some other type of structure containing different parts of speech in the TT (for instance, 'Me es simpático' into 'I like him'). Many other writers designate this phenomenon simply as 'transposition'; we have used the full term 'grammatical transposition' here in order to prevent confusion with 'cultural transposition' (see above, pp. 20–7). Chapter 16 deals with an issue that is a frequent source of difficulties for English-speaking learners of Spanish: the difference made in Spanish between a verb in the subjunctive mood expressing the purpose or aim of an action and a verb in the indicative mood expressing result or effect. Chapter 17 deals with the richly nuanced field of issuing commands or giving instructions in Spanish: sensitive ways of conveying these nuances generally require grammatical transposition or communicative translation. Chapters 18 and 19 explore aspects of two related areas of grammatical transposition particularly characteristic of translation from Spanish to English: alternative tactics for the transposing of phrases containing pseudo-reflexive or pseudo-reciprocal pronouns (in particular the pronoun 'se'), and the grammatical transpositions necessitated by the translation of Spanish passive and impersonal constructions (including uses of the passive 'se').

The choice of just four contrastive topics out of the many that we could have chosen was a difficult, and in the end rather arbitrary, one. We have picked out four of the most common and rich contrastive sources of translation difficulties between Spanish and English, and illustrated each through a variety of classroom exercises.

There are two ways in which the contrastive exercises differ from other practicals in the course. First, students will often be translating sentences taken out of context, so that attention can be focused specifically on the contrastive problems themselves – problems that, in textual context, tend to be masked or blurred by considerations of style or genre. Naturally, we do not mean to imply that context is, after all, less important than we have insisted hitherto. On the contrary, where context and register are felt to be decisive factors, the discussion calls explicit attention to this fact. However, the routine of strategic decisions we are suggesting depends on fostering a contrastive awareness of available translation options, to which strategic considerations involving context can be subsequently applied. The availability of options can only be properly assessed by taking sentences out of textual context.

Second, in the contrastive chapters we frequently reverse the direction of translation to translating from English into Spanish. This is in order to bring into the open certain possibilities *in English* which one can easily overlook when translating *from Spanish*. For some Spanish sentences, the option of translating into English without significant grammatical transposition actually exists, but frequently at the cost of significant translation loss in terms of idiomaticity and appropriate register in the TT. Many of the English STs in the contrastive chapters contain constructions which cannot pass into Spanish without (sometimes drastic) transposition. These are instances of precisely those idiomatic English constructions which it is easiest to overlook as possible options when one is translating a Spanish ST, particularly one whose structure can be faithfully replicated in English. Our hope is that, having come across these constructions as stumbling-blocks in translation *into* Spanish, students will remain aware of their availability as options in translating *from* Spanish.

16

Contrastive topic and practical: subjunctive expressing purpose/aim versus indicative expressing result/effect

This chapter constitutes the material for all or part of a practical. If possible, the following preliminary exercise should be handed in before the practical. It should in any case be completed before going on to the material in the rest of the chapter. Chapter 16 is devoted to a practical problem which is more obvious when translating from English into Spanish, because then the translator is more immediately aware of the range of nuances available in the choice between a subjunctive and an indicative subsidiary verb. On the other hand, the problem is more subtle and insidious when translating from Spanish into English, mainly because the translator is likely to overlook the nuance conveyed by the mood of the verb. Of course, the problematic nature of the translation of the subjunctive mood from Spanish is well known and is too vast a topic for in-depth discussion here. The aim of the present chapter is merely to focus attention on one particular group of conjunctional expressions, and possible ways of translating them.

PRELIMINARY EXERCISE

Offer one Spanish translation for each the following English STs, using only a Spanish monolingual dictionary:

1 I placed the couch so that the light might reach it from the window.
2 Simon positioned the table so that the light reached it from the window.

3 She opened the parcel upside-down so that the contents fell out.
4 She did it so that we would all notice.

5 Little Petra broke the clock and her brother got the blame.
6 Philip put on his best suit and we noticed how handsome he was.

7 I left the room so that no one would notice.
8 Jack dressed in such a way that the others didn't recognize him.
9 After the party Anne cleared up so that her parents didn't realize it had taken place.
10 Paula nudged his back without Ana noticing.

All of the sentences given in the preliminary exercise are in fact translations from Spanish STs. In the course of class discussion, students will no doubt have suggested a wide variety of conjunctional expressions ranging from the coordinating conjunction 'y' to subordinating conjunctions which are frequently found in association with the subjunctive, such as 'para que' or 'sin que'. However, the basic structure which all of the Spanish STs shared was a conjunctional phrase of the type 'de manera/modo/forma/suerte que' followed by a verb in either the subjunctive or the indicative mood. The main point to bear in mind is that the choice of mood of the subordinate verb is determined by whether the speaker wishes to convey that the action in the subordinated verb is the result or effect of the action in the main verb, or whether the subordinate verb is to be construed as expressing the purpose or aim of the main verb.

The choice of the subjunctive versus the indicative mood in structures of the type *main verb + conjunctional phrase + subordinate verb* is one of the principal sources of difficulty for English-speaking learners of Spanish. This is due, in part, to the fact that English – particularly in its spoken varieties – tends to be far less rigorous in distinguishing between the expression of result/effect and purpose/aim. English can in fact differentiate between these two ideas in the choice speakers make between using simple indicatives and the auxiliary verbs 'do/did', 'will/would' or 'may/might'. This point can be illustrated if we compare the following STs:

ST1 I will place the couch so that the light might reach it from the window.
ST2 Simon positioned the table so that the light reached it from the window.

In ST1 it seems quite clear that the subordinate verb describes an intended effect resulting from the action described in the first verb. This is conveyed both through the future aspect of 'will place' and by the fact that the subordinate verb, 'might catch', itself expresses the intention or purpose of the action described in the main verb; the following TT would seem appropriate:

TT1 Colocaré el sofá de modo que la luz le llegue desde la ventana.

In ST2, however, it is unclear whether the speaker intends the action described by the subordinate verb to be seen as the result or effect of Simon's action or whether it should be understood as conveying the purpose of his action. Compare the following Spanish counterparts to the sentence and consider how their nuances can be most accurately conveyed in English in order to underscore the difference in their respective meanings:

(a) Simón colocó la mesa de modo que la luz la llegó desde la ventana.
(b) Simón colocó la mesa de modo que la luz la llegara desde la ventana.

A somewhat exegetical rendering of (a) would be 'in such a way that/so that the light did reach', whereas (b) could more plausibly be translated as 'in such a way that/so that the light might reach'. The translation of either the indicative 'llegó' or the subjunctive 'llegara' as 'would' is more problematic since 'will/would', while often associated in English with the expression of intention or purpose, may equally suggest the result to be expected from an action. This possible ambiguity needs to be borne in mind in translations where the translator considers that the TT needs to make clear whether a subclause expresses result/effect or purpose/aim.

Students will find it useful to edit the TTs they produced in carrying out the preliminary exercise in the light of these observations. Once this exercise has been completed, we suggest that the following class practical is done.

Class exercise

Offer one TT for each of the following STs, using only a monolingual Spanish dictionary. Try to make your TTs as clear as possible with regard to whether the subordinate verb is to be taken as expressing result/effect or purpose/aim:

1 Le guiñó de manera que sus amigos pensaran que tenía algo en el ojo.
2 Tula abrió el paquete de modo que no se derramara el contenido.
3 Doña Paula sonrió de manera que su hijo no lo notara.
4 El Marqués, aún subido al palo más alto de la escalera de mano, no llegaba a coger la barquilla del columpio de modo que pudiera hacer fuerza para descolgarle.
5 Estiró las piernas al lado de las del joven de suerte que las podían comparar los presentes.
6 Empujó demasiado fuerte de modo que se cayó Saturno.
7 Juanito se puso el mejor traje que tenía y nos dimos cuenta de lo guapo que era.
8 María se lo contó todo a su madre de tal manera que ésta no la culpó.
9 Nos hizo una señal de manera que el profesor no lo vio.
10 Salí de la reunión de forma que los demás no se dieron cuenta.

In some cases the exegetical mode of translation outlined above may result in an unidiomatic translation. Consider the following:

TT1(a) He winked in such a way that his friends might think he had something in his eye.

Whilst using 'might' in this construction is grammatically correct, the appropriateness of the formal tone it introduces will depend on the context of the ST. In cases where the context makes it clear that the intended effect of an action is implied, it may be more appropriate to use 'would':

TT1(b) He winked in such a way that his friends would think...

Where in Spanish the indicative is used to express result and effect, an appropriate translation can sometimes be achieved through generalizing or particularizing the conjunctional phrase. It may be generalized by transposition into the coordinating conjunction 'and', which is often used to imply a relation of cause and effect between two clauses, as in 'We shut the window and it got very stuffy'. So, for example, ST6 could be translated as:

TT6(a) He pushed too hard and Saturno fell over.

Alternatively, the conjunctional phrase may be particularized by transposition into a correlative subordinating conjunction which incorporates the adverbial qualifier of the main verb (for instance, 'It was *so stuffy that* she fainted', 'She did it *with such skill that* everyone clapped'). The correlative conjunction therefore has two markers: the first is an adverbial intensifier like 'so' or 'such', marking the main clause; the second is a 'that', marking the subclause. Adopting this approach, one could translate ST6 as:

TT6(b) He pushed so hard that Saturno fell over.

or, more exegetically, as:

TT6(c) He pushed too hard, so hard that Saturno fell over.
TT6(d) He pushed with such force that Saturno fell over.

Of course, the choice of an appropriate translation from amongst the possibilities given could only be determined by the translator's strategic concerns and by the context of the ST. However, the possibility of using the tactic of either generalizing or particularizing in order to attempt to convey the fact that the ST conveys result/effect or purpose/aim is always worth bearing in mind.

Where the ST offers a negative indicative verb after the conjunctional phrase, there are several possibilities for translation. Consider the following renderings of STs 8–10:

TT8(a) María told her mother everything in such a way that she wouldn't get the blame.
TT9(a) He gave us a signal and the teacher didn't see it.
TT10 I left the meeting without anyone noticing.

TT8(a) does express the implied fact that María's intention in telling her mother everything is that she, María, should not be blamed. However, this sentence is clumsy to the point of implausibility. The following alternative makes María's intention explicit, by introducing the verb 'manage to' into the second clause; it is also more idiomatic, thanks to the tactic we used in TT6(a), the substitution of a coordinating conjunction for the ST conjunctional phrase:

TT8(b) María told her mother everything, and managed not to get the blame.

While similar considerations apply to TT 9(a), another tactic which is possible in some contexts is to use the preposition 'without' followed by a gerund. Context permitting, this might offer a satisfactory way of rendering ST9:

TT9(b) He gave us a signal without the teacher noticing.

It should be noted that here, as in TT10, the verb 'notice', as distinct from 'see', or even 'realise', is used to imply the element of intention. As these examples and TT8(b) suggest, the translator's choice of verb is as important as the choice of grammatical construction.

The practical work which follows comprises two stages. At the first stage, each student should draft two rough TTs for each of the STs. At the second stage, students should work in small groups to evaluate each of their TTs in relation to the ST, and draw up a list of preferred TTs.

PRACTICAL 16

16.1 Conjunctional phrases

1 Don Fermín la miró de modo que ella no le vio.
2 Esto lo dijo bastante alto de manera que lo oyese el sereno que daba vuelta a la esquina.
3 Empleaba largos preparativos para colocar los brazos de modo que hiciera la fuerza suficiente para levantar el columpio.
4 Frígilis tosía fuerte de manera que le oyera Ana.
5 Frígilis le advirtió a Álvaro de suerte que se abstuvo de asaltar el parque aquella noche.
6 Quintanar preparaba el reloj despertador de suerte que le llamase a las 8 en punto.
7 El escándalo le salió de modo que se enteró el pueblo entero.
8 Pero otra cosa era seducir a la criada de suerte que lo ignorara el amo.

17

Contrastive topic and practical: orders and requests

This chapter constitutes the material for all or part of a practical. If possible, the following preliminary exercise should be handed in before the practical. It should in any case be completed before going on to the material in the rest of the chapter. The chapter is devoted to a practical problem – the translation of structures conveying requests and commands – which has implications for tonal register. As we saw in Chapter 12, audience expectations of a given genre and tolerance of particular features often vary between SL and TL. This is an issue to which translators should pay serious attention, particularly in the case of commands and requests.

PRELIMINARY EXERCISE

Offer one English translation for each of the following Spanish STs, using only a Spanish monolingual dictionary:

1 Dame una cerveza.
2 Bueno, venga, Paco, déjalo ya, hombre...
3 Y mirame, por favor, levantá la cabeza... Decime que me perdonás.
4 Ve a comprar unas hierbas para preparar una infusión.
5 Oiga, mire, yo es que prefiero no salir, a ver si me entiende...
6 Hágame el favor de ir al grano.
7 ¡Arriba las manos! No se mueva.
8 Quisiera hablar con el médico.
9 Le ruego difunda la información que le envío y coloque el cartel en el tablón de anuncios.
10 En media hora haremos el cambio. Iráis a la playa de Hendaya. Allí os lo entregaremos a cambio del dinero.

It is evident from the preliminary exercise that the range in the formal expression of tonal registers employed in orders and requests in European and Latin American usage of Spanish is wide. In discussing this usage, we use the following terms: the term *imperative* refers to the affirmative second person constructions commonly designated 'imperative' forms, such as 'ten/tened' or 'habla/hablad'; the term *command* refers to constructions which use the subjunctive to give orders. In addition to these categories, there are miscellaneous other constructions which may, in current usage, convey orders, such as impersonal 'se' frequently used in written instructions, but to which we do not give a collective label. We do, however, use *order* as a cover term for all constructions sharing a common illocutionary function, that of issuing instructions.

It should be noted at the outset that the actual tonal register of an order or request in Spanish in spontaneous oral texts is articulated primarily through intonation. In written texts – even those which purport to reproduce oral material, as dialogue in a novel may – tonal register is established to a large extent by the manipulation of illocutionary particles, tags and the like. It should be remembered that tags such as '¿quiere?', '¿eh?', '¿vale?', '¿de acuerdo?', 'cuando puedas/quieras' are more common than expressions based on 'hacerme el favor' or 'por favor', which are markedly formal.

The role of illocutionary particles and other markers to modify the tone of orders and requests in Spanish is a difficult area for translators: one reason for this is the low degree of tolerance in Spanish for expressions based on 'hacerme el favor' or 'por favor', coupled with the fact that the language has developed a wide range of other structures that modify the blunt impact of an order.

The material which follows is divided into three sections. The first deals briefly with certain differences between European and Latin American usage. The second treats the emphatic reinforcement of orders by means of structural devices. In the third we discuss the modification of the tone of the imperative through the use of miscellaneous illocutionary devices.

17.1 Informal 'tú/vos/vosotros(as)' versus formal 'usted/ustedes': European versus Latin American usage

Although the primary distinction between a speaker's choice of 'tú/vos' and their plural forms on the one hand and the appropriate form of 'usted' as a marker of formality on the other is based mainly on the speaker's attitude to the addressee, there is a clear difference between Latin American usage, particularly that of the Southern Cone, and European Spanish usage. First, especially in Argentinian usage, different imperative forms accompany the 'vos' form – some of these can be seen in sentence 3 of the preliminary exercise. In addition to this, there is an increasing tendency in Latin American varieties of Spanish to use the 'usted/ustedes' form when addressing more than one person. This phenomenon is due to the erosion of the use of 'vosotros/vosotras' in Latin America and in no way denotes a particular attitude of respect to the addressees: for example, a father would make use of the 'ustedes' form to address his children, as in 'Estense quietos'.

In European Spanish the situation is no less complex. Forms of 'usted/ustedes' are used mainly in orders addressed to someone older than the speaker, someone in a position of authority, or a respected subordinate. Although 'usted' is often used to address someone unfamiliar to the speaker, in some cases the familiar form may be used to soften the tone of an order directed towards someone unknown to the speaker. For example, a request to a bartender would be likely to have its tone modified by the use of a 'tú' imperative rather than *usted + por favor*.

17.2 Emphatic reinforcement

Consider the following dialogue extract, which was designed to illustrate the gradations in the strength of informal structures conveying an order. Only one side of the dialogue is given. There are, of course, formal alternatives to these milder informal order constructions, such as using imperfect or conditional forms of 'poder' in an interrogative construction, or various manipulations of the verb 'querer' (see sentence 8 in the preliminary exercise). The point here is to illustrate that the scale in tonal range extends from the tone of a mild request, as in *ir + a + infinitive* or *quisiera + infinitive*, to the abrupt and emphatic effect of an order couched in the future tense. Attempt a TT of the dialogue extract which conveys the heightening of its imperative tone:

– Hija, vas a bajar al bar y me subes una botella de gaseosa.
– Baja ahora y súbemela.
ST1 – Que bajes ahora mismo y te dejes de tonterías.
ST2 – Bajarás y me subirás la gaseosa en seguida.

(adapted from the model provided in García Santos, 1990, p. 38)

In this extract students will have noted that the structure *que + subjunctive* functions to strengthen the simple imperative. It has been suggested that the role of 'que' in order constructions signals an implied phrase such as 'Ya te he dicho' ('I've already told you'). Consider the following translation of line 3 of the dialogue extract (ST1):

TT1(a) I've already told you to go down and fetch it.

and compare this with the following:

TT1(b) You've already been told once to go down and fetch it.

Each of these TTs reproduces the idea that the structure *que + subjunctive* reiterates and reinforces the simple imperative; they do this by particularizing *que + subjunctive* into a formula which actually refers to the act of ordering. TT1(a) renders the structure to which the 'que' putatively refers, whilst TT1(b) uses a passive construction to de-emphasize the agent and to highlight the non-compliance of the person to whom the order was addressed. In this respect, TT1(b) can be seen to be faithful to the ST's suppression of an implied main clause preceding 'que'. TT1(b) is the more plausible translation of the two, but the translator may still feel that this rendering could benefit from further reinforcement, for example:

TT1(c) You've already been told once to go down and fetch it. Do I need to tell you again?

or even:

TT1(d) How many times do you have to be told to go down and fetch it?

The order structure which is strongest in tone in the dialogue extract – involving the future indicative – presents few problems for the translator working into English, since the TL permits the use of the future auxiliary 'will' in an emphatic imperative structure. However, once again it is possible that the translator may consider further TL reinforcement necessary in order to convey more clearly the impact of the ST. Compare the following TTs of line 4 of the dialogue extract (ST2):

TT2(a) You will go down at once and bring me up the lemonade.
TT2(b) You will go down and bring me up the lemonade. At once!

17.3 Modification of the imperative tone

As noted above, Spanish uses a whole range of illocutionary particles and expressions – such as '¿puedes?' – to modify the impact of the syntactic forms used in issuing orders. Consider, for example, the difference in tonal register between sentence 8 of the preliminary exercise and the following ST:

ST3 Querría dos kilos de naranjas.

In sentence 8 of the preliminary exercise, the imperfect subjunctive 'quisiera' functions as a mark of considerable formality, possibly translatable as 'I wonder if it would be possible to', while the conditional in ST3 is merely marked as polite: 'I should like...'. The following ST illustrates other, more complex, markers of a softening of tonal register:

ST4 Venga, tío, que nos vamos a casita.
TT4(a) Come on, you, let's go home.

Like sentence 2 of the preliminary exercise, ST4 uses 'venga' as an illocutionary particle to denote familiarity. It may be variously translated as 'come on (now/then)', 'come along' or even 'come off it', depending on the context. TT4(a)'s 'come on' seems plausible; however, 'tío' marks the sentence as being of a low register rather than merely colloquial (in the context ST4 is indeed spoken by a youth in a bar to another youth who is in a drug-induced torpor). In the light of this, 'tío' might be more plausibly rendered as 'man'. The force of 'que' in ST4 seems not to be directed towards emphasizing or reiterating the tone of the order, but rather seems to be explaining events to the addressee – at any rate, any emphatic imperative tone it may have carried is diminished by the use of the first person plural (as opposed to the second person singular) and by the diminutive form of 'casa'. The effect of the latter of these two devices is not directly rendered in TT4(a) and may need some form of compensation. Consider in this light the following TT:

TT4(b) Come on then, man, let's get you home.

ST4, in fact, presents a fairly straightforward example of the use of modifying devices. Both of the STs which follow provide more complex examples; these are quoted from a novel in which the author – Rosa Montero – contrasts the personalities of her characters through their speech habits. ST5 is spoken by an effusive, supercilious and over-polite character, while the speaker of ST6 is over-assertive and sarcastic to the point of brutality:

ST5 Alguna vez, si usted me lo permite, claro está, quisiera ir a visitar a su adorable hermana para presentarle mis respetos.

ST6 Hazme el inmenso favor de dejar de hacer ruiditos, ¿quieres?

ST5 is overloaded with markers of respect and formality. In the first place, the speaker is imprecise in the extreme as to when the request should be fulfilled. The introduction of the phrase 'si usted me lo permite' before the request itself suggests that the speaker is reluctant – perhaps even afraid – to state the object of the request. This phrase, moreover, is marked for such a high degree of formality as to sound somewhat archaic. The tag 'claro está' underscores the speaker's respect for the addressee once again, and is followed up by the imperfect subjunctive of 'querer', which is also marked for a high degree of respectful formality. The overall impression given by ST5 is that its speaker greatly respects – or more likely fears – the addressee and considers himself to be making a very bold request. This overall impact may be conveyed by the following:

TT5 If you would be so good as to permit me, I should very much like to call on your delightful sister and to pay my respects to her.

ST6 is equally complex and also manifests a high density of markers which affect its tonal register. In the first place, although the speaker uses the formal 'hacerme el favor', he is nonetheless using the 'tú' form; so the ST begins with something of a clash in register. This effect is intensified through the use of the adjective 'inmenso' which underscores the emphatic nature of the request, an emphasis heightened again by the illocutionary particle '¿quieres?' at the end of the sentence. This particle carries a much more mundane tone than the speaker's 'hazme el inmenso favor' and thus undercuts the formality of this lofty formula. The clash of registers already noted is also present in the diminutive form 'ruiditos' (instead of 'ruidos'): a modifying technique more commonly associated with informal situations and more mundane requests. Overall, the contrast in tonal register suggests the sarcasm and false politeness of the speaker:

TT6(a) Would you please be so good as to stop making those bloody stupid noises?

The contrast in register between the lexical, syntactic and sentential elements which comprise ST6 is notable, and TT6(a) does not satisfactorily convey this. It is interesting to note that in the context the speaker is addressing his sister, whom he treats with great contempt, and that 'ruiditos' refers to her weeping as a result of his treatment of her.

In the light of this, TT6(a) should be compared to the following alternative TTs, with a view to considering what overall strategy seems most appropriate for rendering ST6:

TT6(b) Would you kindly cut out that bloody snivelling?
TT6(c) I'd be grateful if you would stop that awful racket.
TT6(d) Please stop making that noise instantly.
TT6(e) Look – cut out that racket. It's really bugging me.

18

Contrastive topic and practical: pronominalization

This chapter constitutes the material for all or part of a practical. If possible, the following exercise should be handed in before the practical. It should in any case be completed before going on to the material in the rest of the chapter.

PRELIMINARY EXERCISE

Translate the following passage into English.

> No he querido saber, pero he sabido que una de las niñas, cuando ya no era niña y no hacía mucho que había regresado de su viaje de bodas, entró en el cuarto de baño, se puso frente al espejo, se abrió la blusa, se quitó el sostén y se buscó el corazón con la punta de la pistola de su propio padre, que estaba en el comedor con parte de la familia. Cuando se oyó la detonación, el padre no se levantó en seguida, sino que se quedó durante algunos segundos paralizado con la boca llena, sin atreverse a masticar ni a tragar; por fin se alzó y corrió hacia el cuarto de baño. Cuando llegó allí lo único que se veía desde la puerta fue los pies de la suicida. El padre se echó a gritar.
>
> (adapted from Marías, 1992)

This Spanish ST could, of course, be discussed in a number of respects but we shall concentrate briefly on the specific points related to the topic of this chapter, namely uses of 'se'. The range of uses of 'se' in the ST is evident. For example, the passive 'se' in 'se oyó la detonación' will be familiar to most students, as will the employment of a pronominal form of the verb 'echar' to convey a violent inchoative action, such as bursting into tears, which will most likely have been learned as an item of vocabulary. In this chapter, we will focus on the use of 'se' principally in its capacity to alter the meanings of verbs. We use the term *pronominalization* to denote the use of reflexive pronouns to convey meanings other than true reflexivity or reciprocity. Compare the reflexive and reciprocal uses of 'se' in the sentence:

ST1 (Ella) se resignó a la idea de que se amarían a escondidas.

with the following example of a pronominalized use of 'se':

ST2 En seguida se lanzó a escribir el ensayo.

In ST1, the first use of 'se' is likely to be considered reflexive by a native speaker – the action of the verb (giving up) is clearly operated upon its subject (she) – although a non-native speaker may consider there to be a slight alteration in meaning (give up > resign oneself) due in part to the fact that the verb 'resignarse', as distinct from 'resignar', does not admit of a direct object. In contrast to this, the second use of 'se' is clearly reciprocal (they would love each other). The subtlety of pronominalization in ST2 is perhaps best explored when a TT of this sentence is compared with TTs of the following sentences:

ST3 Lanzó la pelota al aire.
TT3 She threw the ball into the air.
ST4 Se lanzó al torrente.
TT4 She leapt/jumped/threw herself into the rushing stream.

ST3 is an example of the transitive use of the verb 'lanzar'. In contrast to this ST4 presents an example of the use of 'lanzar' with a reflexive pronoun in a manner parallel to that seen in the first use of 'se' in ST1: the subject performs the action of 'throwing' upon herself. Also like the verb in ST1, the verb in question has its direct object in the form of the reflexive pronoun, and therefore cannot take a further direct object. Now let us consider two possible TTs of ST2:

TT2(a) He immediately threw himself into writing the essay.
TT2(b) He got stuck into writing the essay at once.

TT2(a) is faithful in as much as English offers the possibility of employing a metaphoric idiom similar to that employed in the ST – the idea of throwing oneself into an activity; however, given the emphatic force associated with the pronominalization of verbs of motion in Spanish, the rendering of 'lanzarse' offered in TT2(b) might be considered a more idiomatic one. TT2(b) is an example of how a communicative rendering may move the pronominalized form further from the meaning of the verb which is at the core of the structure. However, problems may arise when the meaning offered by the pronominal form moves still further from the verb on which it is based and where there is no parallel metaphoric relationship between the SL and TL. This can be seen in the following pair of sentences:

ST5 Rosalía empeñó el candelabro de plata.
TT5 Rosalía pawned the silver candelabra.
ST6 Se empeñó en pedirme factura.
TT6 He demanded/insisted on asking for a receipt.

As the preliminary exercise and the examples discussed suggest, there are a variety of reasons why the translation of pronominalized verbs from Spanish to English offers problems, particularly when the ST verb is in the third person. The first reason is linked to the complex range of other syntactic functions which are associated with 'se', such as its use in passive and impersonal structures. The second is the variety of effects which may be achieved through the use of pronominalized verbs, and it is this that will be discussed in the following sections. The primary source of difficulty is the use of pronominalization to focus attention on some aspect of the relationship between agent and action rather than that of subject and object, verbal complement, and so on. There are four areas which merit attention. The first is the use of pronominalization to change the meaning of a verb. The second relates to the translation problems which arise from emphatic verbal structures using 'se'. These are twofold: a potential difficulty in the identification of what exactly is being emphasized and, as a direct consequence of this, the failure to find a satisfactory compensatory structure for the TT. A third area of difficulty is the use of pronominal verbs to denote possession or ownership of the following direct object. The fourth is the use of pronominal 'se' with verbs which function as passives. Discussion of the first three of these areas will be followed by a ST for use in class. This practical may also be used as a follow-on exercise for the next topic: impersonal and passive uses of 'se'.

18.1 Pronominalization, transitivity and change of meaning

The verbs which are grouped together under this category vary depending upon which of the standard grammars is consulted – this seems to be due to differences in what is considered as constituting a change of meaning. This point was illustrated in the use of 'resignarse' in ST1. We refer to cases where in pronominal forms associated with reflexivity, a slight change in meaning is perceived by English speakers as reflexive pronominal change, for example that perceived between 'sentar' (to seat) and 'sentarse' (to sit down). It should be noted, as pointed out above, that in many cases native speakers will consider these verbs as truly reflexive (Molina Redondo and Ortega Olivares, 1990, pp. 40–1, 58–9). Where the meaning of the pronominalized form differs radically from the source verb, grammarians usually recommend the memorization of the pronominal form as if it were a separate lexical item. However, the majority of verbs which come into this category offer few problems for the translator because pronominal meaning is quite clearly related to the core meaning of the verb. Consider the difference in nuance between the following two examples:

ST7 ¡No hagas eso, Paco! Que me enfadas.
ST8 ¡No hagas eso, Paco! Que me enfado.

In ST7, the speaker presents himself as reacting directly as the object affected by the action that Paco is performing. A plausible TT might be:

TT7 Don't do that, Paco – you're annoying me.

'Que' is employed here as a co-ordinator between the two phrases. In ST8, however, the function of the pronoun is to reinforce the fact that the verbal action, 'me enfado', is the response of the speaker as subject to Paco's behaviour. Consider these possible TTs:

TT8(a) Don't do that, Paco – it's annoying.
TT8(b) Don't do that, Paco – I'm getting annoyed.

TT8(a) offers a close analogue to TT7 and it is difficult to see where the difference in the two English versions lies, other than in the identification of the origin of the annoyance. In TT7 it is clearly Paco who provokes the reaction whereas TT8(a) suggests that it is the action itself which is annoying. In TT8(b) the idiomatic English use of the verb 'get' with a past participle to describe a process of change or becoming offers a close parallel to the effect of pronominal 'enfadar', and in fact offers a potential solution for a significant number of pronominal verbs, including some of those which have inanimate subjects. Consider the following STs, and discuss plausible TTs in class:

ST9 Se casó con un enfermero.
ST10 La fiebre se cura sin medicina.
ST11 Me perdí en camino al bar Chispa.

ST10 and ST11 are of interest because each has a possible point of overlap with another category of the use of 'se'. The pronominalization which changes the nuance of ST11's verb from 'lose' to 'get lost' may be more accurately thought of as reflexivity such as was seen in the verb 'resignarse' in ST1. ST10, on the other hand, may be interpreted as a passive or impersonal 'se':

TT10(a) Fever is cured without medicine.
TT10(b) One cures fever without medicine.

although the word order suggests otherwise: this will be discussed in the next contrastive chapter.

18.2 Emphatic pronominalization

One of the functions of the use of pronominalization is to convey the fact that what is being described is accidental, unplanned or unexpected. The following example is one in which it is extremely difficult to compensate for pronominal form in translation:

ST12 El trágico suceso se produjo cuando la víctima se encontraba bailando.

The ST is from a popular tabloid article which recounts how a young man, deviating from his normal Saturday routine of a night out with his girlfriend, ended up going for an evening's drinking with his friends, an occurrence which led to a fatal accident. He is portrayed throughout the article – told by his mother to the journalist – as the passive victim of an unfortunate chain of events. The unintentional and coincidental nature of the fact that he found himself dancing when the accident occurred is difficult to convey. Consider the following TTs:

TT12(a) The tragic accident happened when the victim was dancing.

All sense of the coincidental nature of what he was doing is lost from the TT. A slight adjustment of the syntax offers a slightly more emphatic version:

TT12(b) The victim was dancing when he was overtaken by a tragic turn of events.

Here the loss of emphasis on the unfortunate nature of the victim's circumstance (his dancing) is handled by compensation in the form of the English passive ('he was overtaken by'). If further emphasis were required then a direct reference to the coincidental nature of the dancing could be explicitly expressed:

TT12(c) The victim happened to be dancing when he was overtaken by a tragic turn of events.

However, TT12(c) seems to be almost too emphatic and TT12(b) reads more idiomatically when the context of the ST is taken into account: an article in the tabloid newspaper, *El caso criminal*, which specialises in human interest stories concerned with crime.

The use of pronominal forms to convey the accidental, unplanned or unexpected nature of the action is prevalent with verbs of motion:

Se vino pobre de las Américas.	(compare: Vino a casa.)
Se salió del teatro antes de que terminara la obra.	(compare: Salió del cine después de ver la peli.)
Se encontró con Juana en Burdeos.	(compare: Encontró el bolígrafo donde lo dejó.)

and verbs of movement:

ST13	Se abrió la puerta.	TT13	The door was opened.
ST14	La ventana se cerró.	TT14	The window closed.
ST15	Se rompió el vaso.	TT15	The glass got broken.
ST16	Se me cayó de la mano.	TT16	It slipped out of my hand.

In ST13 to ST16 the pronominal verbs have inanimate subjects. This sort of structure is often closely aligned to passive constructions. If the pronominal rather than passive interpretation is intended, then the grammatical subject will precede the verb, as in ST14; however, the verb followed by the grammatical subject in this construction allows both interpretations, although a passive one may be considered more probable, as in ST15. ST16 is an example of a common function of the pronominal form, which is to indicate the accidental nature of the action. (A similar example to this may be seen in TT15, where we translated 'se rompió' as 'got broken' rather than as 'was broken'.) As TT15 suggests, the use of English *get + past participle* often also conveys the idea of an accidental action, or one in which responsibility is not attributed, and in STs in which this is deemed to be the function of the pronoun, care must be taken to include this nuance in the TT.

Emphatic pronominalization is frequently found along with verbs of consumption, knowledge or perception, and tends to denote the totality of the action. Consider the following:

ST17 Se fumó una cajetilla de cigarillos.
TT17(a) She smoked a packet of cigarettes.
ST18 Se leyó tres lecciones en media hora.
TT18(a) He read three lessons in half an hour.
ST19 Se aprendió tres capítulos.
TT19(a) She learned three chapters.

TT17(a) and TT18(a) are quite faithful to their respective STs in all but that they fail to capture the emphatic nature of the action as conveyed through the use of pronominalized forms. In each of these cases this can be adequately compensated for through the addition of the adjective 'whole' before the object described, giving us the following more pointed versions:

TT17(b) She smoked a whole packet of cigarettes.
TT18(b) He read three whole lessons in half an hour.

ST19, on the other hand, does not lend itself so readily to this method of translation, and it is only through the addition of a verbal complement that the loss of meaning conveyed by the pronominal form can be compensated:

TT19(b) She learned three chapters (off) by heart.

18.3 Possessive pronominalization

It has been noted that Spanish has a lower tolerance than English for possessive pronouns in contexts in which the owner or possessor is clear from the verbal context or from the presence of pronominal forms. Consider again the function of pronouns in lines 3–4 of the ST given at the beginning of this chapter:

ST20 ... se abrió la blusa, se quitó el sostén y se buscó el corazón...

As the woman in the text was described as 'una de las niñas' it is possible that 'abrirse' is functioning reflexively to signal on the one hand that the action is performed by the woman upon herself and, second, that the object of the action, 'la blusa', is worn by the subject of the verb. That the pronouns here signal possession of the objects described is emphasized by the use of a pronominalized form of 'quitar' and 'buscar'. This is a minor point in translation but one which nonetheless repays consideration and care.

Marías has taken care to build up a series of parallel structures of the type *se + third-person singular preterite verb*, and this calls for a similarly structured TT, even if the verbs do not all have the same syntactical function. The following rendering:

TT20(a) ... she unbuttoned her blouse, took off her bra and sought out her heart [with the muzzle]...

to some extent loses the effect of the parallelism in the ST by cutting out the syntactically unnecessary repetition of the personal pronoun 'she'. Likewise the choice of 'sought out her heart' seems unidiomatic in comparison with the more prosaic choices of 'unbuttoned' and 'took off'. The key to this passage is to develop a strategy which attempts to take into account what the translator perceives to be the effect of the repetition of the structure *se + verb + definite article + object*. The reader will have noted that the use of simple, unadorned verbal structures throughout this passage and the lack of adjectives build up a stark picture of the events which suggests they are of a rather mundane nature and which offers few clues as to possible motivation. There is a clear contrast between the horror of the events described and the author's selection of uncomplicated grammatical structures and simple lexis suggestive of shock. The repetitive pattern is then broken down when more complex grammatical structures are reintroduced in the form of a verbal complement followed by a relative clause. The following rendering:

TT20(b) ... she unfastened her blouse, she took off her bra and she aimed at her heart [the muzzle]...

is disjunctive inasmuch as its final phrases present the unidiomatic syntactic order of *verb + adverbial complement + direct object* over the preferred English *verb +*

direct object + adverbial complement. However, this allows for the sentence to continue in a manner permitting the introduction of the relative clause which is necessary to the continued development of the narrator's description of the action:

ST21 ... buscó el corazón con la punta de la pistola de su propio padre, que estaba en el comedor con parte de la familia.

TT21 ... she pressed to her heart the muzzle of a pistol which belonged to her own father, who was in the dining room with some of the family.

PRACTICAL 18

18.1 Uses of 'se'

Assignment

(i) Examine the uses of 'se' printed in bold in the ST and consider what their contextual communicative effect is.

(ii) Paying particular attention to 'se', compare the ST with the TT, and edit the TT where your comments are critical.

Contextual information

La Regenta, by Leopoldo Alas, 'Clarín', was first published in 1885. The novel is a satirical exploration of the mores of a dilapidated provincial town. The ST extract is part of an extended scene set in the Casino, which is the regular meeting place and club of the town worthies. The TT below is an extract from the Penguin Classics translation of *La Regenta* by John Rutherford (1984). Rutherford is a British academic whose area of speciality includes the works of Alas. His translation has been very well reviewed.

Source text

De los periódicos e ilustraciones **se hacía** más uso; tanto que aquéllos desaparecían casi todas las noches y los grabados de mérito eran cuidadosamente arrancados. Esta cuestión del hurto de periódicos era de las difíciles que tenían que resolver las juntas. ¿Qué **se hacía**? ¿**Se les ponía** grillete a los papeles? Los socios arrancaban las hojas o **se llevaban** papel y hierro. **Se resolvió** últimamente dejar los periódicos libres, pero ejercer una gran vigilancia. Era inútil. Don Frutos Redondo, el más rico americano, no **podía dormirse** sin leer en la cama el *Imparcial* del Casino. Y no había de trasladar su lecho al gabinete de lectura. **Se llevaba** el periódico. Aquellos cinco céntimos que ahorraba de esta manera, le sabían a gloria. En cuanto al papel de cartas que desaparecía también, y era más caro, **se tomó la resolución** de dar un pliego, y gracias, al socio que lo pedía con mucha necesidad. El conserje había adquirido un humor de alcaide de presidio en este trato. Miraba a los socios que leían como a gente de sospechosa probidad; les guardaba escasas consideraciones. No siempre que **se le llamaba** acudía, y solía **negarse** a mudar las plumas oxidadas.

Target text

More use was made of newspapers and illustrated magazines. So much so, that the former disappeared almost every night and any prints of merit were carefully torn out of the latter. The theft of newspapers was one of the difficult questions to be resolved at meetings. What was to be done? Chain the papers up? The members would tear the pages out or carry off both newspaper and chain. In the end, it was resolved to leave the newspapers unfettered, but to exercise the utmost vigilance. It was to no avail. Don Frutos Redondo, the richest of the Americans, could not sleep at night without first reading the Club's copy of *El Imparcial* in bed. And he was not going to transfer his bed to the reading room. He took the newspaper away with him. The five céntimos which he saved in this way smacked to him of glory. With regard to the writing-paper, which also kept disappearing, and was more expensive, it was resolved to give one sheet to any member who made an urgent request for it – and he could consider himself lucky to get even that. The porter had acquired the attitude of a prison warder in these dealings. He regarded members who were fond of reading as people of dubious probity, and treated them with scant respect. He did not always come when he was called, and he often refused to replace rusty nibs.

19

Contrastive topic and practical: passive and impersonal constructions

---

This chapter constitutes the material for all or part of a practical. If possible, the assignment at the end of Chapter 18 (pp. 205–6) should be handed in before the practical as a preliminary exercise. It should in any case be completed before going on to the material in the rest of this chapter, where we shall concentrate on the use of passive and impersonal constructions. By passive constructions we mean those in which the grammatical subject of the verb is not the agent or the producer of the action, and we shall limit discussion to that group of passive constructions formed by verbal periphrasis with the past participle, and to the use of the passive 'se'. **Verbal periphrasis** is the grammatical term given to the structure comprising an auxiliary verb, which usually loses some or all of its original semantic content, and an infinitive, gerund or participle: passive periphrasis always employs a past participle. The problems associated with the translation of *estar + past participle* passive constructions will not be dealt with in detail here. In the course of our discussion we shall use the abbreviation SP to refer to the passive expressed in the terms of verbal periphrasis with 'ser', EP to refer to passives with 'estar', and RP to refer to the passive reflexive.

The commonplace view that Spanish has a low tolerance for the use of passives in the form of SP is gradually losing ground. Recent research has shown on the one hand that, partially under the influence of Anglo-American agency journalism, SP is increasingly coming to be used in journalistic writing and, on the other, that when RP is considered along with SP, the use of passive constructions turns out to be more widespread than is generally appreciated. In fact it appears that these two structures and the use of *estar + past participle* are currently converging (Pountain, 1993). In addition to this, there is some evidence which suggests that SP is becoming increasingly common in unscripted, spontaneous oral texts – and consequently also in fictional representations of dialogue – in the Spanish of the Americas.

Most of the problems experienced in the translation of passive constructions actually arise when working from English into Spanish; however, although more limited, the difficulties which arise when translating from Spanish cause serious interpretative problems, and we shall focus on these in the current chapter. One of the primary problems associated with RP is related to the variety of other functions performed by the reflexive pronoun 'se'. Indeed, students experience particular difficulty with constructions which cannot be easily identified as either RP or impersonal active statements, such as 'los de la hora del café no son más que unos intrusos a los que se tolera' and 'la fiebre se cura'. Related to the question of the use of RP are the problems posed by the frequent use of periphrastic passives, for example 'se quedó paralizado' and 'nunca se le veía con nadie'. Each of these passive constructions and the problems they pose will be discussed below. Particular consideration will be given to the question of tonal register.

19.1 SP constructions

In most cases the translation of SP offers few difficulties. Examine the following typical examples and discuss possible TTs in class.

ST1 [*newspaper article on business matters*] Günter Rexrodt fue propuesto como nuevo ministro de Economía alemán.

ST2 [*technical document*] El agua salada es enfriada hasta la formación de hielo.

ST3 [*Spanish textbook on grammar*] La construcción pasiva es poco usada en castellano.

ST4 [*tabloid newspaper picture caption*] Un joven es asesinado a golpes por un vigilante de discoteca.

ST1 can be plausibly rendered into a passive construction in English:

TT1 Günter Rexrodt was proposed as the new German Minister for the Economy.

Because of its technical register, ST2 can also be rendered by a passive:

TT2(a) The salt water is frozen until ice forms.

However, in the ST the passive construction fulfils the function of describing a general process, that is to say a timeless/habitual action, in which the use of a definite article (suggesting specific salt water) may not be appropriate. This function of the passive may be more readily conveyed by suppressing the direct article:

TT2(b) Salt water is frozen until ice forms.

This conveys the instructive, formal and generalizing tone of the ST, an extract from a technical scientific text, more idiomatically than TT2(a). As with ST2, ST3 is likely to be read as descriptive and rendered accordingly:

TT3(a) Passive constructions are little used in Spanish.

If ST3 is accepted as descriptive, use of the passive in the TL is certainly appropriate although it could be construed as a little pompous. If only for reasons of register, an active construction may be more plausible:

TT3(b) Passive constructions are infrequent in Spanish.

However, when the context of this text is borne in mind – the 1931 edition of the Real Academia Española's *Esbozo de una nueva gramática* – then its ideological function as proscriptive becomes clear and it could be argued that in this context a passive construction is more appropriate.

The examples considered so far suggest that any difficulties arising from the translation of the SP from Spanish into English are associated with features such as the register, ideology and generic classification of the ST. ST4 is a particularly good example of this. Discuss the following versions in class and consider their appropriateness to the context of the ST:

TT4(a) Teenager is killed by bouncer.
TT4(b) Teenager is murdered by bouncer.
TT4(c) Teenager is beaten to death by bouncer.

All three TTs render the passive into English. Each deals with the connotations of the verb and its complement differently. TT4(a) neutralizes the negative connotations of the verb 'asesinar' by generalization and omits detail from its complement which, in the ST, contributed to the sensationalizing tone; TT4(b) also generalizes the verb and its complement, but renders their connotations more faithfully; TT4(c) maintains the detail in the form of the idiomatic English expression 'beat to death' which carries with it the sensationalizing tone of the ST, and consequently is the most convincing communicative rendering. However, when the contextual function of the ST is considered – a picture caption in a tabloid newspaper – the TTs' translation of the ST passive structure 'es asesinado' as a full passive in English is seen to be inappropriate given the conventions and restrictions of the genre to which the ST belongs. The version which follows fulfils generic expectations by suppressing the auxiliary verb in the periphrasis which forms the passive:

TT4(d) Teenager beaten to death by bouncer.

19.2 EP/SP nuancing

The question of EP/SP nuancing will be considered only briefly because the difficulties presented in translating these two structures become most apparent only when EP/SP constructions with parallel semantic content are placed side by side. Nonetheless, it is as well to be aware of the difference in nuance which is occasionally marked. Discuss the following STs in class and offer plausible TTs. The example is adapted from Gili Gaya's (1989) discussion of the problem:

ST5 Las casas son edificadas con mucho cuidado.
ST6 Las casas están edificadas con mucho cuidado.

ST5 indicates that care has been exercised in the construction of the houses since building began – and it may not yet be complete – whereas ST6 refers to the completed process of building. We offer the following exegetic TTs in order to convey the difference in nuance as fully as we can:

TT5 The houses are being built with great care.
TT6 The houses have been built with great care.

A contrast can be seen here in the imperfective aspect of TT5 – which refers to an activity which is incomplete at the time the statement was uttered – and the perfective aspect of TT6, in which the process of building has clearly been completed. In fact, there is a tendency to read ST6 as if 'edificadas con mucho cuidado' were an adjectival phrase describing the houses. Consider the following examples from Molina Redondo and Ortega Olivares, 1990:

ST7 El coche es destrozado.
ST8 El coche está destrozado.

The difference in nuance here is so slight as to be almost unidentifiable. ST7 and ST8 are both clearly passive according to the definition we supplied above: in each case the grammatical subject of the sentence, 'el coche', is not the agent or producer of the action. ST7 presents a text which is readily construed as, for example, providing a commentary on an event as it occurs:

TT7(a) The car is destroyed.

or perhaps as a newspaper photograph caption:

TT7(b) Car destroyed.

This reading is feasible, although, of course, familiarity with SL journalistic style would normally lead the reader to expect the indefinite article 'un' in a newspaper caption. In contrast, ST8 highlights the fact that the destruction of the car is a state which came about as the result of a process, and it could easily be interpreted as *estar + adjective*. An appropriate idiomatic rendering of ST8 which fully conveys this nuance is difficult to achieve. Consider the following versions:

TT8(a) The car is destroyed.
TT8(b) The car is wrecked.

The point to observe here is the degree of overlap between TT8(a) and TT8(b) and the possibility of using either of them as an English rendering of ST7.

19.3 Reflexive passive/Impersonal constructions

In this section, rather than offer a series of strategies for translation, we shall examine the constructions under discussion and consider possibilities for their translation. Occasionally ambiguity may arise as to whether a particular sentence should be construed as an example of RP or as an impersonal active construction. This ambiguity is virtually non-existent when the grammatical subject of the passive verb is transitive and in the plural. Consider the following examples:

ST9 Según la sentencia los hechos ocurridos en marzo se llevaron a cabo en establecimientos comerciales.
ST10 Los gritos que se oían alarmaron a una vecina.
ST11 Se calificaron las entrevistas de 'vital' [sic] y 'transcendentales'.

However, in popular speech there is a tendency to render a passive verb which precedes the grammatical subject as singular, and student translators should remain aware of this possibility (note that this construction sounds unacceptable to educated speakers and, in some cases, may be a marker of sociolect (Butt and Benjamin, 1994, p. 370)). Consider the following example and discuss TTs which make clear the contrast between it and ST11:

ST12 Se calificó las entrevistas de 'vital' [sic] y 'transcendentales'.

Where the grammatical subject of the main verb is singular, the possibility of interpreting the construction as either RP or impersonal is open, and greater care should be taken. Where the grammatical subject is animate, interference from other uses of 'se' may adversely affect interpretation. Consider the ambiguities inherent in the following examples and discuss plausible TTs in class:

ST13 ¿Qué se hacía?

Without further contextual information, ST13 is difficult to translate and it could be rendered equally convincingly as either of the following:

TT13(a) What was one to do?
TT13(b) What was to be done?

If TT13(a) is considered more appropriate, it will be read as an impersonal statement and the reader will expect contextual clues clarifying the identity of the agent. Depending on the register of the context, further particularization may even be preferable, for example 'What was she to do?' or 'What were they to do?' If TT13(b) is more contextually appropriate, this will be because the agent has been identified with the grammatical subject 'qué'. In fact, ST13 is a quotation from the *La Regenta* passage which was set as a preliminary exercise, and the sentence that immediately precedes it provides sufficient information to guide the reader:

> Esta cuestión del hurto de periódicos era de las difíciles que tenían que resolver las juntas.

TT13(a) now seems an unlikely choice given the fact that the subject of the main clause in this preceding sentence is 'esta cuestión'. The passive rendering offered in TT13(b) fits more idiomatically in the context. (Had the main clause been governed by 'las juntas', an impersonal construction might have been preferred.) ST13 is an excellent example of the ambiguity between passive 'se' and impersonal 'se'.

Another type of ambiguity which is a result of interference from other uses of 'se' can be found in the following example:

ST14 Se asesinaron dos argelinos.

In ST14 the pressure of reading the 'se' construction as reflexive outweighs the latent passive structure:

TT14(a) Two Algerians murdered one another.
TT14(b) Two Algerians were murdered.

Fortunately, translators only occasionally encounter ambiguities such as those in ST14 because Spanish offers a widely used construction *se + third person singular transitive verb + personal 'a'*, which resolves the ambiguity. In simple sentences these seldom offer the translator any problem:

ST15 Se encerró a setecientas prostitutas para moralizarlas.
ST16 Se condenó a dos vigilantes.

However, when these occur in more complex sentences where they are accompanied by other pronoun combinations, student translators often fail to recognize them as passive. Consider the following examples:

ST17 No siempre que se le llamaba acudía.

In ST17, the pronoun 'le' clearly refers to the subject of the second verb, 'acudía', which also seems to be the main verb of the sentence:

TT17 He did not always come when...

At this point the translator needs to have recourse to the context before being able to make a decision as to whether 'se le llamaba [a él]' should be rendered as passive or impersonal. Here is the preceding sentence:

> Miraba a los socios que leían como a gente de sospechosa probidad; les guardaba escasas consideraciones.

From this it transpires the object in 'se le llamaba' is the same 'he' who is being described in the preceding sentence, and is the subject of the verb 'acudía'. It is clear, then, that a passive rendering would be more appropriate to the ST context. In our experience, it is with these more complex sentences that students have most problems, and they are likely not to recognize them as passive at all. Consider the following example:

ST18 No parece comprensible que se le cerrara acceso a la Real Academia de la Lengua.

Here the grammatical subject of the verb in the subclause is clearly 'acceso' whilst the logical object is 'le' (that is, in context, 'a ella') thus indicating that a passive rendering is appropriate:

TT18 It is incomprehensible that her admission to the Royal Academy of Language should be blocked.

Discuss plausible and appropriate TTs of the following in class:

ST19 Se le niega año tras año este 'Noble de las letras españolas'.

19.4 Periphrastic passives

By the term periphrastic passive, we mean a passive construction which is created through the combination of an auxiliary verb and a past participle. Consider the following examples and discuss appropriate TTs in class:

ST20 Más de 56.000 personas se veían afectadas por el corte del agua.
ST21 Se quedó paralizado.
ST22 Queda dicho ya que la construcción pasiva es poco usada en castellano.
ST23 Un vecino de Santo Paolo resultó herido a causa del atropello.

20

Summary and conclusion

The idea of translators as active and responsible agents of the translation process has played a constant and central part throughout this course. Indeed, the personal responsibilities of translators are, in our view, of paramount importance. Although loyalties may genuinely be divided between responsibilities to the author of the ST, to the manifest properties and features of the ST (in particular, with a view to what is there in black and white in a written ST, as opposed to what its author may have intended), to the 'paymaster' by whom a TT has been commissioned, and to a putative public for whom the TT is meant, it is, in the end, the translator alone who is responsible for submitting a particular TT. Responsibility entails decisions, and it is with this in mind that we have insisted at every juncture on the key notions of *strategy* and *decisions of detail*, stressing the idea that decisions of detail should be rationally linked to the prior formulation of overall strategy for translating a particular text in a particular set of circumstances.

The adoption of an appropriate translation strategy implicitly means ranking the cultural, formal, semantic, stylistic and genre-related properties of the ST according to their relative textual *relevance* and the amount of attention these properties should receive in the process of translation. The aim is to deal with translation loss (see especially Chapter 2), and the attendant necessities of compromise and compensation (see the discussion in Chapter 3), in a relatively rational and systematic way: in short, by sanctioning the loss of features that have a low degree of textual relevance, sacrificing less relevant textual details to more relevant ones, and using techniques of compensation to convey features of high textual relevance that cannot be more directly rendered.

To return briefly to the idea of 'textual relevance', this is a qualitative measure of the degree to which, in the translator's judgement, particular properties of a text are held responsible for the overall impact carried in and by that text. In a sense, textually relevant features are those which stand out as making the text what it is. This is not as trivial and circular as it might sound. On the contrary, it is the basis for the only reasonably reliable test of textual relevance. No such test can, of course, escape a degree of subjectivity, but the most objective test of textual relevance is to imagine that a particular textual property is omitted from the text and to assess what difference this omission would make to the overall impact of the text as a whole. If the answer is 'little or none', we may take it that the property in question has a very low degree of textual relevance. If, on the other hand, omission of a textual property would mean a palpable loss in either the genre-typical or the individual (perhaps even deliberately idiosyncratic) character of the text, we may attribute a high degree of relevance to the textual property in question.

Ideally, developing a translation strategy by way of assessing textual relevance in a ST entails scanning the text for every *kind* of textual feature that might conceivably be relevant to formulating an appropriate TT. For such scanning to be systematic yet speedy, it is vital to have in mind a concrete 'check-list' of the *kinds* of textual feature one needs to look out for. It is with this in view that we suggest the schema of textual 'filters' sketched out in Figure 20.1. The overall schema summarizes practically the entire framework of the course, and, for the most part, follows the order of presentation in the main body of the text. The only exception to this is in the inclusion of 'grammatical transposition' among the options listed in the 'cultural' filter, where it occupies a position between 'calque' and 'communicative translation'. It can be argued that grammatical transposition is, indeed, a cultural matter and has important implications in the presentation of different world-views favoured by SL and TL respectively (for instance, the tendency for Spanish to express the shaping of substances into forms by *noun + de + noun* constructions, as against the tendency in English to express the same message by a *noun-on-noun* construction, compare 'cristales de hielo' with 'ice crystals'). It can also be argued that as an option grammatical transposition is intermediate between the rather more SL-oriented creation of calqued expressions (which retain much of the cultural flavour of their SL models) and the considerably more TL-oriented choice of communicative translations (which retain none of the cultural flavour of their SL counterparts). Consequently, the position accorded to grammatical transposition in our schema of textual filters is fully justified. The reason why this does not match our presentation in the main body of the course is a tactical one: grammatical transposition forms the subject matter of four contrastive chapters (Chapters 16–19), which we have chosen to use as movable course components, and which, by sheer size alone, could not be incorporated in the chapter on cultural issues (Chapter 3) without disrupting the modular structure of the course. For reasons of practical usefulness, grammatical transposition has been taken out of its logical place in Chapter 3 and given extended treatment in the form of contrastive exercises. The schema of textual filters restores this issue to its logical place.

For the rest, the contents of the 'cultural' filter correspond to issues discussed in Chapter 3. This component calls attention to textual features that present choices between 'extra-cultural' and 'indigenous' elements (see the discussion in Chapter 3). As such, it invites the translator to assess – when considering a ST in this light – the degree to which features of the ST are detachable from their cultural matrix, that is to say the extent to which their culture-specificity is textually relevant.

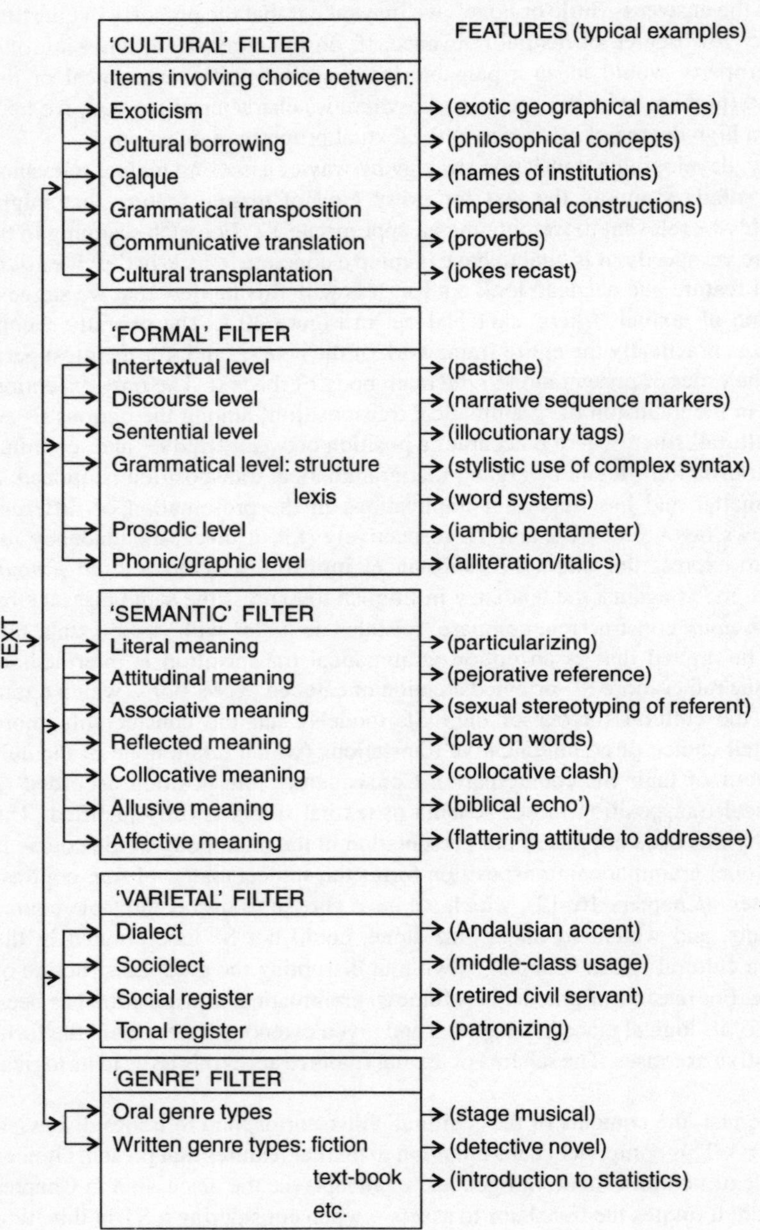
SCHEMA OF TEXTUAL 'FILTERS'
TEXT
'CULTURAL' FILTER
FEATURES (typical examples)
Items involving choice between:
Exoticism
(exotic geographical names)
Cultural borrowing
(philosophical concepts)
Calque
(names of institutions)
Grammatical transposition
(impersonal constructions)
Communicative translation
(proverbs)
Cultural transplantation
(jokes recast)
'FORMAL' FILTER
Intertextual level
(pastiche)
Discourse level
(narrative sequence markers)
Sentential level
(illocutionary tags)
Grammatical level: structure
(stylistic use of complex syntax)
lexis
(word systems)
Prosodic level
(iambic pentameter)
Phonic/graphic level
(alliteration/italics)
'SEMANTIC' FILTER
Literal meaning
(particularizing)
Attitudinal meaning
(pejorative reference)
Associative meaning
(sexual stereotyping of referent)
Reflected meaning
(play on words)
Collocative meaning
(collocative clash)
Allusive meaning
(biblical 'echo')
Affective meaning
(flattering attitude to addressee)
'VARIETAL' FILTER
Dialect
(Andalusian accent)
Sociolect
(middle-class usage)
Social register
(retired civil servant)
Tonal register
(patronizing)
'GENRE' FILTER
Oral genre types
(stage musical)
Written genre types: fiction
(detective novel)
text-book
(introduction to statistics)
etc.

Figure 20.1

The 'formal' filter corresponds in content and organization to Chapters 4–6, with the proviso that it is to be read from bottom to top (see the discussion at the beginning of our Introduction), and constitutes a component for scanning the formal properties of texts, which are discussed in detail in these chapters.

The 'semantic' filter summarizes the contents of Chapters 7 and 8, focusing the translator's attention on the important decisions relating to the translating of literal meaning, as well as of textually relevant features of connotative meaning.

The 'varietal' filter sums up the stylistic aspects inherent in the use of different language varieties, and invites the translator to pay due attention to the textual effects of sociolinguistic variation. The contents of this filter correspond to Chapters 9 and 10 in the course.

Finally, the 'genre' filter serves as a brief and necessarily sketchy reminder of the vital importance of assessing the genre-membership of texts, and discovering their genre-related characteristics. This filter corresponds to the entire contents of Chapters 11–15.

Although analogies can be misleading when used in explanation, we risk an analogy by suggesting that the schema visualizes the methodological framework of translation as a 'battery of filters' through which texts can be passed in a systematic attempt to determine their translation-worthy properties. In terms of this analogy, textually relevant properties find their level by being 'collected' in the appropriate filter; the importance of the various levels can be ranked according to the nature of the text (for example, the prosodic level will probably rank as minimally important in scientific texts, but as maximally important in some poetic genres); and certain filters or levels will be found to contribute no textually relevant features (for example, a particular text may contain no detectable allusive meanings).

It should also be said that STs are not the only texts that can be passed through the elements of the proposed battery of filters: both tentative and published TTs can be similarly processed before they are finalized, and their features compared with those of the ST, as a means of evaluating their success.

The analogy of filters is a mechanical one, and in this lies a serious danger of misunderstanding. We do not wish to imply that our schema is intended as a means of mechanizing the process of translation; on the contrary, we believe this process to be an intelligent and 'humanistic' one involving personal, and in the final analysis subjective, choices made by the translator. The schema of filters is not a mechanical device but a mnemonic one: it reminds the working translator of what features to look for in a ST, as well as of the need to rank these features in order of relative textual relevance, as part and parcel of working out a strategy for translating the ST. It also serves to remind translators of options and choices when tinkering with details in editing a provisional TT. But the decision and choices remain entirely non-mechanical: they are for the translator to make.

A further point to be made about the schema of textual filters concerns the time element. Scanning a text in the kind of detail that a full use of the filters would seem to imply is unrealistic when the translator is working against a time limit. In such cases, a more perfunctory use of the schema is still useful in speeding up the process of adopting a translation strategy, and in spotting and handling particular problems of detail. It is worth remembering that the usefulness of the schema is not dependent on making a full and exhaustive use of its scanning potential: it performs a useful function even in speed translation. The translator simply has to make as much, or as little, use of it as time will allow.

Finally, it is worth noting that, through practice, the scanning of texts in the manner suggested by the schema quickly becomes habitual, so that the translator comes to perform the process automatically and rapidly, without having to consult the check-list.

Glossary

affective meaning the emotive effect worked on the addressee by the choice of a particular **linguistic expression**, in contrast with others that might have been used to express the same literal message; affective meaning is a type of **connotative meaning**.

alliteration the recurrence of the same sound/letter or sound/letter cluster at the beginning of two or more words occurring near or next to one another in a **text**.

allusive meaning the **connotative meaning** of a **linguistic expression** which takes the form of evoking the meaning of an entire saying or quotation of which that expression is a part. (NB If a saying or quotation appears in full within a **text**, that is a case of citation; we speak of allusive meaning where only a recognizable segment of the saying or quotation occurs in the text, but that segment implicitly carries the meaning of the entire 'reconstructed' saying or quotation.)

anaphora in *grammar*, the replacement of previously used **linguistic expressions** in a **text** by simpler and less specific expressions (such as pronouns) having the same contextual referent; in *rhetoric*, the repetition of a word or phrase at the beginning of successive clauses.

associative meaning the **connotative meaning** of a **linguistic expression** which takes the form of attributing to the referent certain stereotypically expected properties culturally associated with that referent.

assonance the recurrence of a sound/letter or sound/letter cluster in the middle of words occurring near or next to one another in a **text**.

attitudinal meaning the **connotative meaning** of a **linguistic expression** which takes the form of implicitly conveying a commonly held attitude or value judgement towards the referent of the expression.

calque a form of **cultural transposition** whereby a TT expression is modelled on the grammatical structure of the corresponding ST expression.

code-switching the alternating use of two or more recognizably different language variants (varieties of the same language, or different languages) within the same **text**.

cogency the 'thread' of intellectual interrelatedness of ideas running through a **text**.

coherence the tacit, yet intellectually discernible, thematic development that characterizes a cogent text, as distinct from a random sequence of unrelated sentences.

cohesion the explicit and transparent linking of sentences and larger sections of **text** by the use of overt linguistic devices that act as 'signposts' for the **cogency** of a text.

collocative meaning the **connotative meaning** lent to a **linguistic expression** by the meaning of some other expression with which it frequently or typically collocates in a grammatical context; that is, collocative meaning is an echo of the meanings of expressions that partner a given expression in commonly used phrases.

communicative translation a style of **free translation** involving the rendering of ST expressions by their contextually/situationally appropriate cultural counterparts in the TL; that is, the TT uses situationally apt target culture counterparts in preference to **literal translation**.

compensation the technique of making up for the **translation loss** of important ST features by approximating their effects in the TT through means other than those used in the ST – that is, making up for ST effects achieved by one means through using other means in the TT.

compensation by merging condensing the features carried over a relatively longer stretch of the ST into a relatively shorter stretch of TT.

compensation by splitting distributing the features carried in a relatively shorter stretch of the ST over a relatively longer stretch of the TT.

compensation in kind compensating for a particular type of textual effect in the ST by using a textual effect of a different type in the TT (for instance, compensating for **assonance** in the ST by **alliteration** in the TT).

compensation in place compensating for the loss of a particular textual effect occurring at a given place in the ST by creating a corresponding effect at a different place in the TT.

connotative meaning the implicit overtones and nuances that **linguistic expressions** tend to carry over and above their **literal meanings**. (NB The overall meaning of an expression in context is compounded of the literal meaning of the expression plus its contextually relevant connotative overtones.)

crossover the conversion of a written **text** into a corresponding oral text, or, conversely, of an oral text into a corresponding written text. (NB The correspondences are a matter of degree, and are never more than approximate.)

cultural borrowing the process of taking over a SL expression verbatim from the ST into the TT (and, ultimately, into the TL as a whole). The borrowed term may remain unaltered in form or may undergo minor alteration or **transliteration**.

cultural transplantation the highest degree of **cultural transposition**, involving the replacement of source-cultural details mentioned in the ST with cultural details drawn from the target culture in the TT – that is, cultural transplantation deletes from the TT items specific to the source culture, replacing them with items specific to the target culture.

cultural transposition any degree of departure from a maximally **literal translation** – that is, the replacement in a TT of SL-specific features with TL-specific ones; cultural transposition entails a certain degree of TL orientation.

decisions of detail in translating a given **text**, the decisions taken in respect of specific problems of grammar, lexis, and so on; decisions of detail are ideally taken in the light of previously taken **strategic decisions**.

deictic a **linguistic expression** (for instance, a demonstrative, a pronoun, a temporal expression) designating a specific referent which the hearer/reader is required to identify relative to context of situation.

dialect a language variety with non-standard features of accent, vocabulary, syntax and sentence formation (for example, **illocutionary particles**, intonation) characteristic, and therefore indicative, of the regional provenance of its users.

discourse level the textual level on which whole **texts** (or sections of whole texts) are considered as self-contained, coherent and cohesive entities; the ultimate discourse structure of texts consists of a number of interrelated sentences, these being the lowest analytic units on the discourse level.

editing the last stage of the translation process, consisting in checking over the draft of a written TT with a view to correcting errors and polishing up stylistic details.

exegetic translation a style of translation in which the TT expresses and explains additional details that are not explicitly conveyed in the ST; that is, the TT is, at the same time, an expansion and explanation of the contents of the ST.

exoticism the lowest degree of cultural transposition of a ST feature, whereby that feature (having its roots exclusively in the SL and source culture) is taken over verbatim into the TT; that is, the transposed term is an ostensibly 'foreign' element in the TT.

foot a prosodic/metric unit in versification, consisting of a rhythmic pattern of stressed and/or unstressed syllables; in certain languages (for example, English or Latin, but not Spanish), feet are the basic units of poetic rhythm.

free translation a style of translation in which there is only a global correspondence between units of the ST and units of the TT – for example, a rough sentence-to-sentence correspondence, or a still looser correspondence in terms of even larger sections of text.

generalizing translation, **generalization** rendering a ST expression by a TL **hyperonym** – that is, the **literal meaning** of the TT expression is wider and less specific than that of the corresponding ST expression; a generalizing translation omits details that are explicitly present in the literal meaning of the ST.

gist translation a style of translation in which the TT purposely expresses a condensed version of the contents of the ST; that is, the TT is, at the same time, a synopsis of the ST.

grammatical level the level of linguistic structure concerned with words, the decomposition of complex (inflected, derived or compound) words into their meaningful constituent parts, and the patterned syntactic arrangement of words into phrases, and phrases into yet more complex phrases.

grammatical transposition the technique of translating a ST expression having a given grammatical structure by a TT expression with a different grammatical structure containing different parts of speech in a different arrangement.

hyperonym a **linguistic expression** whose **literal meaning** is inclusive of, but wider and less specific than, the range of literal meaning of another expression: for instance, 'parent' is a hyperonym of 'mother'.

hyponym a **linguistic expression** whose **literal meaning** is included in, but is narrower and more specific than, the range of literal meaning of another expression; for example, 'younger sister' is a hyponym of 'sibling'.

illocutionary particle a discrete element which, when added to the syntactic material of a sentence, informs the listener/reader of the affective force the utterance is intended to have – for example, 'alas', 'for God's sake!', '¿qué sé yo?', '¿no es cierto?'

interlineal translation a style of translation in which the TT provides a literal rendering for each successive meaningful unit of the ST (including affixes) and arranges these units in their order of occurrence in the ST, regardless of the conventional grammatical order of units in the TL.

inter-semiotic translation translating from one semiotic system (that is, system for communication) into another. For a translation to be inter-semiotic, either the ST, or the TT, but not both, may be a human natural language.

intertextual level the level of shared culture on which texts are viewed as bearing significant external relationships to other texts (for example, by allusion, by imitation, by virtue of genre membership).

intralingual translation the re-expression of a message conveyed in a particular form of words in a given language by means of *another* form of words in the *same* language.

linguistic expression a self-contained and meaningful item in a given language, such as a word, a phrase, a sentence.

literal meaning the conventional range of referential meaning attributed to a linguistic expression (as abstracted from its **connotative** overtones and contextual nuances).

literal translation a word-for-word translation, giving maximally accurate literal rendering to all the words in the ST as far as the grammatical conventions of the TL will allow; that is, literal translation is SL-oriented, and departs from ST sequence of words only where the TL grammar makes this inevitable.

partially overlapping translation rendering a ST expression by a TL expression whose range of **literal meaning** partially overlaps with that of the ST expression – that is, the literal meaning of the TT expression both *adds* some detail *not* explicit in the literal meaning of the corresponding ST expression, and *omits* some other detail that *is* explicit in the literal meaning of the ST expression; in this sense, partially overlapping translation simultaneously combines elements of **particularizing** and **generalizing**.

particularizing translation, **particularization** rendering a ST expression by a TL **hyponym**; that is, making the **literal meaning** of the TT narrower and more specific than that of the corresponding ST; a particularizing translation adds details to the TT that are not explicitly expressed in the ST.

phonemic translation a technique of translation that consists in an attempt to replicate in the TT the sound sequence of the ST, while allowing the sense to remain, at best, a vague and suggested impression.

phonic/graphic level the level of linguistic structure concerned with the patterned organization of sound-segments (phonemes) in speech, or of letters (graphemes) in writing.

prosodic level the level of linguistic structure concerned with metrically patterned stretches of speech within which syllables have varying degrees of *prominence* (in terms of such properties as stress and vowel-differentiation) varying degrees of *pace* (in terms of such properties as length and tempo) and varying qualities of *pitch*.

reflected meaning the **connotative meaning** lent to a **linguistic expression** by the fact that its *form* (phonic, graphic, or both) is reminiscent of a homonymic or near-homonymic expression with a different **literal meaning**; that is, reflected meaning is an echo of the literal meaning of some other expression that sounds or is spelt the same, or nearly the same, as a given expression.

rephrasing the exact rendering of the message content of a given ST in a TT that is radically different in form, but neither adds nor omits details explicitly conveyed in the ST.

script a written **text** intended as a basis for the performance of an oral text realized in spontaneous (or apparently spontaneous) form.

sentence markers linguistic devices that, over and above the syntactic basis of words and phrases, endow sentences with a specific type of communicative purpose and intent; the principal types of sentence marker are intonation or punctuation, sequential focusing (that is, word order) and **illocutionary particles**.

sentential level the level of linguistic structure concerned with the formation of sentences as complete, self-contained linguistic units ready-made to act as vehicles of oral or written communication. (NB Over and above the basic grammatical units – which may be elliptical – that it contains, a sentence must be endowed with sense-conferring properties of intonation or punctuation, and may in addition contain features of word order, and/or **illocutionary particles**, all of which contribute to the overall meaning, or 'force', of the sentence.)

social register a style of speaking/writing that gives grounds for inferring relatively detailed stereotypical information about the social identity of the speaker/writer. (NB 'Social identity' refers to the stereotypical labelling that is a constant feature of social intercourse.)

sociolect a language variety with features of accent, vocabulary, syntax and sentence formation (for example, intonation, **illocutionary particles**) characteristic, and therefore indicative, of the class affiliations of its users.

source language (SL) the language in which the **text** requiring translation is expressed.

source text (ST) the **text** requiring translation.

strategic decisions the general decisions taken, in the light of the nature of the ST and the requirements of the TT, as to what ST properties should have priority in translation; **decisions of detail** are ideally taken on the basis of these strategic decisions (though, conversely, decisions of detail may have an effect on altering initial strategic decisions).

synonymy the highest degree of semantic equivalence between two or more different linguistic expressions having exactly identical ranges of **literal meaning**. (NB Synonymous expressions usually differ in **connotative**, and therefore in 'overall', meaning; that is, they are unlikely to have perfectly identical meanings in textual contexts – compare 'automobile' and 'jalopy', for instance.)

target language (TL) the language into which a given **text** is to be translated.

target text (TT) the **text** proffered as a translation (that is, a proposed TL rendering) of the ST. (NB 'Publishing' a target text is a decisive act that overrides the necessarily relative and tentative success of the target text.)

text any given stretch of speech or writing produced in a given language (or 'mixture of languages' – see **code-switching**) and assumed to make a self-contained, coherent whole on the **discourse level**.

textual variables all the ostensible features in a **text**, and which *could* (in another text) have been different; that is, each textual variable constitutes a genuine *option* in the text.

tonal register a style of speaking/writing adopted as a means of conveying affective attitudes of speakers/writers to their addressees. (NB The **connotative meaning** of features of tonal register is an **affective meaning**. This connotative meaning is, strictly speaking, conveyed by the *choice* of one out of a range of expressions capable of conveying a particular literal message; for example, 'Give me the money, please' versus 'Chuck us the dosh, will you?')

transcript a written text intended to represent and record (with a relative degree of accuracy) a particular oral text.

translation loss any feature of inexact correspondence between ST and TT. (NB Where a TT has properties, effects or meanings that are *not* represented in the ST, the addition of these counts as a translation loss. That is to say, translation loss is not limited to the omission from a TT of properties, effects or meanings present in the corresponding ST.)

transliteration the use of TL orthographic conventions for the written representation of SL expressions; for example, Russian 'спутник' transliterated as English 'sputnik'.

transposition see **grammatical transposition**.

verbal periphrasis grammatical structure comprising an auxiliary verb, which usually loses some or all of its original semantic content, and an infinitive, gerund or participle.

word system a pattern of words (distributed over a text) formed by an associative common denominator and having a demonstrable function of enhancing the theme and message of the text (for example, an alliterative pattern emphasizing a particular mood).

References

Alas, L. 1984. *La Regenta*. Rutherford, J. (trans.). Harmondsworth: Penguin.

Alas, L. 1991. *La Regenta*. Madrid: Cátedra.

Allende, I. 1984. *De amor y de sombra*. Barcelona: Plaza & Janés.

Alonso, D. 1980. *Letras*. La Habana: Letras Cubanas.

Alvar, M. 1960. *Textos hispánicos dialectales: antología histórica*, II. Madrid: Revista de Filología Española (Anejo LXXIII).

Anderson, V. 1972. *The Brownie Cookbook*. London: Hodder & Stoughton.

Aphek, E. and Tobin, Y. 1988. *Word Systems: Implications and Applications*. Leiden: E. J. Brill.

Baker, M. 1992. *In Other Words: A Coursebook on Translation*. London: Routledge.

Bécquer, G. A. 1961. *Rimas, Leyendas y Narraciones*. New York: Doubleday & Company (Colección Hispánica).

Beeton, M. 1962. *Mrs Beeton's Family Cookery*. London: Ward, Lock & Company.

Bonavia, D. 1984. 'La importancia de los restos de papas y camotes de época precerámica hallados en el valle de Casma', *Journal de la Société des Américanistes*, Tome LXX. Paris: Musée de L'Homme.

Butt, J. and Benjamin, C. 1994. *A New Reference Grammar of Modern Spanish*. 2nd edn. London: Edward Arnold.

Calderón de la Barca, P. 1960. *La vida es sueño*, Cortina, A. (ed.). Madrid: Espasa-Calpe.

Collins Concise English Dictionary. 1992. 3rd edn. Glasgow: HarperCollins.

Collins Spanish–English English–Spanish Dictionary. 1992. Colin Smith in collaboration with Diarmuid Bradley [*et al.*], 3rd edn. Glasgow: HarperCollins.

Cortázar, J. 1976. *Los relatos: juegos*. Madrid: Alianza.

Cortázar, J. 1981. *Los premios*. Barcelona: Bruguera.

Cortázar, J. 1984. *Rayuela*. Madrid: Cátedra.

Cortázar, J. 1986. *The Winners*, Kerrigan, E. (trans.). London: Allison & Busby.

Darío, R. 1987. *Prosas profanas y otros poemas*, Zuleta, I. M. (ed.). Madrid: Castalia.

Enciclopedia Universal Ilustrada Europeo-Americana. 1993. Suplemento Anual, 1991–1992. Madrid: Espasa-Calpe.

En español; materiales video; guía didáctica, 4. 1988. Madrid: Ministerio de Cultura.

García Lorca, F. 1980. *Obras completas* (revised edition), del Hoyo, A. (ed.). Madrid: Aguilar.

García Lorca, F. 1987. *Yerma*, Macpherson, I. and Minett, J. (eds and trans.). Warminster: Aris & Phillips.

García Santos, J. F. 1990. *Español: curso de perfeccionamiento*. Salamanca: Universidad de Salamanca.

Gili Gaya, S. 1989. *Curso superior de sintaxis española*. Barcelona: Biblograf.

Góngora, L. de. 1964. *The Solitudes of Luis de Góngora y Argote; the Spanish Text with an English Translation by Gilbert F. Cunningham*. Alva (privately printed).

González Muela, J. and Rozas, J. M. (ed.). 1986. *La generación poética de 1927*. Madrid: Istmo.

Goscinny, R. and Uderzo, A. 1965. *Astérix et Cléopâtre*. Neuilly-sur-Seine: Dargaud.

Goscinny, R. and Uderzo, A. 1966. *Astérix chez les Bretons*. Neuilly-sur-Seine: Dargaud.

Goscinny, R. and Uderzo, A. 1967. *Asterix en Bretaña*, Perich, J. (trans.). Barcelona: Grijalbo-Dargaud.

Goytisolo, J. 1976. *Señas de identidad*. Barcelona: Seix Barral.

Goytisolo, J. 1988a. *Marks of Identity*, Rabassa, G. (trans.). London: Serpent's Tail.

Goytisolo, J. 1988b. *Reivindicación del conde don Julián*. Barcelona: Seix Barral.

Guillén, J. 1950. *Cántico*. Buenos Aires: Sudamericana.

Guillén, J. 1968. *Aire nuestro; Cántico, Clamor, Homenaje*. Milan: All'Insegna del Pesce d'Oro.

Guillén, N. 1974. *Obra poética 1920–1972*. La Habana: Editorial de Arte y Literatura.

Guillén, N. 1976. *Motivas de son*, in *Sóngoro Cosongo; Motivos de son; West Indies Ltd.; España: poema en cuatro angustias y una esperanza*. Buenos Aires: Losada.

Halliday, M. A. K. and Hasan, R. 1976. *Cohesion in English*. London: Longman English Language Series.

Hickey, L. 1977. *Usos y estilos de español moderno*. London: Harrap.

Huidobro, V. 1964. *Obras completas*, Arenas, B. (ed.), Vol. I. Santiago de Chile: Zig-Zag.

Hulme, J. 1981. *Mörder Guss Reims*. London: Angus & Robertson.

Jakobson, R. 1971. *Selected Writings*, Vol. II. The Hague: Mouton.

Jovellanos, G. M. de. 1858. 'Memoria sobre educación pública, tratado de enseñanza con aplicación a las escuelas y colegios de niños', in *Obras*, Biblioteca de Autores Españoles, 49. Madrid: Rivadeneyra.

Leech, G. 1974. *Semantics*. Harmondsworth: Pelican.

McCluskey, B. 1987. 'The chinks in the armour: problems encountered by language graduates entering a large translation department', in Keith, H. and Mason, I. (eds). *Translation in the Modern Languages Degree*. London: Centre for Information on Language Teaching and Research.

Machado, A. 1982a. *Poesías completas*, Alvar, M. (ed.). Madrid: Espasa-Calpe.

Machado, A. 1982b. *Selected poems*, Trueblood, A. (trans.). Cambridge, Mass.: Harvard University Press.

Machado, A. 1987. *Solitudes, Galleries and Other Poems*, Predmore, M. (trans.). Durham: Duke University Press.

Malof, J. 1970. *A Manual of English Meters*. Bloomington, Ind.: Indiana University Press.

Marías, J. 1992. *Corazón tan blanco*. Barcelona: Anagrama.

Martín-Santos, L. 1985. *Tiempo de silencio*. Barcelona: Seix Barral.

Molina Redondo, J. A. de, and Ortega Olivares, J., 1990. *Usos de 'ser' y 'estar'. Problemas Básicos del Español*. Madrid: Sociedad General Español de Librería.

Moliner, M. 1975. *Diccionario de uso del Español*. Madrid: Gredos.

Navarro Tomás, T. 1991. *Métrica española*. Barcelona: Labor.

Newmark, P. 1982. *Approaches to Translation*. Oxford: Pergamon.

Ortega, Simone. 1972. *Mil ochenta recetas de cocina*. Madrid: Alianza.

Oxford Spanish Dictionary/Diccionario Oxford. 1994. Oxford: Oxford University Press.

Pereda, J. M. de. 1965. *Sotileza*, in *Obras completas*. Madrid: Aguilar.

Pérez Galdós, B. 1971a. *Lo prohibido*. Madrid: Castalia.

Pérez Galdós, B. 1971b. *Miau*. Puerto Rico: Universitaria.

Pérez Galdós, B. 1991. *La de Bringas*. Madrid: Cátedra.

Pountain, C. J. Spring. 1993. 'Aspect and voice: questions about passivization in Spanish'. *Journal of Hispanic Research*, 1, 2. London: Impart Publishing.

Pring-Mill, R. c.1990. *'Gracias a la vida'; the Power and Poetry of Song*. Department of Hispanic Studies, Queen Mary and Westfield College, University of London.

Rommel, B. 1987. 'Market-orientated translation training', in Keith, H. and Mason, I. (eds)

Translation in the Modern Languages Degree. London: Centre for Information on Language Teaching and Research.

Sastre, A. 1969. *Escuadra hacia la muerte*. Colección Teatro, Madrid: Escelicer.

Sieiro del Nido, C. 1993. 'La Espectroscopía de Resonancia de Spin Electrónico (RSE) en España', *Política Científica*, 37. Madrid: Comisión Interministerial de Ciencia y Tecnología.

Snell-Hornby, M. 1988. *Translation Studies: An Integrated Approach*. Amsterdam: John Benjamins.

Teresa de Jesús. 1957. *The Life of Saint Teresa of Avila by Herself*. Cohen, J. M. (ed. and trans.). Harmondsworth: Penguin.

Teresa de Jesús. 1978. *Su vida*. Colección Austral, 8th edn, Madrid: Espasa-Calpe.

Tracy, M. 1965. *Modern Casserole Cookery*. London: Studio Vista.

Unamuno, M. de. 1962. *The Tragic Sense of Life*, Elguera, A. (trans.). London: Collins.

Unamuno, M. de. 1982. *Del sentimiento trágico de la vida*. Madrid: Espasa-Calpe.

Van Rooten, L. 1968. *Mots d'heures: gousses, rames*. London: Angus & Robertson.

Voces de España; BBC Radio for Schools and Colleges, Modern Languages Student's Workbook. 1990. Falmer: Brighton Polytechnic, The Language Centre.

Voces Hispánicas; Spoken Documents for Advanced Learners of Spanish. 1992. London: Birkbeck College.

Whitley, M. S. 1986. *Spanish/English Contrasts: A Course in Spanish Linguistics*. Washington, DC: Georgetown University Press.

Zukovsky, C. and L. (trans). 1969. *Gai Valeri Catulli Veronesis Liber*. London: Cape Goliard.

Index